Written
on the
Wind

Anuradha Kumar-Jain is a writer and an astrologer. A PhD in Geography from Panjab University, she is also deeply interested in ornithology, cloud spotting and embroidery. She currently lives in Delhi with her husband, daughter and son.

Written
on the
Wind

Anuradha Kumar-Jain

RUPA

Published by
Rupa Publications India Pvt. Ltd 2020
7/16, Ansari Road, Daryaganj
New Delhi 110002

Sales Centres:
Allahabad Bengaluru Chennai
Hyderabad Jaipur Kathmandu
Kolkata Mumbai

ISBN: 978-93-90356-78-2

First impression 2020

10 9 8 7 6 5 4 3 2 1

Printed at Gopsons Papers Ltd, Noida

The moral right of the author has been asserted.

For
Anil
Motivator, goader, irritator, editor

Chapter 1

Harjeet
Lahore 1929

Harjeet had not been able to sleep the whole of last night. The baby kept wailing, probably disturbed by the unseasonal storm that had made the wind howl in the trees outside, and had sent shivers up her spine as well. But it was morning now, the morning of the Basant Panchami festival, and forgetting her tiredness, she hurriedly got out of bed and walked to the window of her room on the first floor. It was still very early, and although the cold winter night had frosted the glass over, she could make out the faint glow emanating from the box kites which were flown in the pre-dawn, with a lighted candle in them, to mark the start of the festivities. The storm had abated, but there was a light wind, and the day promised to be perfect for kite flying. The Basant festival marked the start of the spring season and was held on the fifth day of *Magha*, which usually corresponded with the beginning of February, and even after so many years in Lahore, she was still amazed at the fervour with which the entire city joined in the festivities. Kites were flown from every rooftop and melas were held at Sufi shrines across the land. The whole world seemed to have taken on a golden hue, the flowers of the sarson painted entire fields yellow, people wore the same bright colour and ate sweet rice tinged with saffron and cardamom. Halwai shops were piled high with mithai and decorated with garlands of marigold.

From downstairs, she could hear the first stirrings of the household coming to life; the opening and closing of the front door as her father-in-law left for his morning walk, the tinkling of Champa's anklets as she swept the angan. Dispiritedly, she thought of the routine chores that awaited her today, as on all other days, 'the daily grind of life', as she listlessly thought of them. At least the festival would bring some cheer to this awful humdrumness.

Turning back from the window she looked at Inder, two years old and angelic, sleeping peacefully in his cot. Poor kid, he had had a bad night as well. And she thought of Gautam, who had probably slept soundly through the disturbance, oblivious of the storm, in his room next door. 'I need a full night's undisturbed sleep to be able to attend office in the morning,' he had declared as soon as Maya, now four, was born, shifting his things to the smaller room adjoining their bedroom.

Nervous, gentle Gautam, who did not excite her at all, and whom she had so desperately wanted not to marry. If her parents had been alive, would they have forced her to spend the rest of her life with someone she didn't want? Even the God she had worshiped for all of her nineteen years had sided with her conniving bhabhi in getting her married to a stocky, balding man ten years her senior. When she had gone to the Gurudwara the last day before her marriage, she had finally decided to switch Gods; all her praying, cajoling and even threatening had not melted His heart. So although she would continue to love Guru Nanak, she would put her faith in Lord Krishna. Maybe, the God of love would infuse some magic into her life, some sorely needed sorcery to lift it from the morass of boredom and inertia it had got trapped into.

Or maybe there was something the matter with her, she thought morosely. This was not how a young woman barely into her mid-twenties, married into one of the most prominent families of Lahore, should be feeling. 'What more do you want,' her bhabhi had rebuked her once. 'Money, status, educated in-laws, a kind husband, Lahore, you have it all.'

The last part was certainly true. She welcomed the chance to continue living in Lahore, and had she not been so dissatisfied with her life in general, would have enjoyed its charms even more. Although she had lived in Lahore for many years, she had only fallen in love with the city during her years at Kinnaird College, when in spite of having to live with her maternal aunt, who had since passed away, the freedom from regimented boarding school had come as a breath of fresh air. She loved everything about Lahore, the Mall Road, the hustle and bustle of Anarkali, the beautiful Lawrence Gardens and the Gymkhana Club. Her in-law's house was located in a four *kanal* plot at the very entrance to Birdwood Road in a quiet part of the city. It was an imposing structure, one of the very few double storeyed buildings in the area, and from the road gave a stately look, with its fluted columns, deep verandah and long tree-lined driveway. The front door, made of heavy Burma teak, led into a small passageway which opened into a big, light-filled drawing room. The three bedrooms were located to one side of the passageway while the kitchen and the storeroom were on the other. A door from the drawing room led to the study cum office, one of whose walls was entirely lined with book-filled shelves. The house had been renovated just before Gautam's marriage, and the two refurbished bedrooms on the first floor were given to the newlyweds, delighting Harjeet who was grateful for the distance it put between herself and her mother-in-law.

But by far, the biggest advantage of Lahore was that it was more than a hundred miles from her village, with its small town familiarity. The village was named after her family, who had been the landlords for generations. Benevolent and philanthropic, the family traced its descent from the Gurus and was much revered in the region. Their house, built in the nature of a homestead, was located on the outer fringes of the village, in the middle of lush green fields. Everyone knew everyone, and made everyone's business their own. On her infrequent visits to the village, to her only friend's house, there would be much bowing and calls of 'bibaji', from the small shops lining the only paved road. Obsequiousness did not make her uncomfortable, she had grown up with it. It was the invasion of her privacy, the constant prying eyes of her brother, and later of her bhabhi as well, that she resented. And her widowed aunt, her father's sister, who had come to live with them after their parents' death nearly fifteen years ago, although weak and ineffectual in front of her brother, nonetheless kept a hawk's eye on her movements.

As it was, she had not spent much time at home for the last several years. Packed off to an elite residential school in Lahore soon after her parents had died when she was just nine, she had spent most summer vacations at a hill station with the Christian nuns and other children like her, who either could not or did not go home. Her brother would come to pick her up during the Christmas holidays, and that one month would sometimes be the only time she spent with her family.

Family; she had often pondered over the word. Did it mean her aunt and brother whom she seldom met, or the British children she spent most of the year with? Her brother was very proud of the fact that she was one of the few Indian girls at the school, and reminded her of it whenever she expressed a desire to leave. So, family for many years had meant only Isabella, the Swedish nun who taught them English, and was also in charge of their dormitory. Kind and gentle, she was the recipient of all Harjeet's childish fears and teenage longings. Isabella, with the twinkling blue eyes, who promised to pray for her before every test, and who lit a candle with her in the chapel whenever she was upset.

But now suddenly, the word family had expanded to include her husband, his parents and siblings plus an assortment of aunts and uncles. Although it had seemed strange at first, she had gradually got used to being part of such a large group. And to give them due credit, it had not been that difficult at all.

Forward looking and liberal minded, her father-in-law was a very active member of the Arya Samaj, and eschewed ritualism of any sort, often in the face of stiff opposition from his more conservative wife. Belonging to a prominent Khatri Malhotra family of Lahore, Justice Lal Chand or Lalaji, as he was popularly called, had resigned from his post as Judge at the High Court over a disagreement with his senior, and now ran a very successful law firm, which Gautam had joined after finishing his studies. Lalaji was the first member of his family to have become an Arya Samaji, introduced while still in college, to the Hindu reform movement that swept through the Punjab, attracting to its fold a large number of Khatris and the more prosperous members of the trading classes. The Samaj had been founded by Dayanand Saraswati in 1875, and in its ethos of social reform Lalaji found a reflection of his own beliefs, becoming a great advocate of women's education and widow remarriage, and a patron of the Dayanand Anglo Vedic colleges and schools set up by the organisation, to which he gave monetary support. But the Arya Samaj did not confine itself only to reform and welfare activities; it very vigorously encouraged nationalism and a larger Indian identity, and it was through association with the Samaj that Lalaji discovered his political leanings, and like many other Samajis, joined the Punjab Congress. Over time the Congress and the Samaj became his two great passions, and whilst his son Gautam inherited his intense nationalism, he was ambivalent about the Samaj, having been somewhat influenced by his deeply Sanatan Dharami mother.

Lalaji's patriotism was not confined to any one faction or organization, and although personally favouring the moderate group or Naram Dal within the Congress party, he was nevertheless shattered when a leader of the opposing or extremist faction, Lala Lajpat Rai, a personal friend of his, died in November of the previous year, beaten with lathis while leading a peaceful protest against the Simon Commission. Lalaji, always in favour of non-violent means of demonstration, was not part of the procession, but many of his friends were, and for days afterwards this was the only topic of discussion in their house, which had somehow attained the status of permanent meeting place for such gatherings. The Simon Commission, comprising of a group of British Members of Parliament, who had been sent to suggest further constitutional reforms needed for India, faced strong opposition right from the start because it had no Indian as a member.

Such was the anger at the British administration that even Harjeet's mother-in-law, normally prone to disapprove of these meetings, now showed her support through an endless stream of hot tea and snacks, made by their excellent cook Bachhu, who also for once did not complain about how overworked he was. The fact that the government disowned any responsibility for Lajpat Rai's death fuelled further heated discussions, resulting in these meetings continuing well into the new year. Harjeet particularly recalled that day towards the end of the year, when two young nationalists who had been part of the procession, killed J. P. Saunders, probably mistaking him for Scott, who it was rumoured, was the one who had personally beaten Lajpat Rai. It was a period of much drama and whispered speculation, and it seemed as though the entire house had been taken over by her father-in-law's friends. Every hour brought a tonga to stop at their gate, from which would alight a white kurta-pyjama clad man of distinguished age.

It was during this period that Rukmini, her best friend and biggest support in Lahore, motivated her to join the All India Women's Conference, which had been started two years previously by Sarojini Naidu, Annie Besant and Margaret Cousins, all very active social reformers.

'Women like you and me are needed by the organisation, Jeeto,' Rukmini had said. 'We need to think beyond our own selves. Besides, it will give you a chance to get out of the house more.'

Rukmini, belonging to a prominent family of Amritsar, where her parents still lived in their sprawling ancestral bungalow, had been with her at school, and later at Kinnaird College. Their lives had followed an almost amazingly parallel course, with both of them getting married within an year of each other, and even having children at the same time, a boy and a girl each, although Harjeet had an older girl and Rukmini an older boy. But there the similarity ended; Ruku was much in love with her dashing banker husband, who had further polished up his charm in London, from where he had started his career. Gautam had also done his bar-at-law from London, but had not been able to imbibe any of the suaveness that the city had bestowed on Ranjeet. The only lasting habit he had picked up was smoking, and now could not do without his two packets of Rothmans a day. He had hated England, finding the weather cold and the people even colder, and had returned to

India immediately on finishing his education, not even stopping to spend some days at Devon with his older half-brother and his English wife.

Lalaji had been initially very distressed when his eldest child, Krishan—born from his first wife—who had gone to England to finish his studies, had ended up marrying Kate, a farmer's daughter, who was a part-time librarian at the college. Gradually however, the progressive and liberal side of his nature took over, and the process of forgiveness and acceptance was complete after the birth of his first grand-child, a girl whom he named Gauri after his first wife. Now, his second wife took great pride in showing off her British daughter-in-law, and on the one occasion that Harjeet had met her, she had seemed a very pleasant person. Not that it stopped her mother-in-law from talking derogatorily about her behind her back and taunting Lalaji about his eldest son.

'How could Krishan do this to us in our old age? Did I not love him like my own son, looking after his every need and nursing him when he was sick? How could he have married a firangi, and become a ghar jamai?' she would say, referring to the fact that Krishan and his wife had shifted to be with her mother in Devon upon her father's death shortly after their marriage.

But Gautam had not disappointed his parents, marrying the girl they chose for him without questioning. She was beautiful, tall and slim, with green flecked brown eyes and skin like porcelain, the right companion for the son of such a distinguished family. Well educated at an elite school, but with sufficient traditional values, she could be shown off both at British gatherings and at family weddings. The only jarring note was that she had aspirations of her own, different from those of her mother-in-law, and even of her sister-in-law Kunti, who was only a few years older than her. Kunti was already married, with a baby, by the time Harjeet had come into the family, and was in many ways the perfect daughter-in-law. Always impeccably turned out in French chiffons and diamonds, she was happy looking after her husband's family, giving instructions to the cook, hosting parties and constantly redecorating her in-laws' palatial home in Patiala. She was the one, who on one of her frequent visits to the Continent, had discovered French chiffons, Belgian crystal and Lalique glassware in the Art Deco style.

Harjeet did not like her, and always felt like the poor country cousin in her presence. Even the Cartier bracelet gifted by her to Harjeet on her wedding day seemed to Harjeet to smack of a desire to show her down. 'Oh, Harjeet, I do hope you like it. While crossing the Bond Street, I saw it in the shop window, and just had to buy it for my brother's new bride. Since he doesn't like travelling, I don't know when you will be able to visit London yourself.' Harjeet was furious, although in the nervousness of being a new bride, she just nodded politely. How dare Kunti be so condescending? She did not even like the bracelet, with its rubies set too far apart for her liking. Her own jewellery was far more ostentatious and intricate. The emerald necklace with matching earrings that she had worn for her engagement was a masterpiece of craftsmanship, and she had received many compliments on the way the stones brought out the green flecks in her eyes.

Her brother had certainly spared no expense for her wedding. Her salwar kameezes and churidar kurtas were made of the finest silks and brocades, richly embroidered with *zardosi* work and edged with *gota*. Sarees of the flimsiest chiffons and heavy silks glowed jewel like whenever she moved. Each piece of jewellery had a story to tell. Most had belonged to her mother, who had a special fondness for rubies, while others had been made to order by the family goldsmith, whom many believed to be the finest craftsman in the region. Even her *juttis*, the traditional footwear worn by Punjabi women of her class, were specially made for her and embroidered with threads of real silver and gold.

Besides, what did she care about Kunti? She was far prettier and better educated than her. Standing nearly as tall as Gautam, she was almost a head taller than Kunti. Both Gautam and Kunti had inherited their mother's height, but thankfully, their father's facial structure. Lalaji was fair skinned and sharp featured in contrast to his duskier and more petite second wife. His first wife had been a handsome woman, and his elder son Krishan had inherited her good looks.

Savitri was Lalaji's second wife, the first having died while giving birth to her second child, a baby boy. As soon as the ritualistic thirteen days of mourning were over, talk had started about getting him married again. After all, for how long would his old mother look after the baby? Lalaji had protested strongly; he had loved his wife and was not ready to let anyone else take her place. And he was appalled when he learnt of the prospective bride—his wife's younger sister, more than fourteen years his junior.

'This is child marriage', he had thundered, greatly disturbed by this violation of his personal beliefs, influenced largely by the Arya Samaj. But his mother, made of sterner stuff, had persevered.

'She will love her sister's children and will not discriminate against them when she has her own. Do you want your sons to grow up unloved by their mother?'

However, in the end, when all her pleading and cajoling failed, she resorted to her master plan of giving up food and water, and going on a fast unto death. By the evening of that day, a suitable date for a low key marriage had been agreed upon, and exactly six months later, Lalaji and Savitri became man and wife. Savitri had proved to be a good wife and mother, and had indeed loved her sister's children like her own. Unfortunately, the younger boy died of smallpox when he was only two years old. But having been married at such a young age to a man much older in years and experience, Savitri never got over her father fixation with him, becoming over time, very demanding and highly strung. Used to having her every whim pandered to by a husband who looked upon her as a child, barely ten years older than his first born, she lacked the maturity of most women her age. She was also of a very nervous and delicate disposition, although Harjeet was secretly convinced that half the time when she took to bed with one of her headaches, which she had started doing with increasing frequency, she was just trying to elicit Lalaji's sympathy.

Such weakness, and the playing up of it was totally alien to

Harjeet. Although herself lonely for as long as she could remember, she had mastered the art of keeping her thoughts to herself and presenting an indifferent façade to the world. Such was her skill at hiding her feelings, and so impregnable was the wall that she had built around herself, that often no one, not even Rukmini, would know what she was thinking. Her sharp tongue and brusque behaviour further reinforced her aloof demeanour.

Perhaps if her marriage had been a more fulfilling one, she might have been lured into letting her guard down. Sometimes, sitting alone in her room and brooding, she wondered what it would be like to be totally, passionately in love with someone, to feel the intensity of emotion that she had only read about so far. Maybe she would never know, and would be doomed to die with this vague feeling of restlessness that she had lived with for so long. Lonely in death as in life, she thought despondently, turning to look at the first rays of the sun skimming the top of the tallest trees lining the leafy avenue outside. Time to start the day.

Chapter 2

A couple of hours later, Harjeet had bathed, got Maya and Inder ready and woken up Gautam, who liked to sleep in late on holidays. They had been invited for afternoon tea by Rukmini and her husband, and she welcomed the thought of getting out of the house for a few hours. Wearing a beautiful turquoise and yellow salwar kameez, with a gold edged yellow *dupatta*, and matching glass bangles, a set of which she was carrying for her friend as well, she knew she looked beautiful and was mildly disappointed when Gautam said nothing about her appearance. Never mind, she thought to herself, meeting Rukmini would cheer her up and maybe she would try her hand at flying a kite, something she had never done, initially because of boarding school and now because of the watchful eyes of her mother-in-law. Although the atmosphere at home was a liberal one, and her in-laws prided themselves on being open minded about their expectations from her, there was an unwritten code, a *Laxman Rekha* that could not be crossed. She was expected to adhere to prescribed norms regarding the behaviour of a daughter-in-law, but having spent several years in a school with British children, and having imbibed a great deal of their way of thinking, she often chaffed at these restrictions.

The morning passed in a flurry of activity, with the entire family making several trips to the roof top to see the hundreds of kites flying overhead. Shouts of triumph, followed by collective groans of disappointment, the withdrawl of smaller players with the arrival of the masters with their specially crafted kites, the gradual fluttering down of kites dismembered from their strings, as against the sudden nose dive of those entangled with the opponent's; the almost universal uniform of yellow *dupattas* and *pagris* that looked like a sea of gold set against a technicolour sky; this kaleidoscope of sights and sounds never ceased to amaze Harjeet. Basant in Lahore was like nowhere else, and she was soon caught up in its infectious excitement. After a hurried lunch of sweet saffron rice and yellow halwa, their private buggy was called for, and the five of them, including Basanti, the children's *aya,* left for Rukmini's house. The plush padded seats and the collapsible roof of the buggy, which had been folded back to let them enjoy the balmy February afternoon, coupled with the rhythmic clatter of horse hoofs on the road, almost lulled Harjeet into a doze, but they had only a short distance to cover and soon Rukmini's house, located nearby on Jail Road, came into view.

Rukmini and Ranjeet were waiting for them in a sunny corner of the verandah in front of their house, along with some other guests Harjeet had never met before. 'Jeeto, Gautam, meet our friends Saroj and Subu, who have come from Madras, and Haider, who has recently shifted to Lahore to teach mathematics at the McLeagan Engineering College. Haider was with Ranjeet in school and is a very dear friend, as are Subu and Saroj.'

After the customary greetings and handshakes were over, tea was served in dainty white china cups, accompanied by platters of sandwiches and traditional mithais. All through the desultory conversation with Saroj and Rukmini, Harjeet kept getting more and more restless, until she finally got up and announced her intention of going to the terrace to see the kites. Rukmini, torn between her desire to accompany her friend, and her duty as a good hostess, gave her a pained, accusing look.

'Saroj has a headache and does not want to go to the roof again. She is not used to the cold air.'

'That's alright, I can go alone you know. I'm a big girl now', joked Harjeet.

'I'll come with you', said Haider suddenly. 'I love flying kites myself'.

Harjeet gave Gautam an uncertain look, but he immediately put her at ease.

'Go on', he said adjusting the round glasses he always wore, 'and maybe you can even try your hand at flying a kite yourself. I know how keen you are to do that.'

It was a glorious afternoon, timeless and mellow, the canvas of the sky splattered with flashy colour; blue interspersed with the white of cotton candy clouds and the red, yellow and green of kites, as if a child had carelessly squirted entire tubes of paint onto a pristine surface. Last night's storm had left the afternoon colder than usual and a brisk breeze played with her hair, pushing rebel tendrils across her face. Forcing them back, she noticed Haider watching her intently.

'Let me teach you to fly a kite', he said.

Picking up a red and white kite from a small pile lying in one corner of the terrace, he thrust it into her hand and moved to a distance with the *pinnab* around which the cord was wrapped.

'Hold the kite loosely, give it an upward lift and let it go', he instructed.

Harjeet did as she was told, and the kite began to rise, ascending higher and higher in the sky.

'Now you hold the *doree*, and try to balance the kite. The trick is to let it flow in harmony with the direction of the wind.' Saying that, Haider handed the *pinnab* to her, and giving the kite an skyward lift, let it go. It immediately crashed and fell to the ground.

'Nothing worthwhile ever comes easy,' he joked, 'try again.'

Harjeet did try, but it seemed like a daunting task, and it was only after several attempts, that she finally managed to get the kite to fly at a somewhat respectable height.

'Well done', said Haider, coming in behind her and holding the *doree* from just above her hands.

'No, don't let go,' he said, sensing her moving away. 'Feel the way I turn the string to catch the wind and make the kite fly higher. It's a good thing it has not been much armoured with glass or you would have cut your hands.'

Catching a gust of wind, the kite gave a sudden tug, and started climbing higher and higher, magically transforming into a living, pulsating being in her hands. Filled with exhilaration, she watched it mingle with the clouds, become one with the sea of vibrating, tugging, swooping colour. It was no longer about the kite alone, she was the one flying free, high above every restriction, tasting and smelling weightlessness, floating in a sky of happiness.

If only life could always be like this, full of promise and afloat with dreams. She would remember this day forever, the mellow winter sun, the softly caressing breeze, the feeling of joy in her heart after so long. And most of all, the kites of basant, fluttering like butterflies over a field full of flowers, transforming a mundane rooftop into an enchanted place.

Gradually she became aware of other sensations, and of the man standing so close to her. Turning, she looked at him properly for the first time. Tall and fair, he was quite good looking, with brown eyes and hair and a deeply cleft chin. He was dressed smartly in a blue collared shirt and tan trousers, and she guessed him to be in his late thirties or early forties, and was suddenly curious about him. Where was he from, was he married, did he have children? Appalled at the direction her thoughts were taking, she lowered her gaze before thanking him.

'Thank you Mr Haider, for teaching me to fly a kite. I have been wanting to do so for years.'

'No need for the "Mr". Haider will do. Why did you take so long to do what your heart desired?' he asked, as if knowing instinctively what the experience had meant to her.

She turned away without answering, and said instead, 'we should be going back downstairs. The others will be waiting for us.'

The rest of the afternoon passed quickly, and it was soon time for them to leave. On the way back, Gautam was in an unusually talkative mood. He had been discussing the latest political developments with Ranjeet, and as usual, that had energised him. Bhagat Singh and Rajguru, the two nationalists who had killed J. P. Saunders, had escaped to Calcutta under disguise towards the end of December, followed shortly by Chandrashekhar Azad, who had fled to Delhi. There was much speculation about the future of the Hindustan Socialist Republican Association, of which all three were active members. Now that all of them had escaped, and were probably in touch with other members of the Association, they would have ample time to regroup and plan future protests. Gautam and Ranjeet both agreed that it would not be long before news came of another encounter. 'They are true revolutionaries, and certainly don't shy away from what needs to be done', Gautam said with admiration in his voice. 'Plus they have the courage to own responsibility for their actions. Remember the pamphlet that Pitaji brought home after the shoot-out?' he asked Harjeet, referring to the posters that had been put up all over the city by the Association, accepting responsibility for the killing of Saunders. Lalaji had brought one home, much to the discomfiture of his wife, who had rebuked him strongly before tearing it up.

'Contraband material in this house makes me nervous, you know that, but still you bring this paper home. What if someone should see it with you?' she asked her husband with a pained expression.

Lalaji gave her an indulgent smile, and tried to assuage her fears.

'No one saw me with it, and anyway these posters are all over Lahore and everyone knows about them,' he said.

The ingeneous escape by the revolutionaries, and the possibility of more such incidents occouring in the future, were still being discussed at the women's club meeting that Harjeet and Rukmini attended almost a month later. The idea of starting a women's club was originally Rukmini's, who felt that it would give the ladies a chance to meet up without their husbands and have some girlie fun. But having a strong socialist leaning, she wanted the club to also become a medium of social awareness, especially regarding issues of concern to women. The Wednesday Club, as it was called, met twice a month on every second and fourth Wednesday, and within two years its strength had grown from the original four members to thirty five. The meetings were held in the homes of the members by rotation, and the host, in addition to providing a mid-morning snack, also had to teach the others a skill through demonstration. This could be cooking, sewing or any other craft.

However, this week, the host Yasmeen Inamdar, whose brother-in-law Iqbal, was a very well-known dramatist and short story writer, suggested something different. What if they enacted some scenes from his famous play 'Tasveer', which dealt with issues of female empowerment? Yasmeen had even rustled together some basic costumes for the main characters.

The idea gained immediate acceptance, and theatre became a regular feature of the Club meetings over the next few months, with every member suggesting one scene each from the works of contemporary writers. Harjeet found herself enjoying the enactments immensely, especially since she often got to play the lead role, initially because of her stunning looks, but later because she seemed to have a genuine flair for acting. It felt nice to dress up and behave like someone else, even if for a little while. She was no longer Jeeto, restless and bored; she was Radha, the abused wife of an alcoholic, or Shakina, who wanted to go to school like other girls. And, often at the end of these sessions, she would be forced to look within and count her blessings. After all, there were much worse things than having a non-communicative and dull husband.

But this sense of gratitude would last only for a couple of days, before the familiar feeling of being cloistered returned. She wanted to soar free like the kites of basant, to see how high she could fly, even if it meant crashing down occasionally. But her mother-in-law, the old witch, while pretending to be frail and sick, nevertheless kept track of her movements with as much dexterity as her aunt had. Her whole day was accounted for, from supervising the cooking and cleaning to looking after Maya and Inder, who were the only bright spots in her life. Thankfully, Basanti was very efficient and patient, and genuinely cared for the children. But even so, Harjeet liked to have them around her at all times. Watching them play, hearing their childish laughter, gave some purpose and meaning to her life. And, it was the only common link between Gautam and her these days.

Gautam doted on his children, and would often take them for a walk in the huge garden, pointing out the different flowers and birds to them. He would also indulge them by buying them a toy each, almost every week. But Harjeet, in her usual cynical way, would wonder at this love, which was not willing to put itself out for the object of its affection. Did he not sleep in a separate room every night, just because he felt that they might disturb him? Didn't he ever want to cuddle their small, warm bodies before sleeping, and inhale the baby fragrance of their breath? And what about the way he treated her, the mother of his children. Did he think she enjoyed his brief, twice-a-week visits to her bed at night?

No, she didn't. His quiet, timid ways were not manly enough for her and seldom gave her any physical satisfaction. She did not like the way he dressed either, always in white starched pyjamas paired with boring long coats. At her insistence, he had agreed to wear shorter coats and had even got himself a couple of trousers and collared shirts stitched from Ranken, the famous drapers. On his birthday last year, she had got a suit made for him in the finest material she could find, and much preferred his wearing it to the achkans he normally favoured. Even his beautiful pocket Rolex looked better with such clothes. And his glasses were wrong for his face, round on round, making him appear more rotund than he actually was. Physical appearance apart, she did not like the way he never argued with his parents, never took her side against his devious mother, never said no to anyone. The conversations they had were always about him, his work, the cases he handled, his highs and lows. Never did he think about her, her needs and desires. The only time he would be free of his pompous, stuffed expression was while discussing the latest political situation, like today, when since the morning, he had been in an animated discussion with her father-in-law and his friends over the bombs thrown in the Central Assembly by two revolutionaries.

Although, the incident had taken place on the 8 April, almost a week ago, the arrival yesterday of Madan, one of Gautam's friends, who had been present in the Assembly that day, had rekindled already simmering passions, and as usual their house had become the rallying point for such discussions. The High Court was located nearby, and all day, there had been a steady stream of Lalaji's friends and colleagues, who wanted to hear the account first-hand. The two Bills which were to be passed that day, The Trade Disputes Bill and the Public Safety Bill, had already generated much public resentment, and before the result of the former could be announced, there was an explosion in the Assembly. The amazing part, explained Madan, was that the two revolutionaries, Bhagat Singh and B. K. Dutt, made no attempt to run away. After raising slogans and throwing pamphlets in the Assembly, they stood their ground while Sergeant Tracy and his colleague arrested them. They insisted that the bombs they had thrown at Sir Chester, were not with the intention to kill, but to make the British Government listen to the voice of the people. Madan claimed that throughout the ensuing chaos, and rush to leave the hall, he saw many prominent persons like Motilal Nehru, Madan Mohan Malviya and Mohammad Jinnah remain calmly seated at their places.

The discussion then veered towards the outcome of this act, with the various possibilities being hotly debated. Harjeet attributed this habit of her father-in-law and her husband of discussing things threadbare and at length, to their being lawyers. Although these concerns were shared by her brother as well, the discussions were never as animated or as passionate in the village. Maybe it had something to do with bigger towns, and especially with Lahore, where the very air seemed to be thought-provoking and intellectual. Every major newspaper, like the *Tribune* and *Milap* carried big news items and editorials criticising the bills and glorifying the revolutionaries. And even though Lalaji was personally not in favour of the violent means being adopted by the revolutionaries, he helped the chief reporter of the *Pratap*, an influential Hindi newspaper that had faced government displeasure several times, to write the main report regarding the incident, inspite of strong protests by his wife.

'Why do you want to get involved with controversial issues? What if someone should find out that you helped with the legal aspects of the write-up?' she asked.

'I have to be true to what I believe in. And, anyway every

single person in Lahore is angry and involved. Will the British Government catch all of us?' answered Lalaji, fanning himself with the offending newspaper.

The weather had gradually become very warm, with April signalling the beginning of the uncomfortably hot months. Although it was not yet May, Savitri had already got the bamboo-chicks enclosing the back verandah replaced, in spite of her husband protesting that they were in a perfectly good condition, and could easily last for another couple of summers. The thick blue chicks made the verandah pleasant, even during the midday heat, making it the favoured spot for both lunch and dinner all through the scorching summer months. While the chicks were being replaced, a ramshackle nest that a pair of pretty pink doves had painstakingly made on top of the rolled up portion—which made a convenient platform about five inches broad—came tumbling down. It was the same story every summer. As soon as the chicks were rolled down, one nest was sure to break, sometimes with two white eggs still in it.

Harjeet found herself thinking about the doves, and wondering whether they were tenacious beyond the call of duty, or just plain stupid. From her room upstairs, and while walking in the garden during the morning hours, she would see the birds pick up twigs and stalks of grass one by one to build their home, and while most of their attempts at rearing a family in the verandah were successful during the winter months, this was seldom the case from March onwards, when the chicks had to be rolled down. The almost habitual breaking of their nest might have put off many from trying to rebuild another at the same place again, but not the doves. Harjeet liked to think that it was strength of character that made them try again and again in the face of adversity. However, when she mentioned this to Gautam, he looked at her blankly for a minute, before muttering something about doves being bird-brained. It seemed to Harjeet, from the manner in which he looked at her, that the remark was not just directed at the birds. Why was he always so pompous and unimaginative? Never could she enjoy a lighter moment with him.

Rukmini, on the other hand, was always bubbly and full of life, so when she proposed a trip to Anarkali, the biggest bazaar in Lahore, Harjeet readily agreed. She loved Anarkali, and never missed an opportunity to be part of its delightful liveliness, even though such occasions were far less frequent than she would have liked. Her mother-in-law, like her aunt before her, disapproved of frequent visits to bazaars, and much preferred having the goods brought home. All through her growing years, right upto the time she got married, her aunt had insisted that she send a measurement of her foot, outlined on a piece of paper, to the shoe shops, rather than visit them personally. Her mother-in-law had also tried to enforce the same rule, but Harjeet had objected strongly. When Hillary, who was with her in school, could work in a senior capacity at a famous shoe store on Regent Street, could she not even visit one?

Her mother-in-law gave in to this uncharacteristic display of defiance, and the issue was not raised again openly. But the silent disapproval and the sullen glances continued whenever she planned a trip to the market. Harjeet blamed Gautam for this and was convinced that her mother-in-law would have been more considerate of her wishes, if she knew that her son also desired the same. Since Gautam left her to fight her own battles, neither did his agreeing with her stance later when they were alone assuage her feelings, nor did the fact that he also did not side with his mother give her any comfort.

Since the days had become very warm, Harjeet and Rukmini left for Anarkali in the early evening, and as soon as their buggy entered through the Lohari Gate, they were greeted by the heady fragrance of summer flowers. Vendors selling mogra, jasmine and rose petals lined the narrow road on both sides, alongside fruit sellers with their brightly coloured wares heaped precariously in huge baskets. A young man, crouched low in front of a flower seller, painstakingly picking out the freshest blooms, filled Harjeet with a momentary pang. Who was he buying the flowers for? Would he weave them through her hair at night?

Brushing aside such thoughts, she turned to Rukmini and asked, 'in the excitement of coming to Anarkali, I didn't even ask you the reason for this visit. I personally don't have anything much to buy, but since we are here, I'll pick up some clothes for Maya, and some groceries from Kwatra's.'

'Remember the play we are staging for the September meeting of the Wednesday Club, the one in which the husbands are also invited? The costumes are being designed by Shaukat, the author himself, and he wants us to buy the cloth from Karachi Cloth House', Rukmini replied.

'Do you have a list of all the stuff you need, the exact measurements and colours, or will we have to come back again like last time?' asked Harjeet jokingly, referring to Rukmini's habit of often forgetting what she had set out to buy.

'There will be no confusion this time. Remember Haider, whom you met at my house? He is the younger brother of Shaukat, and is very involved with the entire production. He will be meeting us at the shop in a while,' said Rukmini.

Harjeet felt an unexpected current of excitement run through her body at these words. Of course she remembered Haider, he was inextricably linked with the magic of Basant Panchami this year. But she had forgotten how tall he was. As their buggy stopped outside the cloth shop, he came out to help them get off. Again Harjeet was struck by his good looks, especially his warm brown eyes. Must be some Pathan blood in him she thought, that had given him the height and the light eyes.

Rukmini's voice calling her name brought her back to the present, and realising that she had been staring at Haider, she blushed and lowered her gaze before answering his greeting. But all the while that Rukmini was choosing the cloth, Harjeet was distracted and intensely aware of him sitting next to her. As the shopkeeper proudly showed off his large collection of brocades, voiles, chiffons and georgettes, her eye was caught by a beautiful embroidered dupatta. It was baby pink in colour, and had silver and gold gota work on the edges.

'Sorry Madam, this is not for sale. This is a sample piece we have just received from our workmen in Karachi,' the shopkeeper replied to her query about its price.

'That's all right, I was just asking,' said Harjeet, slightly disappointed.

After having chosen what seemed to Harjeet to be metres and metres of cloth, it was decided that while the shopkeeper got it all packed, the two of them would finish the rest of their shopping at the bazaar. Leaving their buggy behind, they walked some distance before entering a big general merchant's shop, from where Harjeet bought some toiletries, including a new face cream that promised miracles, and some general groceries. Just then she noticed a fortune teller, a *najumi*, sitting with a parrot on the pavement outside the shop. As soon as the door to it's cage was opened, the parrot would hop across and, with it's beak, pick out a card from a pile lying in front of him. Feeling restless, Harjeet had a sudden urge to have the parrot pick out a card for her as well, but when she mentioned this to Rukmini, the latter glared at her before saying a stern no.

'What's the matter with you today, Jeeto. You didn't pay any attention at the cloth shop, and now you want your fortune told by a charlatan' she grumbled.

Harjeet simply smiled and shook her head. 'I just wanted to know what the future holds. Anyway, it's getting late. Let's get back to the cloth shop.'

At the shop, all the cloth had been neatly tied into bundles and put into their buggy, and after Rukmini had settled the bill and they were about to depart, Haider came out holding a packet which he thrust into Harjeet's hands. Before she could say anything, he spoke, 'I don't want you to wait that long for anything you desire ever again,' alluding indirectly to their conversation at Rukmini's house on Basant. Harjeet was surprised and started protesting, but Haider signalled to the buggy driver to move, and before she could complete her sentence and hand the packet back to him, they were on their way.

'What's all this about, Jeeto. What have you been up to?'

demanded Rukmini immediately.

'I don't know myself. I don't even know what's in the packet,' argued Jeeto, just as confused.

'Then give it here and let me see,' said Rukmini, taking the packet from her hands. 'Why, it's the pink dupatta you were admiring. Is there anything going on between the two of you, have you been meeting him?' she asked agitatedly.

'No nothing at all, Ruku, I swear. Trust me. This is the first time I have met him since that day at your house,' replied Harjeet.

'Well maybe we are reading more into it than really exists,' conceded Rukmini. 'But you better be careful around him. And don't tell Gautam about this at all. He won't understand'.

On reaching home, Harjeet hurriedly put the packet away, before going downstairs and attending to the dinner. But after everyone had retired to their rooms, and Maya and Inder had slept, she took out the dupatta, and opening it, draped it around her shoulders. In all her memory, this was the first time anyone had done something like this for her. Although Gautam was very kind, and never refused her anything, he had never given a thought to what she really wanted. Almost nobody, she realised with a start, had ever asked for her preferences, whether it was for mundane things like deciding the menu for lunch, or more serious issues like marriage. Why then had a complete stranger, someone she had met only twice in her life, shown such concern for her? Absently fingering the dupatta, which seemed to have taken on an almost ethereal glimmer, she thought of Haider, and felt a warm glow in her heart. It was nice to have someone caring about her after so long. But almost immediately she felt a pang of guilt. What was she thinking? She was a married woman with two children, and Haider had probably just felt sorry for her. And he was a Muslim. Although both her father-in-law and Gautam had a large number of Muslim friends, after a series of events concerning Hindus and Muslims earlier this year in Bombay and in parts of Punjab, Lalaji had asked them to be more careful in their speech around them.

These thoughts kept her awake most of the night, and in the

morning, restless and guilty, she decided to return the dupatta. Next week, the Wednesday Club was to be held at Rukmini's house. She would reach slightly early, and leave the packet with her to return to Haider whenever she met him next.

On Wednesday, she got ready before time, and leaving the children with her mother-in-law, left for Rukmini's house. She usually liked to take Maya along whenever she visited Rukmini, because the latter's two children, an older boy and younger girl, were almost of the same age. But today she was in a pensive mood, and didn't think she could deal with childish prattle. 'You're looking very pretty and fresh today, Jeeto', Rukmini greeted her, complimenting her on the light pink and silver churidar kurta she was wearing, with matching silver jootis and long pearl and ruby earrings. Her hair she had tied in a loose bun with a rose tucked into one side.

'But I don't feel pretty or fresh at all. Listen Ruku, I have brought the dupatta with me, and I want you to return it to Haider,' she said.

'You can return it yourself. Haider has come to deliver the costumes and to help with the dialogues for the September play,' Rukmini replied.

'I didn't know he was also interested in drama, like his brother. Anyway, I don't want to talk to him. You return it,' said Harjeet.

'Why don't you want to talk to me, Jeeto?' a voice asked from the door, and turning she saw Haider standing there. How long had he been there, listening to their conversation, Harjeet wondered.

'You know it's rude to eavesdrop on the conversation of others. Anyway now that you are here, I'll return the dupatta myself. I don't accept gifts from strangers', replied Harjeet, annoyed.

'I'm not a stranger', said Haider, giving her an intense look. 'I want you to consider me to be your friend, like I am Rukmini's', he added as an afterthought.

Another lady walked in right then, preventing Harjeet from replying, which was just as well, she thought, as she was at a loss for words. Put that way, the gift seemed harmless enough. Maybe she really was reading more into the incident than was called for.

The rehearsals were over quickly, and over the delicious mid-morning snack of sandwiches and samosas with mint chutney, it was decided that the next meeting would be held in the last week of July, after the annual summer break of two months, during which time, many ladies shifted with their children to the cooler environs of the hills. Harjeet and Rukmini, along with their husbands and children and the former's mother-in-law, had gone to Srinagar for the summer last year. Although Gautam and Ranjeet had returned after a week, the women had spent nearly two months in a beautiful house boat on the Dal Lake. To ensure that their stay was a comfortable one, they were accompanied by a retinue of cooks, maids and nannies.

This year it was resolved that they would spend the two summer months in Mussoorie, a hill station near Dehra Dun. There was a very convenient train from Haridwar to Dehra Dun, from where Mussoorie was only twenty-one miles uphill. However, Savitri who had felt cold and uncomfortable throughout her stay in Srinagar, had decided against going with them. Lahore, hot as it would get, would be much better than a damp, spooky hill station. Harjeet was relieved at this news. She would be able to put her feet up and relax without her mother-in-law breathing down her neck, and since Basanti as well as Rukmini's maid would be accompanying them, the children would have someone to keep an eye on them.

Although initially, both Gautam and Ranjeet were to accompany them, a few days prior to their departure, Gautam decided to stay back to hear Bhagat Singh and B. K. Dutt's statements at the Sessions Court in Delhi where their trial had been going on since the first week of May. 'You know how keen I am to accompany you and the children, Jeeto. But Madan will be returning to Delhi tomorrow, and he knows someone at the Sessions Court who has promised to get us the most vantageous seats to hear the proceedings from. I'll join you later during the month.' Harjeet felt a twinge of disappointment at his words. How like him to always put his work, his own interests before that of his family, and even though his company was not particularly scintillating, she would have liked him to have accompanied them and helped them settle in. Moreover, she would feel like an intruder between Rukmini and Ranjeet, especially since the latter, who was probably as interested in the court proceedings as Gautam, had chosen to leave work and spend time with his wife and children instead.

'We can wait for you for a few days if you want,' said Jeeto.

'No you carry on. Anyway you are already late. The *chhota barsat* will start anyday now', replied Gautam, referring to the pre-monsoon rains that would hit Mussoorie in the first week of June, making the roads slippery and occasionally dangerous.

Chapter 3

Gautam was right about the chhota barsat. The rains started the very evening they reached, enveloping the mountains in a cloak of mist. They had rented a cottage in Oak Grove Estate, near Camel's Back, owned by Edward and Emily Woodin, a British couple who taught Western dance during the summer months. The cottage, which was originally built as an annexe, had a lovely wooden floor and a sloping tin roof covered in red tiles. It had three rooms, along with a living room and a cosy kitchen. Harjeet felt at home almost immediately, and unlike Rukmini, didn't mind the rain, loving the wind-swept hillside, and the pitter-patter of raindrops on the roof.

On the evening of the second day, she decided to go for a walk, both for some fresh air and to give Rukmini some time alone with her husband. She knew how much they liked being in each other's company, although out of consideration for her, Rukmini had not left her alone for a minute of the two days they had been there. Picking up her umbrella because of the slight drizzle, she let herself out of the front door, closing it softly behind her. The cottage was set slightly back from the main entrance to the estate, which was located right on the road. Turning left from the gate, she continued along the road, the umbrella giving her the feeling of being cocooned in her own private world, in the midst of, but still distant from the rain. There were a few other people on the road, and a couple of them raised a hand in greeting, her bright pink salwar kameez illuminating the drab greyness of the day. After walking some distance, she stopped near a bench, and looked back the way she had come. It would be dusk in some time, and she certainly didn't want to get lost.

'Aadab Jeeto,' said a familiar voice. Startled, she looked up to see Haider standing next to her. 'Aadab,' she replied. 'What are you doing here?'

'The same as you. I am here on holiday with my mother and sister', he answered. Not knowing what to say next, she turned to leave. What was it about this man that always left her tongue tied?

'Wait for a little while, Jeeto. Your cottage is not far from here. I'll walk you back', he said.

'How do you know where I'm staying?' she asked surprised.

'I know everything about you', he answered, but seeing her expression, added, 'I'm just joking. Ranjeet told me last week that you and Rukmini would be here for the next couple of months. I was on my way to your cottage when I saw you and stopped to say hello'.

For the first time since they had met, she noticed his voice. It was a deep smoky timbre, smooth and rugged at the same time, as though seasoned by the experience of many different worlds. It made her wonder whether every voice reflected the places and experiences the owner had lived through, but somehow his was the only one that she had ever noticed, or whether such inflection was indeed uncommon.

'It's getting dark, and I'm unfamiliar with these roads. I must be getting back', said Harjeet, turning to go. 'I'll walk you home, and meet Ranjeet as well', replied Haider, joining her.

Dusk was falling rapidly now, and as they walked through the mist that was beginning to rise up the valley, she resisted the urge to pinch herself. It all seemed so unreal. 'I wasn't entirely honest with you right now, Jeeto', said Haider suddenly. 'As I was about to reach your cottage, I saw you walking out, and followed you here.' 'Why?' asked Harjeet, with a sinking feeling in the pit of her stomach. She did not need any more complications in her life.

'Because I wanted to talk to you alone. You must know how much I like you, Jeeto. I know you are married and have a life of your own. I don't want to create any problems for you. I just want a small part in your life, and maybe someday, a small part in your heart.' Dazed, Harjeet looked up at him, and a sudden frivolous thought came to her. It was nice to have someone to look up to. Haider towered over her five feet six inches frame, unlike Gautam, who was only an inch or two taller than her.

The thought of Gautam, and then of Maya and Inder, immediately sobered her. What was she doing, letting this man talk to her like this? 'How dare you talk to me like this, Haider? I am sorry you got the impression that I am easy with my affections. It's best if we leave this matter here, outside the cottage, forever.'

They were in sight of the cottage now, and before Haider could say anything else, they heard Rukmini calling out to her. 'Jeeto,' she said agitatedly, 'where have you been, and why didn't you tell anyone where you were going? We have been so worried about you.'

'I went for a walk, and didn't realise it would get dark so quickly,' replied Harjeet.

'It's a good thing I met her on the road and walked her back', said Haider. 'I was on my way to meet Ranjeet.'

'Come on in,' said Rukmini, 'and thank you for escorting Jeeto home. I was worried that she had fallen off the cliff or been kidnapped.'

'Don't be absurd Ruku. I was perfectly alright,' replied Harjeet, as she took the children for their routine bath before they went to bed.

For the rest of the evening, and well into the night, Haider's words played in her mind. In spite of herself, she was excited and a little flattered. Lately, especially since Gautam had shifted to another room, she had begun to doubt her own attractiveness and desirability.

The next evening, Ranjeet proposed that the three of them walk down to the Stiffles Restaurant, where their British landlords taught dance during the summer months, and where it was rumoured that the food, excellent as it was, provided only a small part of the total experience of the night. Although Harjeet, wanting to give Rukmini and Ranjeet some time together, tried to get out of the program, they insisted that she accompany them. The atmosphere at the Stiffles was carnivalesque; tables spilled onto the brightly lit road, people milled around laughing and chatting, while a live band played the latest tunes. There were a number of beautifully dressed European women of indiscriminate age, whom Ranjeet referred to as 'grass widows', women whose husbands stayed on in the plains on duty, while they, along with their children, migrated to the hills, often for the entire summer season. The prettier ones among them were the cynosure of all eyes, with young and dashing men, probably on their annual break, trying to catch their attention, while men of a more advanced age, and presumably posted at Mussoorie itself, looked bored. The Indian population was out in all its finery as well, in lace sarees and expensive jewellery, and Ranjeet frequently pointed out members of the royalty from the neighbouring Punjab States to Harjeet and Rukmini.

Harjeet was dazzled. She was no newcomer to such gatherings, being a frequent visitor to the Gymkhana and the newly opened Cosmopolitan Club at Lahore, but never before had she encountered this spirit of abandon and fun. Therefore, it was in a way befitting that when her eyes met Haider's across the room, she held his gaze for a moment too long while he made his way across to her. Rukmini and Ranjeet were talking to someone they had just met, so his greeting, the smile in his warm brown eyes, was meant just for her. The music had changed to a slow, romantic melody, 'Stardust' by Hoagy Carmichael, and as many couples took to the dance floor, and Ranjeet led Rukmini lovingly by the hand, Haider turned to her with an imploring look in his eyes. Suddenly she was caught up in the gaiety of the evening. Lahore and Gautam seemed so far away. Why should she deny herself some innocent fun for a husband who had not even bothered to spend a week's holiday with her? She was as much a grass widow as any of the other women present there, and like them she was also going to enjoy herself tonight. Surely one dance would not make her an unfaithful wife.

Smiling, she accepted his outstretched hand, and at his touch a current of pure joy ran through her. It felt so right to be so close to him, to feel his body next to hers, his warm breath playing with tendrils of her hair, lifting them up, just as his nearness had lifted her spirits. She never felt like this with Gautam. Even during their most intimate moments, a part of her held back, as though she was making a distinction between oneness of body and togetherness of spirit. But not tonight. Not with Haider. As the music changed to a slower tempo, and the lights dimmed further, he pulled her closer still. Her black saree bespangled with sequins, mirrored the night sky full of twinkling stars, and the pins in her hair sparkled with every move she made. She felt lightheaded with excitement, and so when he suggested that they meet at a quiet place down the road the next evening, she simply nodded her acquiescence.

That night set the pattern for the next few weeks, with the two of them meeting every evening before dusk. Haider would bring along a thermos flask filled with tea, and over cups of the steaming hot brew she found herself telling him things she had never discussed with anyone, not even with Rukmini. It was uncanny how he knew what she was going to say even before the words had left her lips, as if he could read her mind, smell her fears, sense her highs and feel her lows. And as he told her about his life, his widowed mother, famous older brother and their life in Jhang, which was where they belonged, she felt a deep, almost spiritual connection with him that shocked her.

How could she, the ever cautious, almost caustic Jeeto feel such an affinity with someone, and that too so soon? It seemed to her that she had spent a lifetime of loneliness, living in a bleak wilderness where the only source of joy were her two children. Until she met Haider. Talking to him, hearing his deep baritone, sensing how much he cared for her, filled her with a profound sense of happiness. There was something different about him, exotic almost, that captivated her. He was a wanderer and told her tales of faraway places, of the mountains he had conquered and the rivers he had run. He told her of his love of travel and that he taught physics and mathematics at the McLeagan College only to be able to fund his excursions. His other big passion, apart from travelling was cricket, which he had been playing since his school days. In college he was part of the official team, and although he had been playing regularly since, the matches now were of a friendly nature, between clubs or at the workplace. Recently however, he had been offered a chance to play a First Class match in the Lahore tournament to be held in the last week of January, as an extra, and was delighted. Wanderlust and the desire for new experiences were also the reasons why he had never married, fearing that no woman would be able to hold his interest long enough. That was until he met Harjeet.

'Sometimes all you need is a look, Jeeto. Since I met you, I am no longer as keen to travel because that would mean leaving you. And I am not even going to attempt defining my feelings for you, because I can't. All I am saying is that it makes me happy to be with you.'

Harjeet felt warmth spreading through her body at his words, and over the days, started looking forward to their time together more and more, tucking the children in for an afternoon nap well in time and making excuses for not taking the evening tea with Rukmini. However Rukmini, astute as ever, was quick on the uptake and very disapproving, and lost no opportunity to reprimand her.

'What are you doing Jeeto? This is suicidal. What will happen if Gautam finds out?'

'If Gautam finds out what? I would do nothing wrong, you know that Ruku. But I like him, and want to give myself a chance at a friendship that might bring me some happiness,' answered Harjeet.

'That's a very weak argument for a lawyer's wife. I am afraid of the consequences of someone finding out about your meetings. This is totally wrong Jeeto, think about Gautam and the children,' said Rukmini, worried.

'I have spent my whole life thinking about others Ruku—my brother, inlaws, husband. For once, I want to think about myself,' replied Harjeet.

The two months in Mussoorie passed all too soon. Some days

Haider would take them all on a guided tour of the different places of interest around the town. A trip to Kempty Falls took up the entire day, as did the one to Happy Valley and the botanical gardens. Initially Rukmini, anxious and disapproving, refused to go anywhere with Haider, even though the proposal was originally Ranjeet's, who felt that Haider who knew Mussoorie well, would be the best person to take them around. Gradually however, she was won over by his charm and although still critical of his friendship with Harjeet, agreed to let him act as their guide.

During the late afternoon, Harjeet would meet Haider at their appointed spot, and they would walk along the Camel's Back Road towards the Church for about a mile, before turning onto a path that ran alongside a narrow gorge, in which flowed the river Aglar. This was Harjeet's favourite place in Mussoorie; the river a shimmering streak in the rays of the setting sun, with the snowy peaks of the Nag Tiba range glistening golden on the other side. It seemed to Harjeet, as she stood gazing at the river rushing along the steep gradient, that like her, it too was forced to flow within artificial limits, its spirit chaffing against the flesh. Maybe one day it would overflow its banks, and create new channels for itself. Maybe one day she would be free to walk along paths she would choose for herself.

Chapter 4

Gautam did not come at all during the two months that they were at Mussoorie, not even to pick them up. He was too involved in the Bhagat Singh case. However, when she mentioned this to Haider, he was non-judgemental as usual. 'Never mind, he must have been genuinely busy,' he said. 'I don't want us to waste our precious time together in talking about your husband, Jeeto.' Normally, Harjeet never discussed Gautam with Haider; whatever her feelings for him, he was still her husband and it did not feel right to talk about him. She also refrained from mentioning Haider in Rukmini's presence, fearing the latter's continuing disapproval. 'What you are doing is not right Jeeto,' she reprimanded Harjeet every time they met. 'Gautam is a caring husband, you have no business cheating on him like this.' But although prone to severe bouts of guilt at increasingly frequent intervals, Harjeet refused to acknowledge, even to herself, that she was being unfaithful to Gautam. Haider was just a friend, they hadn't touched each other even once, had never even held hands. Surely spending some time with a person who made you happy did not amount to infidelity.

And in any case, their meetings had become much less frequent since returning to Lahore. It was not easy to get away from the prying eyes of her mother-in-law, and she was becoming increasingly reluctant to use Rukmini as an alibi every time. The choice of venue also had to be made with great dexterity, to avoid both the elite areas of the city where she ran the risk of being recognised, and the lower class ones where she would stand out because of her attire and demeanour. Consequently she was beginning to experience a Lahore she had never seen before, the sights and sounds so different from what she was used to that it was almost like being in a different city.

Haider also started visiting their house more often, bringing with him a relative who was involved in a land dispute, and whose case Gautam had agreed to take on. Being a good friend of Ranjeet's, he was given access to the inner quarters, usually out of bounds for clients. Recently his mother had come to visit as well, with some *kalakand* she had made especially for Gautam. During these social occasions, whenever Harjeet's eyes met Haider's across the room, she felt a mixture of emotions: excitement, along with a pang of guilt. Somehow the growing familiarity between their families compounded the wrong further, making social niceties seem so farcical, and she resolved each time, to put an end to their relationship. But as the months passed she found herself unable to do so, becoming on the contrary, more and more captivated by him. They had been meeting for nearly six months now, and finally, although still refusing to acknowledge to herself that she was in love with Haider, but desperately needing someone to discuss things with, she confided to Rukmini that she liked him a lot, but promised to put an end to their meetings soon.

But that was easier said than done. Being with him was like being touched by the wind from distant lands. Exotic, fragrant, with an almost zephyr like quality, it had the power to lull her into an intoxicating stupor, where she was aware of nothing else but his presence. Of late, he had casually started to take her hand into his own, and it seemed so right, so exciting that she wondered what it would be like to be with him always. On one occasion, while sitting in a secluded corner of the Shalimar Gardens, he told her about his life and the village he belonged to.

'My forefathers belonged to Takht Hazara, by the banks of the river Chenab, the same village where Ranjha spent his childhood. There is something about the very air in the village—once we fall in love, it is for ever,' he said with an intense look in his eyes.

'But Ranjha had to leave the village before he found his true love. And anyway, it is a love story that ended in tragedy,' replied Harjeet, jokingly.

'Ranjha left Takht Hazara to find love, the same way I left to find you. He travelled to Jhang, and I to Lahore,' he said, taking her hand in his. 'And in the version of the story popular in our village, Ranjha and Heer spent the rest of their lives together, happily married.'

'But Lahore has never been lucky for lovers. Prince Salim lost Anarkali here, and Mehr-un-nisa her husband,' reminded Harjeet.

'But Jeeto, don't forget that Mehr-un-nisa found love a second time and became Noor Jehan,' replied Haider.

'Look at us quibbling over the facts of history', said Harjeet with a laugh. 'Anyway, I must be getting back now. My father-in-laws' friends are home the entire time these days to discuss the Simon Commission, and my mother-in-law gets anxious, upsetting the cook as well. Poor fellow must be getting tired of making endless cups of tea and pakoras.'

'You should stock up on Khatais and other snacks' said Haider, amused.

'We have started doing that. For the last few days, my mother-in-law has started ordering the Japani samosas from Lahori gate every evening. I love the way they flake into thin layers,' answered Harjeet.

'All this talk about food has made me hungry. I just might drop in to discuss politics one evening and to eat the samosas,' quipped Haider.

When Harjeet got home there was much excitement. The British Government, under a compromise formulated with the Congress, was to agree to the demand for Dominion Status as the basis for the new constitution, by the end of 1929. It was already the last week of December, and the Government had not yet accepted the recommendations made in the Nehru Committee Report of August last year. The Simon Commission, constituted to study constitutional reforms needed to govern India better, had been a bone of contention right from its inception in 1927, primarily because there was not a single Indian among its seven members, all of whom were from the British parliament. Wherever the Commission travelled, it was met with angry protests, and it was during one such demonstration at Lahore, that Lala Lajpat Rai had been fatally injured. The argument put forth by the British Government for not including any Indians in the Commission, was apparently the failure of the latter to reach a consensus as to what would be best for the country. This prompted the formation of a committee of the All Parties Conference, under the leadership of the Congress President, Motilal Nehru, to propose constitutional reforms. The Nehru Report, among other things, demanded that India be granted Self-Government under Dominion status within one year. Now that the year was nearly over Lalaji could talk of nothing else but the Congress Session to be convened the following day.

Next day, braving the bitterly cold weather, Lalaji, Gautam and Ranjeet, along with some other friends, left for Mochi Gate to attend the meet. It was 31 December, New Year's Eve, and Savitri waited till late to have dinner with Lalaji and Gautam, but they did not come home at all that night. Harjeet was not particularly concerned, she would have much rather spent the day with Haider. How nice it would have been if they could have ushered in the new year together. Instead, she spent the afternoon with Rukmini at her house, watching Maya and Inder play with their friends, reminding herself what a pleasure it was to see her children growing up so well. A pleasure denied to Gautam, who was as usual, too busy to even spend the last day of the year with them.

'Today is different, Jeeto, even Ranjeet is not at home. Everyone has gone for the Session,' said Rukmini, when Harjeet mentioned this to her. 'And anyway how does that matter to you,' she added accusingly. 'You have Haider to keep you company.'

Rukmini made no attempt to hide her displeasure at Harjeet's relationship with Haider, and lost no opportunity to admonish her, but such was the depth of their friendship that this had in no way impinged on their closeness.

'But to come back to the Session' continued Rukmini, 'I am very curious to know what is going on, and hope that Ranjeet doesn't miss any of the details.'

'Well, you can be sure that Gautam will stay till the very end, and will discuss every minute happening for days to come,' replied Harjeet.

And indeed, Gautam could talk of nothing else but the personal charisma of Jawaharlal Nehru—elected Congress President at the meet—as he hoisted the flag of India, the tricolour, on the banks of the river Ravi at midnight and the palpable excitement of the huge crowd consisting of Congress delegates and leaders from all political parties as well as members of the public. Passions rode high, infusing the bitterly cold night with warmth, and after the Pledge of Independence was read out, the assembled congregation was asked if they agreed with it, and it was Gautam's belief that there was not a single person who did not raise his hand in concurrence. Subsequently, in a meeting of the Congress Working Committee in January, it was decided to observe 26th of the month as Independence or Poorna Swaraj day.

26 January was also the start of the Lahore cricket tournament, in which Haider was playing for the Muslim team. This was Haider's debut First Class match, and although he was older than most of the other players, and was a last minute entrant against a player who had been injured in an accident, he was genuinely good at the game, having played local matches several times. The tournament was being held at the Lahore Gymkhana, located in Lawrence Gardens, and was to continue over three days. Harjeet, desperate to see it, but unable to explain to the family her sudden interest in the game, finally decided to seek Rukmini's help. Accordingly, Ranjeet was told of his wife's desire to see a cricket match, and being the devoted husband that he was, he personally escorted the two women to the venue. At the end of the match, Haider who had made an impressive debut of sixty-one, came to meet them, and whispered to Harjeet, 'you are lucky for me, Jeeto. I played for you, and look how well I did.' The finals of the tournament were held in February, with the Hindus and Muslims playing against each other. Haider, who had played well in the previous match, was retained in the side, and again managed an impressive score.

The tournament finished two days before basant, almost a year to the day Harjeet had met Haider for the first time. A year, during which her life had changed irrevocably; although never close to Gautam, she felt even more distant now. However, paradoxically, in an attempt to overcome her sense of guilt, she made more of an effort to talk to him about his work, and to involve herself in his life. If Gautam was surprised by this change in her attitude, he did not show it, although sometimes Harjeet caught a look of bewilderment in his eyes. At such moments, she felt almost sorry for him, even though she accepted that her feelings for Haider were now more intense than ever. She found herself wanting to be with him at all times and the days they could not meet seemed empty and meaningless. A gap of a week or more made her restless, and in a strange way, claustrophobic, and she was relieved when Gautam announced that he would be travelling to Gujrat to take part in the Salt Satyagraha.

The Satyagraha started on 12 March, with Mahatma Gandhi leading a group of followers from his ashram near Ahmedabad to Dandi, a village on the sea coast almost 400 km away, to protest against the tax imposed on salt. The Declaration of Independence read out by Jawaharlal Nehru a few months earlier had hinted at the readiness of the people to stop paying salt tax, and in continuation of that agenda it was decided by the Congress Working Committee to launch acts of non violent civil disobedience. The first such protest was the Salt Satyagraha led by Mahatma Gandhi. Under the Salt Act of 1882, the British Government had complete monopoly over the collection and manufacture of salt, and also levied a salt tax. Even those who lived along the coast had to buy it from the government. By making this issue the visible face of the Satyagraha movement, Gandhi had struck a chord with many Indians, and as he traversed the 400 km to Dandi, he was joined by an ever increasing band of followers, including leaders like Sarojini Naidu. One of Lalaji's friends, Gokul, who had accompanied the protesters from Sabarmati, but had to return a few days later due to a sudden bout of high fever, described in detail the surging crowds, the donation and food offered at every village they passed through, the village officials who resigned and joined them. They slept every night in the open, and it was probably there that he developed the infection that forced him to turn back.

Hearing his story, Gautam was also inspired to join the march. Although Mahatma Gandhi had already broken the salt laws on the morning of 6 April, almost ten days back, by raising a lump of salty mud and boiling it in sea water, the group was marching on southwards along the coast, and Gautam wanted to join them wherever he could. As on a few earlier occasions, Harjeet was surprised to see this passionate side of her usually placid husband. Maybe there were some things he felt really strongly about, and maybe it was just her luck that she was not one of them. However, her sense of relief at his going was short-lived as he was back within a few days. Gandhiji was arrested on the night of 4 May from the temporary ashram he had set up at Dandi. Gautam, who had wanted to accompany him on the proposed march to Darsana salt mines, 25 miles further south, did not want to be part of the protest without him, and returned home.

By now, summer was at its peak in Lahore, and in the cool darkness of her bedroom, shaded from the worst of the sun by chicks hung outside the windows, Harjeet spent the long sultry afternoons thinking about Haider. Every couple of days, Basanti would make a paste from the leaves of the mehandi bush, and Harjeet would apply the cooling concoction to her palms and wish Haider was there to see the rich colour staining them. Even the mehandi applied to her hands and feet in an elaborate paisley design on her wedding day had not left such an intensely dark colour. Maybe it was true that the colour of mehandi was the colour of love, and darkened according to the depth of emotions.

In the early evening, the front and back porch would be cooled by the *bhishti*, who carried water in his *mashk*, a bag made from goat skin. The fragrance of wet mud mingled with the equally heady perfume of the evening flowering mogra, and reminded Harjeet of the man she had seen buying flowers in Anarkali. She wondered how the flower sellers kept the flowers so fresh in the heat which had enveloped the city in a shimmering haze. The days were imbued with a languorous monotony in which the rhythmic tuk-tuk of the barbet, heralding the advent of summer, had been drowned by the call of the cuckoos, especially the Koel, who was at his most active during the hottest months. His call, growing shriller in an ascending pitch, would often continue till late in the evening. But it was the call of the papiha that Harjeet waited to hear the most. Its high pitched screeching call, sounding uncannily like 'pee-kahan', could be heard well into the night, especially when moonlight cast its silvery, shimmering web on the tree tops outside her room, before sneaking inside and blanketing her bed. At such times a strange longing took possession of her, making her stand by the window for hours, tracking the passage of the moon as it rose higher in the sky, going to sleep only when it was no longer visible from her room.

The mornings were not much better. The oppressive heat restricted movement during the day; the hot, dry, dust laden loo scalding her skin like the blast from a furnace the moment she stepped out, and very often the evenings would be blighted by dust storms, common during this time of the year. Ordinarily she would have taken the children to the hills for a couple of months, but Rukmini's mother was unwell, and their plans to visit Murree had to be shelved. She could have gone alone with the children and Basanti, but neither did she want to go without Rukmini, nor did Lalaji encourage it. Instead, it was decided that she would visit her brother and bhabhi for a few weeks, after which Maya would be starting school.

Harjeet was glad of the chance to get away from Lahore for a while. Of late, especially since she had sensed in Haider a desire for greater physical intimacy, her mind had been in a turmoil. Maybe putting some distance between them would help her take a better view of their relationship.

Her brother and bhabhi were very welcoming, her bhabhi unusually so. Maybe it was because she was visiting after many months, or maybe because she was learning to control her caustic tongue. She attributed this change in herself to Haider, his easy-going ways had obviously rubbed off on her as well. The slow pace of life at the homestead imbued her days with a sense of calm and added to the general feeling of restfulness. The locals, including her brother, were slow to passion, and while they were quick to respond to any perceived personal imputations, other matters left them largely untouched. This may have been why there were hardly any discussions on the national issues that were so alive in Lahore. Dandi March and its fallout seemed so far away, and unimportant in the face of local concerns. Or maybe there was something about Lahore that made great leaders and orators out of ordinary men like Lala Lajpat Rai, that gave to the country poets like Mohammad Iqbal, and motivated young men like Bhagat Singh and Rajguru to risk their lives for a cause.

However, even after a month at the homestead, in salubrious and tranquil surroundings, where the silence was broken only by the wind whistling through the crops standing in the fields, and the quiet seemed to seep into the bones, she was no closer to getting an answer. She was still torn between heart and head, between her desire to be with Haider and the long indoctrinated urge to do what was right. On her last day in the village, feeling particularly restless, she decided to take a walk through the fields, to a small seasonal stream that marked the boundary of their land towards the south. It was late afternoon, the sun had not yet set, and in the golden integrum between day and night, she was suddenly filled with a deep sense of stillness. The August sky was a riot of colours; bands of azure and lilac juxtaposed with pewter, incandescent white cotton clouds scattered around like small balls of fire, and to the west, the horizon dark with incoming rain. The culvert over the monsoon nallah was at some height, and from where she stood she could see emerald green fields of paddy stretching far into the horizon.

Suddenly it came to her, the reason for the vague restlessness that had dogged her for so many years. All her relationships, each one of them, had left her unfulfilled. Father, mother, brother, husband, none of them had been able to give her what she was searching for: her parents because of their absence from her life and the rest probably because of a disconnect between the proferred and the desired. Or maybe she wanted more than what life was willing to give, and it was time for her to wrest whatever happiness she could from its grasp. Haider made her happy, he made her want to believe that it was possible to live beyond set boundaries, just like the rain-swollen stream beneath the culvert was flowing renewed and strong after breaching its banks.

Her disquietude somewhat settled, she returned to Lahore to find a surprise in store for her. Lalaji had decided to buy a car, and there was much discussion on which would be the most suitable one. Kunti's husband had just bought a Ford model-T, but Gautam was keener on an Austin, arguing that since Ford had already launched a new model-A with an all steel body in America, there was no point in their buying the older one. Eventually they decided on a Chevrolet A B Touring, which was cheaper and simpler to run.

Harjeet was happy at the timing of the purchase. Maya had started nursery school just before the summer holidays—a private one run by two friends, Susan Jones and Kamal Bhandari. The school, small and exclusive, with classes only upto the Junior Cambridge level, was considered to be one of the best in Lahore and admission to it depended largely on parentage. Rukmini's son had joined the same school last year, while her daughter had just taken admission with Maya, so the two girls would be classmates. The car would be dropping and picking up the three children from school every day, and an efficient chauffeur was accordingly engaged.

The car generated much interest, and many of their friends, including Rukmini and Ranjeet, who planned to buy one of their own, came to see it. But for Harjeet it created a problem of a different kind. Whenever she needed to go somewhere, her mother-in-law expected her to take the car. Apart from it being an issue of social prestige and one-upmanship, it seemed to Harjeet that the old witch used it to spy on her movements. Now her meetings with Haider had to be fixed for that time of the day when the car would be busy with Lalaji or Gautam and she could go out on her own. Haider was accommodating as usual, but one afternoon when he had to rush between classes to meet her, he suggested that staging another play at the Wednesday Club would perhaps give them more opportunities to be together. Rukmini, who had been proposing the same thing ever since the success of the play they had last performed, was very enthusiastic, and wanted to go a step further and organise it under the aegis of the All India Women's Conference. The Conference had gradually extended its mandate to diverse social issues such as women's political rights and untouchability. Rukmini, sensing a growing closeness between it and the national movement, was suddenly very keen to join the Indian National Congress in order to play a more active role in the freedom struggle.

'Most of the members of the Conference are members of the Indian National Congress as well. Look how active Sarojini Naidu was at the Dandi march. Let us also join the Congress, Jeeto,' she tried to persuade her friend.

However, Harjeet was totally uninterested in doing so. Just a few days ago, Haider had told her how his elder brother Shaukat had wanted him to join the Muslim League. Shaukat, himself a poet and dramatist, was greatly influenced by Muhammad Iqbal, the charismatic philosopher and poet, who was an active member of the League. Shaukat, also a member for some years now—although a largely passive one—was much inspired after reading Iqbal's recently published *Reconstruction of Religious Thought in Islam*—a collection of six lectures he had delivered at different places in the country—and tried to convince Haider about the merits of a political revival of Islamic civilisation and thought.

'I am a devout Muslim,' Haider said to Harjeet, 'but I refuse to identify myself with any one community or religion. And how can I support the formation of an Islamic State when I know that you won't be part of it?'

Harjeet was humbled by his love. Never before had anyone made her feel so special, and she spontaneously reached up and kissed him. His face lit up with pleasure, and she finally acknowledged to herself how much she cared for him. He pulled her close and whispered in her ear, his breath caressing her cheek. 'I love you, Jeeto,' he said, cupping her face in his hands and giving her a deep kiss, arousing in her a storm of conlicting emotions; fear and excitement and desire. She had never felt this way before, had never wanted a man so desperately, and frightened by the intensity of her feelings, she found herself panicking. Resisting the urge to put her arms around him and kiss him back, she pulled away, her body trembling.

'I have been wanting to do that for a long time, Jeeto, so I'm not going to say sorry', Haider said. 'No, don't say anything,' he added before she could reply, 'unless you're going to tell me how much you love me.'

Harjeet turned away without answering, and they walked the rest of the way in silence. At home that night, lying alone in bed, she was plagued by feelings of guilt. Had she really become an adulterous wife, falling into the arms of the first man who showed her love? However, by the time the first rays of the sun were lighting up the sky outside her window, she had reasoned with herself that neither was she a woman of easy affections, nor was Haider a philanderer. Yesterday he had kissed her for the first time in nearly a year. Maybe what they shared really was special, and she would be a fool to trivialise it by thinking it commonplace.

Chapter 5

The entire summer of 1930, Gautam and Lalaji had been kept busy with the trial of the Lahore Conspiracy case, and even before Gautam told her of his father's involvement, Harjeet had guessed from the hush-hush meetings that were held in his office almost every day, that the two of them were helping draft the arguments for the revolutionaries. By now both Bhagat Singh, who was lodged in the Mianwali Jail, and B. K. Dutt, who along with several others, was in the Lahore Jail, had been on a hunger strike for some time in protest against the terrible food and general lack of amenities in the prisons, and things had got to the point where Bhagat Singh, who had been without food for more than three weeks, had to be brought on a stretcher for the start of the court proceedings. At the court of the Sessions Judge Delhi, in the first week of June, Bhagat Singh read out his statement, which although detailed, was not able to save him, when the judgement was finally delivered in October, from being sentenced to death by hanging, along with Rajguru and Sukhdev.

The whole family was saddened by the judgement. Even Harjeet, who usually kept away from political issues, was disturbed. It seemed as though the three men had become the most visible face of the revolution. Young and patriotic, they had infused the entire city with nationalistic fervour. The trial before the Special Tribunal constituted to hear the case had begun in July, and Lalaji had been apprehensive about the outcome right from the start. But once the judgement was delivered he rose to the occasion and began to talk about appealing against it to the Privy Council. It was the first time that he openly admitted to helping the revolutionaries with their legal matters. Gautam started spending even lesser time with Harjeet and the children, and would remain closeted with Lalaji and their munshi for hours together. Lalaji's lawyer friends and fellow sympathisers would be in and out of the house the whole day, and Harjeet was convinced that their house had irrevocably attained the status of being the permanent meeting place for all matters of national importance. Maybe that was why Lalaji indulged his wife so much. Other than the occasional complaint about his being busy all the time and the house always being full of guests, she left him largely undisturbed. What was more, she ensured that the guests never went back without partaking of Bachhu's delicious cooking.

Bachhu belonged to the hill state of Chamba, and was the third generation of his family to be associated with Harjeet's. His father had served at the homestead in the village, as had his father before him. His older brother was presently the cook and personal butler to her brother, and both he and her bhabhi were totally dependent on him. After marriage, Harjeet found the food at her in-laws' house to be tasteless and overcooked and not at all to her liking. Savitri, always down with some imagined illness, had left the affairs of the kitchen to a burly Parachinari, whose cooking skills were far overshadowed by his expertise as a ladies' man. Consequently, on her next visit to the village, Harjeet requested the cook to send his younger brother, who was also living at the homestead, with her to Lahore. Bachhu was excited at the thought of getting away from his brother's constantly watchful and interfering vigil, and once in Lahore, quickly made himself indispensable to the whole family. His loyalty to Harjeet was so unflinching that she had even toyed with the idea of using him to deliver messages to Haider, because with Lalaji and Gautam spending so much time at home, it was getting increasingly difficult for her to get out and meet him.

The rest of the year passed in much the same way, with Gautam busy and Harjeet restive and edgy, wishing for the umpteenth time that her husband had a job which required him to be out of the house for a fixed number of hours every day, thus giving her some time for herself. For even though he was cloistered in the office with his father and other lawyers the entire time, she could neither leave the house nor go upstairs to her room, her mother-in-law insisting that she stay close by to ensure that every guest was looked after properly.

But sadly, in spite of all the effort put in by so many peope, the three revolutionaries were hanged in March 1931. Till the end Lalaji and his friends had hoped against hope, waiting for a miracle that would save them. But the appeal to the Privy Council by the Defence Committee had been dismissed, as had the mercy petition filed by the Congress party president, Madan Mohan Malviya, before Lord Irwin in February. There was much anger in the country following their execution, and even Mahatma Gandhi, who had been requested to intervene with the Viceroy, faced black flag demonstrations outside Karachi.

This incident made Harjeet ponder over an issue that she had been thinking about a lot these days: the passions that drove men. What drove some men to risk their lives for their country, and others to test their skills against hostile snow covered peaks, to swim against the current? What was that special ingredient which distinguished men from boys, or more specifically, Haider from Gautam? Haider had a zest for life that was infectious, and since meeting him, she had noticed a gradual recasting of her world view, as if she had shifted to the window on the other side of the train and the landscape had totally changed. She had become more observant, had started noticing so many things; the wind in the trees, clouds drifting overhead, the chorus of birds at dawn. It was as if she had suddenly become more alive.

In contrast, Gautam was so staid and boring. The only thing he was interested in was his work. Father and son could sit and discuss the legal nuances of each case for hours, as they had done first during the Bhagat Singh trial and later during the appeal. But even in this, Gautam was never assertive, and Lalaji would have the final say about the way each case was to be dealt. This system seemed to be working fine though, and they had one of the largest and most successful law firms in the region, getting cases from many far flung villages of the Punjab as well. They had a fine division of labour, in which Gautam would pour over the law books, and write the arguments with the help of their very efficient munshi, which were then discussed at length with Lalaji. Gautam was also the one who usually visited the Court to hear the cases, and would even travel to Delhi for the more important ones. Lalaji spent his time meeting up with his lawyer friends, both at home and in the bar room, and it was Harjeet's suspicion that being the strong patriot that he was, he gave free legal advice to whoever asked for it, even helping to draft arguments. Gautam had hinted at this more than once, and she had also heard Savitri protesting to her husband about the possible ramifications of such actions.

But Lalaji was unfazed, and Harjeet had often heard him arguing about the latest political happenings with his British friends at the Gymkhana, although he was always careful not to let the discussions get heated. Harjeet respected him for this; at least he had the courage to say what he wanted to, unlike Gautam, who although very vociferous at home, usually kept quiet in mixed company, and in connection with this an incident from last year flashed in her mind. It was the end of September, and the evenings had become somewhat pleasant again. Some lawyer friends of Gautam had come from London for a few days, and all of them, including Ranjeet and Rukmini, had gone for dinner to the Gymkhana. Jatin Dass, an undertrial in the Lahore Conspiracy case, had died a few weeks earlier, after being on a hunger strike for more than two months. This had led to much heated discussion at home, with Gautam joining in to criticise the British Government in no uncertain terms. But when the matter was raised by Ranjeet over dinner, Gautam maintained a studied silence, leaving his father to argue with the foreigners alone, further reinforcing the impression in Harjeet's mind of his being a timid man.

Unlike Haider. Self assured Haider, who was her open blue sky, the wind rustling in the leaves, the feeling of freedom. Completely non-judgemental, he did not allow anything, not even their different religions, to create any discord between them, preferring instead to call himself a Sufi. 'Next week the Mela Chiraghan will be celebrated at Baghbanpura, near Shalimar Gardens,' he said to Harjeet on their next meeting. 'Although I would love to go there with you alone, I know it won't be possible. Why don't both you and Gautam come with me? It will take his mind off the unfortunate Bhagat Singh case and besides, Ranjeet and Rukmini will also be there.'

Mela Chiraghan, or the Festival of Lights, was celebrated each year towards the end of March, on the occasion of the Urs of the Sufi saint Shah Hussain, who had died in AD 1599. Harjeet had been wanting to visit the mela for a long time, ever since a class fellow from college had recounted in detail the almost magical feeling of devotion pervading the atmosphere for the entire three days of celebration. She had heard of the twinkling clay lamps lighting up the night, the smell of burning hashish, the heady beat of the drums which reverberated in the heart for long afterwards.

The actual experience lived up to all that she had imagined. It was a beautiful night, with the wind, stronger than usual, carrying the sound of beating drums a long way off. Closer to the mela, music of another kind, more melodious and soft, caressed the ears. People sat around mendicants, hearing them recite the Kafis written by the saint, or watched another group singing his qawwalis. Haider took them to a corner where dervishes were whirling in pure ecstasy. Harjeet was struck by their passion, their oblivion to everything else around them. A fire was burning at the shrine, into which devotees were throwing candles. Making his way through the throng of people, Haider walked up to the fire and stood very close to it, and the next time they were alone, he told her that the closer you got to the fire, the greater the chance of your prayers being answered.

'I prayed for us to be together forever, Jeeto. I don't know how to define our relationship, what name to give this thing that exists between us. All I know is that I feel incomplete without you,' he said, pulling her to him. It was the first time since the kiss that he had made a move to get close physically, and Harjeet was taken aback. From this near, she could smell his distinctive fragrance, a mixture of his aftershave—one of the fancy ones available in Anarkali—and his own special manly scent. Gautam never smelt so good, he was not fond of any toiletries and had not even used the after shave she had bought for him on their anniversary last year. Although he claimed he liked it very much, it continued to lie nearly untouched in his cupboard.

Seduced by his nearness and revelling in her power over him, she whispered, 'let's go to your room Haider.' He became absolutely still, but she could see the nerve in the hollow of his neck beating furiously. Quietly he asked her, 'are you sure, Jeeto?' Nodding, she took his hand in hers, surprised at her own uncharacteristic boldness. His room, in a quiet leafy lane, had a separate side entrance through which they entered unobserved. Once inside, she started to lose her nerve, but Haider's touch was like fire, and before long she was caught up in an inferno of love and desire.

Back home, she looked at herself long and intently in the mirror. She saw a tall, fair woman, with green flecked brown eyes and long dark hair. She was good looking, but not earth-shatteringly so, and wondered for the hundredth time what it was about her that had attracted Haider. Her beauty had certainly not been able to enamour her husband, who did not even want to share a room with her. The intimacy with Haider had left her face flushed, and she wondered whether the others would be able to notice anything different about her today. For she felt different, felt more alive than she had in a long time, and even the niggling sense of guilt did little to dampen her happiness.

The feeling of well-being stayed with her for many days: she was no longer so lonely, thoughts of Haider occupied her the entire time. The pleasure she got from her children was multiplied manifold, while the nagging of her mother-in-law seemed less irritating. And although the Wednesday Club had started working on a play—an adaptation of one of Shaukat's short stories—which was being directed by Haider, the rehearsals were held only twice a week, and other than the satisfaction of seeing him and sharing furtive glances, these meetings served no purpose. As a result, whatever time they got together was spent in his room, with Harjeet exploring a side of herself she had never known existed. It was nice to feel desired, to have her every wish fulfilled. Although gentle, Gautam was largely indifferent to her needs while making love, not even lingering to savour the feeling of intimacy afterwards. Not like Haider, who took his time over every inch of her body, loving her with passion and tenderness.

Chapter 6

With intimacy came comfort, a sense of belonging. Harjeet found herself talking to Haider about everything, her childhood, life with Gautam, her dreams for her children. 'What about your own dreams, Jeeto,' he asked her once. 'Surely you must have had some aspirations for your life as well?' Harjeet was quiet for a long moment, before giving vent to feelings pent up for too long. Her thoughts fell over each other in her haste to articulate them all at once. She told him of her classmates at school, most of whom had gone back to England, her desire to study further and finish her last year of college which had been interrupted by her marriage. She spoke about two of her friends who were working in Delhi, and of Susan, Gautam's brother's wife, whom she had met only once, but who seemed to lead a charmed, independent life.

Haider did not interrupt her even once, but when she had finished said, 'it's never too late, Jeeto. Our dreams are what sustain us, our vision of what we can become makes us hopeful, even in the face of all odds. Dreams are meant to be boxed only when we are in the final box, the coffin.'

Fighting back the tears welling in her eyes, Harjeet answered, 'it is too late, Haider. What can I do now, with two small children and a hawkish mother-in-law?'

'Why don't you do some social service, Jeeto?' Haider said, after thinking for a few minutes. 'Both Rukmini and you are already members of the AIWC, but other than the occasional play, you have very little to do with the organisation, which is getting increasingly involved with issues relating to women's education and emancipation. Why don't you start volunteering as a teacher in some school or charity? You know you don't need to work for money.'

At first Harjeet did not give much importance to his suggestion, but after one particularly depressing weekend, she decided to talk to Gautam and Lalaji about it. Rukmini had told her about a Parsi trust which held free sewing and embroidery classes for widows and women who had been deserted, and also helped them sell the cushions, doillies, napkins and handkerchiefs they made, through a small retail outlet. The teachers were paid a token amount, but most of them were well-to-do Parsi women who volunteered for free. Harjeet's suggestion that she also become a volunteer with the trust, invoked a mixed reaction. Lalaji was enthusiastic, Savitri was aghast, and Gautam true to his nature, vacillating. Ultimately, Lalaji was able to convince his wife that Harjeet's involvement with such work was something to be proud of, something that would give Savitri an edge over her friends. Women from several leading families were involving themselves with social issues, and there were increasing demands for gender equality and universal adult franchise. Many of the prominent women leaders were also members of the Congress party, thus making women's issues a part of the larger national movement.

Lalaji was happy that his daughter-in-law wanted to get involved with social work, and would have even encouraged her entry into politics, had she so desired. He was greatly appreciative of the role of political parties, especially the Congress, in mobilising public opinion against the British Government. Of late, however, the increasingly vitriolic communal agendas that were shaping the ethos of different parties had left him very disturbed. Last year in November, the Round Table Conference held in London, at the recommendation of the Simon Commission, had been boycotted by the Congress because most of its leaders were in jail, having been arrested during the Civil Disobedience movement. After the failure of the first Round Table Conference, senior Congress leaders had made an effort to bring about a rapprochement between the Government and Mahatma Gandhi, which had resulted in the British Government releasing the latter from prison and the signing of a pact between him and Lord Irwin, the Viceroy, a few months ago. Although Lalaji was sceptical about the terms of the agreement, which included Mahatma Gandhi promising to give up the Satyagraha movement and the British agreeing to the release of prisoners arrested during the movement, while also allowing Indians to make salt for their own use, he was happy at the release of political prisoners, especially two brothers from Jallandhar who were his clients. The Civil Disobedience movement was discontinued, and the Congress agreed to attend the second Round Table Conference in London in September, where it sent Gandhi as its sole representative. At the conference, he was made a member of two committees, one on federal structure and the other on minorities. It was the latter that worried Harjeet, because its failure to reach a consensus had given the British Government a valid reason to present its own unilateral communal award, which seemed to have opened the proverbial Pandora's box, with each community wanting some part of the spoils for itself. The Anglo-Indians, Muslims, Sikhs, Indian Christians and even the Depressed Classes were all demanding separate electorates, and these constant discussions made Harjeet unsettled and anxious about a future in which she and Haider may not be together any more.

Talks of differences between the Hindus and Muslims had become commonplace, and she was worried about the fallout of this on Haider's acceptability in their house. Not that he came to visit very often, preferring to keep his distance from her family, although he was always very warm towards Lalaji and Gautam, and was ever willing to go the extra mile for them. 'I love everything about you Jeeto, your children, even your in-laws. I want them to keep you happy always,' he said to her once, when she questioned him about his deferential attitude towards her family. But lately, she had noticed an occasional streak of jealousy in his behaviour, especially while making love, as if he wanted to erase all memories of Gautam from her body, and she wondered, was it the body that remembered a touch, a caress, or were they marked indelibly on the mind? For Haider's passion stayed with her for long afterwards, warming even the coldest nights.

It was now the middle of winter in Lahore, and the days were beautiful and sunny, although the nights often became bitterly cold. Harjeet loved Lahore in winter, the hazy mornings, the cold pressing clammy against her face in the evenings, the warmth of her quilt at night. Although Inder had his own cot, she would bring him into the bed she shared with Maya, and the three of them would snuggle into the *shaneel razai*. This was her favourite time of the day, giggling and playing with the children, enjoying the softness of their bodies, the warmth of their breath. Maya was a chubby six year old, while Inder seemed to have inherited Lalaji's leaner frame. In a way she was glad that Gautam did not sleep with them and she did not have to share the children with him. For this brief interlude of time they were all hers, their dimpled hands reaching out to clasp hers, their eyes struggling to keep open. They also served, unwittingly, to deter Gautam from his nightly visits. Finding both the children in her bed, he would signal to her to come into his room, and would mention deviously in front of his mother that Inder needed to sleep in his own cot, and that even Maya needed a separate bed of her own. Harjeet disliked this habit of his. Why was he not man enough to say what he wanted to directly, instead of hiding behind his mother, especially when he knew that she was always nagging Harjeet about the proper way to bring up the children? Even his sister was the same, always trying to behave like an English memsahib, creating trouble between her mother and Harjeet over the correct manner of doing things. Her visits always meant tension for Harjeet and Bacchu, the dinner napkin had to be folded properly, the knives and forks crossed just so.

But not anymore. Harjeet, who had joined the Parsi charity on 1 January 1932, wanting the new year to herald a new beginning for her, was not home for the better part of the mornings, and was spared the constant comparisons and tiresome tirades. She was volunteering at the charity three days a week, teaching cross-stitch and Sindhi threadwork embroidery. Her initial hesitation had given way to enthusiasm, and she looked forward to her time at the centre, and had even made friends with some Parsi women her age. Her very neat hand at embroidery was much appreciated, as were her cooking skills. The latter was a surprise for her because she had never thought of herself as being a good cook. Bachhu managed the kitchen very efficiently, and she didn't need to get involved with the day to day cooking at all. Last week, however, at the insistence of her friends at the centre, she made Yakhni Pulao in the small but well-stocked kitchen, and the succulence of the meat, coupled with the exotic spices, won her many compliments. But when she casually mentioned this at home, Savitri was caustic, and wondered why whatever she cooked at home never tasted so good. Gautam, who was sitting next to her, just smiled weakly and looked away. He probably found nothing wrong with his mother's comment, which was delivered in a sweet, sugary tone. Harjeet was amazed, as always, by Savitri's cleverness. She never spoke a harsh word to Harjeet in Lalaji's presence, and when Gautam was around, she was careful to veil her barbs.

But Harjeet was upset, both at the remark and Gautam's indifference to it. Quickly supressing a pang of guilt at her own conduct, she thought self-righteously that it was just as well that she had Haider in her life, to love her and make her feel special. Because it was not that Gautam, although mild, could not take a stand if he wanted to. Of late, he had developed an interest in poetry, and inspite of Lalaji's subtle disapproval, would often be away till late in the night, attending poetry symposiums. He also loved music and dramatic performances, and when the first 'talkie' *Alam Ara* was released in Lahore towards the end of April, he was one of the first ones to get tickets for the show. Munshi ji was sent on ahead for this purpose; it was not for Gautam to get himself jostled in the crowd.

Harjeet found the movie to be a very exciting experience, especially since Haider was accompanying them, as were Rukmini, Ranjeet and some of their other friends. Harjeet was keen to sit next to Haider, but was preempted by Rukmini, who glared at her before taking the seat. Harjeet was saddened; was their love doomed to be forever played out surreptiously, like the movie playing in the darkened hall? In the movie at least, Alam Ara was united with her prince in a dramatic but happy ending, which was more than what she could ever hope for. Marriage, for whatever it was worth, was permanent and reassuring. Her relationship with Haider, on the contrary, was like a sieve through which time could leak out love, drop by drop. What if he found someone else? He was young and good looking, and his mother was very anxious to get him married. He could get transferred to another town, or decide to go on one of his journeys and never come back.

Harjeet felt panic welling up at the thought of losing him, and tried hard to fight the tears gathering in her eyes. Although they had the most vantageous seats in the hall, right in the centre under a fan, it was taking them time to get to the exit once the movie finished. Fearing that her tears would get noticed, she rubbed her eyes, and complaining about cigarette smoke irritating them, made her way to one of the numerous peanut vendors who had come into the gallery even before the show had ended.

'It is not always necessary to give every relationship a name, Jeeto', Haider said from behind her. 'There will be a time for us someday, and I'll be waiting for that day.' Harjeet, who had not heard him coming, was again struck by the uncanny way he could read her mind. But how could the thought of a day somewhere in the future give her succour, when life itself was so uncertain. What guarantee could time give her, an insignificant being, when even lead players, who were willing to challenge fate headlong, were left by the wayside?

Chapter 7

The Basant this year, 1932, was subject to much political unrest. Mahatma Gandhi had been arrested in the first week of January, on his return from London after attending the second Round Table Conference, which had yielded nothing much. Disappointed at what he felt was an overarching concern with vested interests by the different parties, and the demand for separate electorates by the minorities, which pushed the larger issues concerning the country into the background, he gave a call for resumption of the Civil Disobedience movement. This was followed by large scale arrests in Bombay, Calcutta, Delhi and many other cities. Kasturba Gandhi was arrested, as were several other leaders. These disturbances continued for the next few months, during which the British Government bore down heavily on the Congress, banning many of its organisations and sessions. Lalaji was distressed. Many of his friends who were prominent leaders had been arrested, and the organisation of which he was such a loyal member was being victimised.

At home also, there was a sudden sense of emptiness. The law practice had been slack for some time now, and the hectic parleys for Bhagat Singh had come to an end several months earlier, enabling Gautam to get most of his old routine back. But of late, he seemed to be displaying an uncharacteristic lack of interest in political matters, not showing much concern even when Gandhi and his wife were arrested. There was a preoccupied air about him, and he started to spend more and more time outside the house with one of his friends from Atchison College. Ranveer was the eldest son of one of Doaba's richest landlords, and wore both his customary turban and attitude with great style. Bored with life in the village, he spent most of his time at Lahore, leaving his wife and three children at home with his parents. While at college, it was widely acknowledged that he had the largest retinue of servants, and the food made by his cook was legendary. Unfortunately, his grades could not match up to the same exacting standards, and he left without completing the last year of college, having failed to clear the final exams two years in a row. It was said that when he returned home thus disgraced, his mother had their halwai prepare special moti choor ladoos, which were then distributed to the entire village. She had never been in favour of her son going to Lahore to study, and was relieved when he came back without getting involved with a girl from an unsuitable family.

Harjeet always felt uncomfortable in his presence; there was something shifty about him, but since his visits were rather infrequent, she did not give the matter much thought. Lately, however, he had started visiting their house much oftener, and the usually reticent Gautam would wait eagerly for him. After the customary exchange of pleasantries with the family, the two of them would drive off in the car, only to return late in the evening. This sudden change in Gautam's behaviour did not go unnoticed, and one night when Lalaji questioned him about his new found friendship, he was taken aback by the reply, a couplet of Ghalib's, delivered in a perfectly metred verse.

'I didn't know you were so fond of poetry,' said Lalaji, surprised.

'I didn't know much about poetry myself, until recently, when Ranveer introduced me to it,' answered Gautam. Lalaji gave him a sharp look.

'Is Ranveer a poet?' he asked.

'No, but he is deeply appreciative of poetry, and a regular at many sessions held in the city,' Gautam said with some pride.

Lalaji said nothing, but Harjeet knew that he held a poor opinion of Ranveer, and was not happy with Gautam's association with him. Nevertheless, as the weeks passed, the friendship between the two men only grew stronger, and Harjeet was convinced that this was probably the reason for Gautam being so unusually enthusiastic about the proposed visit to Murree during the coming summer. With Harjeet and the children away for two months, he would be able to spend more time with Ranveer, and hence dismissed Lalaji's suggestion that he spend at least four weeks with them at Murree.

'One month,' he said, aghast. 'What will happen to our clients? You know there are some important cases coming up for discussion soon.'

'Never mind the cases', answered Lalaji. 'I will attend to them with munshiji's help.' But eventually Gautam had his way, and after settling Harjeet and the children into the cottage they had rented in Murree, he came back within a week. Ranjeet, who was also accompanying his family, stayed longer, making another trip towards the end to bring them all back to Lahore.

Murree was relaxing but boring, and by the time they came back, the monsoon had set over Lahore. Harjeet thought of the endless cycle of life, the ever changing seasons. It was now three years since Haider had come into her life. Three winters, four summers and now, the fourth monsoon. Dense indigo clouds crowded the horizon, darkening the afternoon and making the dusk come on early, and at such times a stillness would descend over everything, the proverbial lull before the storm, which Harjeet found stifling. She did not like the season; the grey, overcast days made her restless and depressed. She missed Haider, who had not been able to visit Murree because of his mother's sudden illness. Had she known that he would not be able to take any time off at all, she would not have agreed to go, preferring instead to brave the summer in Lahore.

Now that she was back, and Haider's mother was better, the rain was making it impossible for her to venture outdoors. Was it her imagination, or was the monsoon wetter this year? The rain would start suddenly, falling in sheets, and would continue for whole weeks at a time. Lazily watching a storm cloud drifting overhead one day, she wondered which roof it would pour down on. Would the droplets of water fall on lovers enjoying the season of intimacy on some terrace in a crowded *gali* or would the rain drench flowers that fell from hair caressed in the clouded dark in some outlying mohalla? Hearing frogs croak in puddles by the roadside, watching the wind-swept branches dancing with the raindrops, listening to the joyous call of the chataka or the pied cucoo, she felt jealous. All life rejoiced in this season which she disliked, in which she should have been with Haider, instead of her dumpy husband, whom Rukmini's son had started calling 'Uncle Dunlop', because of the similarity between the cushy mattress and his own plumpness. His gentle nature encouraged the children to clamber all over him, pulling at his glasses, bouncing on his lap, but his round face with the rapidly receding hairline made her think about Haider's much thicker hair, through which she loved running her fingers, and his much leaner frame, which felt so taut to the touch. Being with him was so heady, sweeping her along in a tide of passion, much like rain water swept away everything in its path. Maybe she would just take life one day at a time, and be grateful for the hours she could spend with him, without always worrying about the future.

But how could she not worry? She remained uneasy about the tension between the Hindus and Muslims, which although decades old, seemed to be growing rapidly of late, and found it difficult to remain immune to the whispers and innuendos that grew louder each passing day. What made her especially nervous was the Communal Award that had been passed by the British Government in August. The Award granted separate electorates to the minority communities, including Muslims, Sikhs and the Depressed Classes, and seemed to Harjeet to be the nadir of the events of 1932. Soon after the Award was passed, Gandhi went on a fast to protest against the allocation of separate electorates for the Depressed Classes, which he felt would drive a wedge within the Hindu community. However, Dr B. R. Ambedkar, a prominent leader of the Depressed Classes, supported the Communal Award, and finally an agreement was reached between him and Mahatma Gandhi in September, under which the provision of separate electorates for the Depressed Classes was withdrawn, but not before several concessions had been granted to them.

Lalaji was pleased with this development. He had long objected to the class-based discrimination prevalent in society, a view wholeheartedly supported by Gautam. However, his wife and daughter were not convinced, and continued to hold onto their more rigid beliefs. Harjeet recalled more than one incident in which Lalaji's generosity had led to a fight with Savitri, the latest being last year, when Lalaji had made a seriously ill Chand Ram, the gardener, sit on the charpoy next to him. It was a winter afternoon, and the mellow sunshine gilded the gaily painted legs of the charpoy, placed in Lalaji's favourite corner of the angan. Seing Chand Ram, who had come to borrow some money, sway unsteadily on his feet due to high fever, Lalaji took his arm and made him sit on the bed. Bachhu, who was watching from the kitchen window, immediately tattled to Savitri, who had the entire navar replaced and the legs repainted. Lalaji, although upset, was as usual ineffectual against his wife, and Harjeet wondered what his Arya Samaj friends would say if they came to know about the incident. Even Gautam was not spared his mother's displeasure some days later, when he gave his new lohi to the same gardener on a particularly cold evening. However, the new, more defiant Gautam did not accept her domineering ways so meekly anymore, and had got into an argument with her on more than one occasion recently.

Harjeet, whose family was part of a rigid class and caste based hierarchical system, was nevertheless, very liberal in her views, the years at school having left a much stronger influence on her than any indoctrination by her aunt and bhabhi. However, she was becoming increasingly skeptical about men like Lalaji and Gautam, with their selective broad-mindedness. Why did no one protest against the growing divide between Hindus and Muslims? Why this overarching concern only with one's own community? Hindus and Muslims had been living in the same cities, although in different mohallas, since historical times, and she did not want the situation between the two to reach a point where it would become difficult for Haider to visit Rukmini's house, or to interact with them socially.

But during their next meeting, when she tried discussing her fears with Haider, he laughed and brushed her concern aside.

'You are my religion Jeeto, I search for my God in you,' he said, cupping her face in his hands.

They were sitting in a small ante room in Rukmini's house, which had just enough space for two chairs and a table piled high with costumes and props. Rukmini, although still disapproving, had begun to reluctantly accept their relationship, and would leave them alone when they met at her house once a week, in the guise of working on the script of the latest play to be staged at the quarterly meeting of the ladies club. The Wednesday Ladies Club started by Rukmini, had branched out to include a Quarterly Club which met every four months. Motivated by the All India Women's Conference held in January this year, which had recommended primary education for every child and fixing of the age of marriage at eighteen years, Rukmini had persuaded Harjeet to help set up an organization, which she named the Quarterly Club, to work towards the education of girls from poor families. Although most of the members of the Quarterly Club were originally drawn from the Wednesday Club, as word spread about the excellent work being done by it, membership grew rapidly. Rukmini gave the credit for much of this success to Harjeet, whom she had talked into becoming the General Secretary. Most of the income to the club came through donations, but the members used other novel ways to garner more funds, including putting up plays that dealt with social issues. As in the case of the Wednesday Club, the plays were usually adaptations of the works of contemporary writers, who were, in most cases, also directly involved with the production.

Haider, who had proved to be very efficient and hardworking, had been retained as the in house director. That he worked for free, and helped with the accounts, was an added bonus, although Rukmini was aware that much of this philanthrophy stemmed from a desire to be with Harjeet. Harjeet, on her part, although grateful for his clerical help, was more thankful for the opportunity this

gave them of meeting at least once a week in the relatively safe
confines of Rukmini's house. Ranjeet, always looking for ways
to make his wife happy, had got one room in his office on Fane
Street refurbished for the use of the organisation, and it was
here that all formal meetings were held and all the accounts and
correspondences housed. However, Harjeet preferred to work out
of a small room in Rukmini's house, which was used to store
costumes and props, but which she had cleared to make place for
a small table and two chairs. Here she spent every Wednesday
morning with Haider, going over the accounts and sundry activities
of the organisation during the past week. Haider had no classes in
the mornings on Wednesdays, and for those few hours, the bare
room, long and narrow, with only one small window, would take
on an enchanted aura. Love would seep into its mortar covered
walls, the air would hold a thousand whispered secrets and the
chairs would transform themselves into gilded chinoiseries. The
coffee Rukmini sent would taste no less than ambrosia, especially
since Haider would want to drink from her cup, placing his lips on
the exact place hers had been, and it seemed to Harjeet that she
lived only for these meetings, with the interregnum filled with a
haze of love punctuated by the presence of her children.

With the coming of winter, the three of them, Harjeet, Maya
and Inder, would spend the afternoon in a sunny corner of the
garden, sprawled on chatais spread out on the warm grass, and
Harjeet would feel a deep sense of satisfaction on seeing the children
growing so well. Maya was enjoying school and had something
new to tell her every day. Even Inder, who had joined nursery last
year, would pick up the pencil and try to copy his sister in writing
the alphabet. With Gautam out of the house most of the time,
Harjeet had the children almost entirely to herself. Savitri was too
frail and highly strung to tolerate the exuberance of young kids,
and their interaction with her was limited to the customary hug.
Lalaji on the other hand, loved to spend time with them, and
would take them for an outing every weekend, buying them toys
and something nice to eat. On the way back home they would stop

at Nathu halwai, from where Lalaji would get jalebis and ladoos. With the advent of basant, the halwai shops were full of mithais like gajrela and gulab jamun and saffron coloured halwa.

But the new year, 1933, did not appear to be agreeing with Lalaji; he seemed disturbed and ill at ease, and even though Savitri attributed it to something that the Pandit who came every year to make his Varshphal had said, Harjeet suspected that much of his disappointment stemmed from the change in Gautam's attitude and his growing indifference towards national issues. He would no longer take part in the discussions held with Lalaji's friends, and any effort to elicit his views on the current happenings would be met with silence, or at best, non-committal replies. Harjeet knew that Lalaji enjoyed spending time with his son, and was worried about this change in his behaviour, especially since Gautam's indifference often extended to family matters as well. Although still respectful, his interaction with Lalaji was now largely work related. Most of his evenings were spent outside the house with Ranveer, and on several occasions during the last few months, he had come home very late. Harjeet would go to bed with the children without waiting for him, and much later she would hear the sound of the car pulling into the driveway. It amazed her that Lalaji waited up for his son, dozing fitfully in the armchair in the drawing room, when the duty could easily have been given to Bachhu or to one of the other domestic staff. Savitri mentioned it to Gautam once, rather accusingly, suggesting that he be back at a reasonable hour to avoid inconveniencing his old father.

'No one needs to wait up for me, especially Pitajee. I'll come in through Bachhu's room', he replied.

But Savitri was not one to give up so easily. 'But where do you stay till so late? I knew Ranveer was bad news the moment I saw him. God knows where he takes you,' she said angrily.

'He takes me nowhere, I go of my own will and as I have told you before, we attend poetry readings', Gautam replied in an uncharacteristically sharp voice.

Savitri was too taken aback to say anything further, but Harjeet was pleased at this turn of events. Served Savitri right for clinging to her son, and always trying to fill his ears against her, his wife. Not that she herself minded Gautam's daily absences; it meant his frequenting her bed that less often, but she did miss the chance of going out with him. She enjoyed her visits to the Gymkhana Club, especially on long sultry summer evenings, when she could dress up in her floaty chiffon sarees, or show off her daintily embroidered chunnis. She would put her hair up in a chignon, with pretty side-pins, a popular style to which she would give her own twist by adding a sprig of motia just above her ear. But now with Gautam spending his evenings with Ranveer, she was left to stroll alone in the garden, which was braving the scars of a harsh summer. Only the gulmohar and her favourite, the amaltas, added some colour to an otherwise burnt sienna landscape. The gardener had planted some seasonal flowers in the neatly aligned beds, but they were hardly noticeable, except for the motia, which perfumed both the dusk and her thoughts, sending a wave of longing through her heart. She envied Gautam his freedom, his ability to do as he pleased, go where he wanted to. She wished she could walk out of the house with equal ease whenever she wanted to be with Haider, instead of having to make excuses all the time.

It was the first Sunday of October, a beautiful bright day and Harjeet was taking a stroll with the children in the garden, when she heard Gautam's voice raised in argument, followed by the unmistakeable sound of Savitri sobbing. Leaving the children with Basanti, she hurried inside in time to see Gautam exiting the drawing room in a huff. Savitri was crying and Lalaji was sitting in his favourite armchair in stony silence. The tension in the room was palpable, and Harjeet was filled with a sudden feeling of dread. Calling for Bachhu to get water for Savitri, she asked Lalaji what had happened.

'I'll tell you,' said Savitri agitatedly, in a surprisingly non-teary voice. 'Gautam has been betting on horses every week, and losing money consistently. That no good Ranveer goes with him, and had it not been for his poor wife sending a message to Lalaji, we would never have found out.' Harjeet was shocked, this was something she could never have imagined. But it explained a lot of things, including Gautam's sudden interest in the Civil and Military Gazette, which carried the dates and complete details of all forthcoming racing events, and his long absences from home every Saturday.

The Lahore Race Club was set up in 1924, although the sport had been popular for many years before that. It was located on Jail Road, not far from where they lived, and Harjeet had been there a couple of times with Gautam, the latest being last year when they went as special guests of the secretary of the club. It was on the occasion of the Punjab Governor's Cup race, and from their very vantageous seats in the Grand Stand, Harjeet was able to observe the fashionably dressed women in their shimmering silk sarees and dark glasses, accompanied by equally dapper men. She herself was wearing an emerald green chinon saree, which highlighted the green of her eyes, and even Gautam had traded his customary white pyjamas—always spotless and starched to perfection—for a short English coat worn over a collared shirt and trousers. The weather was perfect for the occasion, the afternoon sun warm and mellow and the breeze gently caressing. Towards the left most corner of the ground there was a lot of hectic activity, and Harjeet wondered why so many men were hurrying about, some even getting into arguments.

'Those are the punters who are placing bets on their favourite horses with the bookmakers,' Gautam said.

'How do they know which horse to bet on?' asked Harjeet, surprised.

'The horses are paraded before the actual race, and the experienced punters know what to look out for—gait, health and general well-being. People also bet on horses that have a history of winning or on horses with their favourite jockeys', explained Gautam.

Harjeet had found nothing untoward in his answer, but she realised now that the depth of his knowledge was backed by direct experience. The racing season lasted from December to April, after which time it became too hot for both man and beast, and throughout those months this year, Lalaji remained uneasy. Harjeet often caught him looking at Gautam anxiously, as if wanting to say something, but stopping short of actually uttering the words. The two of them had argued at length on the subject, with Gautam insisting that it was a harmless pursuit.

'This is not gambling in the real sense. It is more of an informed risk and adds excitement to the sport,' he argued. Lalaji was not convinced, and liked to remind him of the Pandavs, who had lost an entire kingdom over a game of dice, and not stopping there, had even bet on their wife Draupadi. 'It's an addiction Gautam, and once it gets into your blood, there is no escaping its consequences. Your grandfather used to say that bad habits can empty out even a bottomless well full of money,' he said. Finally, however, Gautam buckled under the intense pressure, and agreed not to bet any more money on the races. Savitri, given to histrionics as she was, made him swear on the Gita, but Harjeet could see that Lalaji was still not reassured, and come Saturday, would try to involve Gautam in one of his various meetings, either at the Arya Samaj or at home with his friends.

Chapter 8

The political situation in the country was still unsettled, and there was much discussion regarding Mahatma Gandhi suspending the Civil Disobedience movement once again. It was now the beginning of 1934, and the Civil Disobedience movement had been on and off for more than three years, during which time hundreds of protesters had been arrested. The Congress party had been banned from holding its meetings several times during this period, the latest being in March, when in defiance of the ban, a thousand strong delegation collected in Calcutta to reiterate the demand for full independence. Harjeet was sceptical about the impassioned utterances by leaders of different political parties, regarding them to be mere rhetoric and big talk, powerless in the face of the deteriorating communal situation. Haider would often tell her about the growing disenchantment of most Muslims with the Congress party, which they felt was being unduly influenced by Hindu religious and nationalist groups, a claim contested by most Hindus, including Lalaji.

Gautam, annoyed over what he perceived as unwarranted interference in his life, started to keep totally out of these discussions, often not even making the effort to meet Lalaji's friends when they came home. Ranveer, exposed to Savitri's hostility on more than one occasion had also stopped coming home, preferring instead to meet Gautam at some predetermined location in the city. Harjeet, with a woman's intuition, instinctively felt that there was more to Gautam's aloofness than mere annoyance with the family. He was by nature a gentle, forgiving person, and she had never known him to wilfully hurt his parents. But now he was seemingly oblivious to his father's anxiety and disappointment, and had, once or twice, even answered him back sharply. He was also distracted most of the time, often leaving his cigarettes lying around openly in his room for everyone to see. Harjeet found it difficult to believe that he had become such an ardent lover of poetry overnight, especially since his reading habits were largely confined to patriotic literature. The only time he seemed genuinely happy was while playing with the children. His face would light up, and for that brief interlude of time it was as if the old Gautam had come back. Harjeet felt she could see Lalaji age some more every day, he had developed deep worry lines on his forehead, and seemed less agile all of a sudden. Savitri, on her part, started relying on the family pandit more and more, and last week alone he had visited the house twice. Special ghee ladoos were made by Bachhu to be distributed among the poor, cows were fed every day, and Harjeet was given a *tabiz* to put under Gautam's mattress. All this was done in secrecy, for Lalaji frowned upon such ritualistic practises.

However, none of these *upaays* seemed to be working. Gautam remained the same as the year wore on, withdrawn and irritable most of the time, and his visits to her bed all but stopped. Lately she had been tempted to ask him if he had found someone else to warm his heart and bed, but stopped short of actually doing so, thinking to herself that it would be good if he was in love with another woman. It would lessen her guilt about Haider and who knew, maybe she could use the knowledge to her advantage someday.

There was an air of melancholia about the house now, as if someone had forgotten to switch on the lights at dusk. Lalaji seemed worried and tense the entire time, and did not even try to persuade Gautam to take the family somewhere for the summer. On the contrary, he requested Harjeet to not go as well, saying that Gautam needed to have his family around him at times like these. Harjeet could not understand why so much fuss was being made over Gautam; everyone had their highs and lows, and in all probability he would soon return to his old self again. Why had no one ever made a fuss over her? She had been so unhappy for so long, but neither her brother nor her husband had ever sensed it.

It was Haider, an outsider for both her family and her community, who had realised how lonely she was, and how much love she was capable of. Over the years her happiness had become inextricably entwined with his, and she felt herself bound to him by ever-tightening ties of love and passion, bonds that had held tight in the face of all obstacles, seemingly making them disappear as if by magic, and any talk of tension between their two communities made her fearful of his moving to a farther off locality, or even worse, of his not being able to meet her anymore. 'You are silly to worry, Jeeto. Don't you know that wherever I might be, whatever I might be doing, I live in your house with you, walk the road outside several times a day, and go to sleep with you in my arms,' he would say whenever she mentioned her fears to him, and for those brief moments all her anxiety would fade away just as the winter sun dissipated the early morning mist that enveloped the house.

But her unease was not without reason. The communal situation was indeed deteriorating, and every small incident threatened to become a new flashpoint. Tension had been brewing between the Sikhs and Muslims over a mosque located in the Shahidganj Gurudwara for over a year but in June 1935, matters reached a head. Harjeet had often visited the gurudwara, located in Naulakha Bazaar, with her mother's cousin during her college years. Her aunt's husband was very active in the gurudwara committee, and was at the forefront of a prolonged litigation with the Muslims. The Sikhs had won the legal battle, but tension continued to simmer under the surface, culminating in a decision by them to demolish the adjoining mosque. Accordingly, towards the end of June, thousands of Muslims assembled in front of the gurudwara, passions ran high, and a catastrophe was averted only by the huge presence of the police. Subsequently, leaders of both communities made efforts to reach a compromise, but it seemed to Harjeet that the entire exercise was one of deceit and back stabbing. Shaukat was one of the negotiators, as was her uncle, so she knew first-hand the dichotomy between word and deed.

Suddenly Lahore did not seem such a safe place any more, she worried for the safety of her children and family, and especially for Haider, whom it was becoming more and more difficult to meet. The anxiety continued through much of the year, increasing and decreasing intermittently, peaking in July when the police opened fire on a crowd, and again in November. In the volatile relations between the Hindus and Muslims, everything was tinder, and even disturbances that started out with a political overtone took on a communal twist.

Although Lahore had, like the rest of the region, a long history of Hindu-Muslim conflict, the two communities had managed to co-exist by and large peacefully, living side by side, but distinctly separate from each other, in clearly differentiated localities. Their mutual dependence and personal friendships had ensured the continuation of the very workable relationship they had formulated over the decades. Lalaji, ever suspicious of the British, was convinced that the real trouble had started after the Christian missionaries became active during the early years of the present century, creating insecurities among the already existing faiths. The rising number of converts to Christianity motivated religious reform movements like the Arya Samaj, of which he himself was a devout follower. This insecurity, however, made the Hindus and Muslims close ranks against each other, as well as against other communities. Lalaji was also of the opinion that the weakening of the larger Punjabi identity had resulted in growing religious parochialism, and over the decades it had become common for both communities to give calls for greater unity among their followers, always citing the example of the other religion as having more solidarity. This mutual fear and heightened sense of communalism had been fanned, in the case of Lahore, by the rapidly increasing number of periodicals and newspapers.

Lalaji, always impartial in his observations, was privately of the opinion that in the present circumstances, the Civil Disobedience movement, while no doubt serving a very important purpose, may have heightened tensions between the two communities. However he, unlike Shaukat, refused to blame the Congress for trying to coerce the Muslims into joining the movement. 'Shaukat is very resentful about the Congress trying to portray itself as the sole representative of all Indians, and feels that the Muslim League will give it a befitting reply in the forthcoming elections,' Haider said to Harjeet one day, while they lay together in his bed. They had started meeting more frequently in his room now, and if his old landlord noticed the burqa clad lady accompanying his tenant, he turned a blind eye to it, not wanting to risk the handsome remuneration he received, both for the room and his silence. 'What do you think will happen then?' asked Harjeet, worried. 'I don't know, nor am I concerned,' answered Haider, pulling her close. 'I have more important things to think about right now, like the way your eyes change colour when you are worried.' Although Harjeet disliked the surreptiousness involved in getting into a burqa in a secluded corner of the park near Haider's house, it seemed to be the most sensible thing to do. And the most convenient, for their intimacy had reached a level of no return, and even in her wildest dreams Harjeet had never imagined that she could desire someone so much. It was like being caught in a river in spate, rolling and falling and rushing headlong with the current. Beyond the bolted door and the curtained windows, the world turned at its usual pace, vegetable sellers hawked their wares in a sing song voice, children cried, voices were raised in argument, a horse-driven tonga went by, clip clop. But inside the room all was soft and urgent and hushed, and Harjeet wished desperately each time Haider got up to finally open the door, that she could live in the moment forever, cocooned in a bubble of timelessness.

But she had to go home, to an increasingly petulant husband, and a cantankerous mother-in-law. Inder, now nearly nine years old and Maya eleven, would be back from school by 2 o'clock, and Harjeet made sure she was home before that. Two years ago Maya had moved to Queen Mary College, Harjeet's old school, as had Rukmini's daughter, while last year Inder had joined Atchison College, where Rukmini's son was already a student. The work of both the Wednesday and the Quarterly Clubs had increased, especially since the latter had taken upon itself greater social responsibility, and Harjeet often had to put in long hours in her capacity as General Secretary. This along with the Parsi charity she volunteered for, kept her busy the mornings she was not meeting Haider, and the afternoons she liked to spend with the children, and so time marched on at its appointed pace, the days and weeks and months passing as they must. With Gautam her relationship had reached the stage of an uneasy truce, with neither of them having much to say to the other. Maya, who was born dark and sickly, had blossomed into a very pretty young girl, with thick, waist length hair which she kept tied in two plaits, while Inder's hair was surprisingly curly. Both the children seemed to have taken the best features from both parents, with the girl inheriting Harjeet's eyes and complexion and the boy her height. From their father they had got the family's sharp, almost aristocratic nose, and shape of face. However, unlike Maya, Inder also seemed to have inherited his father's inertia and laid back attitude, which Harjeet fervently hoped was just a passing phase.

The Government of India Act, which was passed last year in 1935, a few years after the third Round Table Conference, provided for independent Legislative Assemblies in all provinces of the country. The electorate was divided into different categories based on social and religious affiliations, and a voter could only vote for candidates from his own category. Lalaji, who prided himself on being a nationalist, was against this concept, but was nevertheless swept up in the general wave of excitement that the announcement of elections had generated. There was much activity in both the Congress and the Muslim League, lists of candidates were drawn and redrawn, manifestoes were discussed at length. Haider was disappointed with the manifesto of the Muslim League, which he felt had little to offer non-Muslims. Lalaji, on the other hand, was very appreciative of the work done by Jawaharlal Nehru while framing the Congress manifesto. Many of the candidates from Punjab were known to him, and it was rumoured that he had also been offered a ticket from Lahore, but had declined from entering active politics.

The results of the elections which were held in Jan–Feb 1937 surprised everyone, even staunch supporters of the Congress like Lalaji. The Congress swept the elections, winning in most of the eleven provinces, including several Muslim dominated areas, thus dampening the aspirations of many within the Muslim League. Lalaji was delighted, even though the Congress had not managed a majority in the Punjab Assembly, where the Unionists won by a huge majority. There was much celebration at home, sweets were bought by the kilo from Nathu Halwai and every hour one or the other of Lalaji's friends would stop by to discuss the results. Even Gautam, who seemed to have got some of his spirit back, would occasionally join in. The euphoria was, however, dampened by the Congress refusing to form the ministries because of a dispute over the use of special powers by the Governor in Legislative affairs. By the time the matter was settled and the new ministries could be formed, it was July and the monsoon had just set in.

Harjeet had taken the children to her brother's house for a fortnight, and although he was generous as ever, and his wife friendly, she was glad to be back. She missed Haider, and even the sight of Maya and Inder enjoying themselves with their cousins on the farm had not prompted her to stay longer. Moreover, she loved Lahore with almost the same fervour with which she disliked the village, and as their car travelled along the Mall Road, past famous landmarks, especially the Zamzama, the huge gun which the children loved, she felt truly blessed, and hoped the success of the recent elections would ease the communal tension somewhat.

On the contrary, however, the communal issue refused to die down. In a series of heated exchanges between Jinnah and Jawaharlal Nehru, the matter was brought to the fore by Jinnah disputing Nehru's claim that there were only two forces at work in India, the Congress which stood for Indian nationalism, and the British Government, arguing that Indian Muslims were a separate and thus the third party. And so, in spite of the Congress claiming that the results proved it did indeed represent the entire country, the Muslim League disagreed, and formulated a report to discuss its major grievances with the former. Shaukat was part of the team that wrote the report, and Haider often discussed with Harjeet his concern at his brother adopting a very rigid and increasingly vitriolic stance against the Hindus as a community. Shaukat found fault with many Congress decisions, he disapproved of the Congress declaring Vande Mataram to be the 'National Song' of India in October, as did the Muslim League as a whole. Vande Mataram, a Bengali poem written by Bankim Chandra Chatterjee in the 1870s had, over the decades, become a symbol of political activism and the struggle for independence. Although banned by the British, it nevertheless continued to be recited by both the Congress and a defiant public. In 1937, sensitive to the fact that some lines contained references to Hindu goddesses, a committee of the Congress adopted only the first two stanzas as the national song to be sung at public gatherings, a compromise which Haider discussed with Harjeet as being perfectly acceptable. But Shaukat was not satisfied, his list of grievances was very long and also included the League's disapproval of Hindi being declared the national language. Even his writing started reflecting his increasingly rigid outlook, and when, towards the end of October, the Wednesday Club got an invite from the Gaiety Theatre in Simla, to stage a play at the start of next year's season, none of his new works were found fit to be dramatized.

Rukmini was delighted at the invitation, taking it to be a big honour, and spent hours deciding on the play and the costumes and props to be used. Simla had a very vibrant amateur dramatic club, which included among its members the Viceroy, several lawyers, military officers, civil servants and even clerks. Plays were staged between April and October, usually at the Gaiety Theatre, and occasionally at the home of a senior officer. The Gaiety Theatre, which was housed in the Town Hall situated on the ridge, had become an integral part of Simla society, and everyone who was anyone had taken part in a play staged there or was desirous of doing so.

After much discussion, the Wednesday Club decided to enact *Karambhoomi*, a play written a few years back by the late author Premchand, whose writing career, spanning more than thirty years, produced nearly three hundred works, including novels, short stories, essays and translations. Surprisingly, the suggestion came from Gautam, who was very appreciative both of Premchand's literary style and of his patriotic zeal. Rukmini, who had not read the novel, borrowed a copy from Gautam, and was immediately enthralled by the contemporary story set in the United Provinces. Overriding dissent from the more conservative members of the club who felt that it might offend the British audience at Simla, she set to work on it at once, enlisting Haider's help with the script. Haider finished dramatizing it within a week, and sprang a surprise when, script in hand, he announced, 'I think Jeeto would be perfect as Amarkant.' There was a long silence; Amarkant was the idealistic but weak hero, who realises in the end that his non-violent attitude, rather than being his weakness, is his greatest strength. At length Rukmini spoke, 'I think you are absolutely right Haider. There could be no better Amarkant than Jeeto.'

However, Harjeet herself was unsure about being able to play the part meant for a man, and even after they had reached Simla she was still jittery, afraid that she might get stage fright or forget her lines, or even worse, be unconvincing in the role of the hero. The weeks of daily rehearsals, costume fittings, reading and re-reading of the script had not been able to lessen her anxiety. The journey from Lahore had been uneventful, the last stretch from Kalka to Simla in coach 14 even enjoyable, with the children squealing every time the train entered a tunnel, but she was not able to shake off the vague, annoying, nagging fear. They were a big party, and took up most of the coach—Rukmini, Ranjeet and their children along with a maid, Harjeet with Maya and Inder, Basanti and a *khansama*. Despite Lalaji's insistent persuasion, Gautam had not accompanied them, although he had promised to come up in time for the opening play of the two day performance, starting a week later. Haider would be accompanying him, along with Shaukat, who Rukmini felt was coming more out of jealousy than a genuine desire to see the play.

The week passed quickly. It was May, the beginning of summer and Simla was at its most glorious, warm but with an energizing nip of cold in the air. The sky remained clear for the duration of their visit, a clear azure flecked with cotton candy clouds, which the wind pulled into ever-changing shapes. They had rented the ground floor of a cottage located by the side of a widish bridle path overlooking the valley, a short distance from the ridge, and Harjeet loved to sit in the wood paneled verandah and hear the sound of the wind rustling in the pines. Even the tea tasted different here, woody and more flavourful. From the cottage it was a short but steep climb to the Mall, and while the children enjoyed taking a stroll and buying tit bits from the interesting looking shops, Harjeet and the other actors finished rehearsing their parts. Gaiety Theatre had no shortage of funds, the seats were plush and the lighting excellent and Harjeet found it a pleasure to work with the fine props and beautiful sets, a pleasant change from the make-shift ones they usually had to use at Lahore.

On the night of the play, the hall was full. Since it was the beginning of the season, there was much enthusiasm among the patrons, and curiosity as well, because normally the theatre was let out to productions from outside only towards the end in September. Harjeet, jittery at the thought of forgetting her lines, or even worse at being unable to enact a scene, was oblivious to the atmosphere of festivity, to the stream of rickshaws running up and down the Mall and to the audience resplendent in full evening dress. But just before she stepped on to the stage, she peered at the darkened hall through a gap in the curtains, and looked towards the first class box Ranjeet had bought to view the play from. She saw Gautam, who had come up the previous day sitting with the children, saw Rukmini with her husband, and then her eye was caught by Haider, who seemed to be looking straight at her, as if he knew magically exactly where she was standing. Suddenly, wondrously, she was caught up in the spirit of the evening and there was no more nervousness, nor any doubt. It did not matter that she was a woman in a man's role, or that her voice was not heavy enough, or her appearance not entirely convincing. As Amarkant she was brilliant, overshadowing all the other actors, making the audience laugh and cry with her.

When it was over, she got a standing ovation, but felt curiously detached from all the applause and the accolades. The local papers made her a celebrity overnight, and the play was extended by a week. Rukmini was delighted, they had collected more money for their charity than she could have ever imagined, and was already making plans to stage the play in other cities as well. Gautam also seemed genuinely proud and extended his stay for the entire week, promising to buy her a piece of jewellery the day they got back to Lahore. The children were pleased but confused, as if they they found it hard to reconcile their mother with the passionate person they saw on the stage. Haider, with whom she was not able to get any time alone, just made a V-for-victory sign with his fingers when no one was watching, but the gesture meant more to her than a thousand spoken words, for the achievement was more his than hers and it was to him that she owed a debt of gratitude; his love had helped her discover her real self, hidden under layers of bitterness and aloneness for years. With him she had found the confidence to step out of the house for the first time, to explore the open sky stretching endlessly from horizon to horizon. To soar like the kite he had taught her to fly that day long ago. They had been together for eight years now, eight long years in which she had changed from a whiny, insecure housewife to a confident, happy woman.

There was a row of trees along the bridle path outside their cottage, and when the sun rose in the morning, it traversed up the slope slowly, illuminating them one by one. The chosen tree, lit up from behind, turned into molten gold, standing out from the rest, enjoying its moment in the sun. Life was like that, Harjeet realised, giving to everyone their moment of glory, and this was hers. The country was in turmoil again, there were rumours of escalating hostilities between Britain and Germany, and sometimes it seemed to Harjeet as though the entire world was at war with itself. Closer home, Gautam was still pensive and Lalaji withdrawn. Her own future seemed humdrum and bleak, the relationship with Haider was permanently doomed to uncertainty and the one with her husband was virtually non-existent. But at that moment, Lahore and her problems seemed so far away, and while waiting at the railway station in Simla for the train back to Kalka, basking in the warmth of a mellow sun and filled with the glow of achievement, Harjeet felt a deep sense of contentment.

All these our lives, she mused, are written on the wind, our futures pre-determined, and everything else just becomes an excuse. We go where the wind takes us, blowing a gale one day and caressing like a zephyr the next, at the mercy of runes that we cannot interpret. Stooping low against the storms that create havoc in our lives, we wait for a change in the wind, for a directional shift in the weather-vane, for the gentle breeze of contentment on our backs. And ultimately our fortunes do change and all the pieces of the puzzle come together to complete the picture. Maybe that was what Haider was, the missing piece that made her life whole. The future would look after itself, right now she had her children and the man she loved with her. She could ask for no more from life.

Chapter 9

AMIYA

Amiya had never met her parents, had no inkling of what they looked like, how they spoke, their likes and dislikes. Her mother had died within a few days of her birth and her father was never mentioned at home. His very name was taboo, and any efforts she might have made as a child, and later as a teenager, to find out more about him, were met with stern disapproval, first by her normally gentle grandfather and later by her aunt. Whatever knowledge she had of him was gleaned through eavesdropping and family gossip, although her mother's cousin, her massi Kamla, did share stories about her mother Gayatri and their carefree life in Delhi. As a child, growing up in rather difficult circumstances, it was soon apparent to Amiya that there were somethings she was not supposed to ask or to know, and her father was one of them, although she had realized fairly early that even the surname she carried was fictious, and that there was probably no Major Bharadwaj, who had died fighting in the Boer war.

However, unbeknown to her, her biological father was indeed an army man, an officer in the British Indian army. Born in the South of England, to a farmer, David joined the newly formulated Indian army in the 1890s, at the age of twenty-two. A smart young man, tall and well built, with a head full of curly hair and deep-set brown eyes, he was always keen on joining the armed forces, and accordingly received his formal education and military training in England, before being commissioned into the City of London Regiment. However, within the first year, nursing a broken heart and an even more wounded ego, he became desperate to move on and look for more exciting and exotic adventures. After two years in the London Regiment, he was commissioned into the Border Regiment of the British army and posted to India. There he joined the 32nd Punjab Pioneers and within a short time was dispatched to the North West Frontier Province, where Chitral, an independent state, was under siege. The state had come under the protection of the Maharaja of Kashmir in 1876, and trouble started when the ruler died in 1892, and there was a scramble among his relatives for the throne. In the confusion that followed, with more than three tribal leaders laying claim to the throne, the British arrested one of them and placed him under custody in the Chitral fort. The other two claimants moved their forces to the fort and laid siege to it in March 1895.

Relief columns were immediately dispatched from Gilgit and Peshawar. David was part of the former and showed exemplary courage throughout. The route from Gilgit to Chitral followed the valleys of three different rivers, and was, in most places, hardly more than a track. In addition, most of the local population was hostile to the British forces, the weather was snowy, with blinding sunshine during the day and freezing cold at night. But David was unfazed throughout, boosting the morale of his fellow soldiers, walking through five inches of snow, unconcerned when a rock thrown down the cliffside by the Chitralis wounded him on the forehead. When they finally reached Chitral in the third week of April, the column was exhausted, but jubilant. David was subsequently awarded a medal for his bravery, and granted six weeks leave to recuperate, which he spent in Delhi with a relative of his mother's, who was posted as a deputy secretary in the Viceroy's office.

It was the first time David had visited Delhi. He was immediately charmed by the city, dazzled by the exciting social life his cousin had access to, seduced by the fragrance of the mogra growing in the houses lining the broad leafy avenues in Civil Lines, where his uncle, like many other Europeans lived. The earliest European settlers in Delhi lived to the south of the fort, but over the years some had moved to the north east, within the walled city. In the early decades of the 1800s, many British troops were moved out of the main city to a settlement some distance away. This new settlement, called Civil Lines, was to the north of the city, and was bounded by the river Jamuna on one side, a ridge of hills on the second, and the northern wall of the city on the third. After the uprising of 1857, things changed even further, and the desire to put physical as well as social distance between themselves and the natives, prompted many Europeans who were still living within the walled city to also move to the Civil Lines. The Civil Lines now became the hub of British life in Delhi and many bungalows were built to accommodate the new arrivals. David's uncle had built his house some years ago, and although it had both gothic and Indian features, somehow it did not look odd. The marble lattice work screen or jaali, as it was called, was both decorative and functional, keeping the house well ventilated during the hot summer months.

David's uncle had a son, George, a serious-minded young man, who had come to India with his parents when he was a baby, and now nearly eighteen years later, was to set sail for England within the next couple of months. A relative had landed for him an excellent paying job in a country estate, and although George was looking forward to his new assignment, he would miss the city he had grown up in. Musically inclined since childhood and an accomplished violin player, he was now learning to play an Indian instrument. David could see no merit in his doing so, he was hardly going to be able to keep it up in England, and privately suspected that it stemmed from a desire on the part of George to keep something of the city with himself forever. That would explain the excitement in his voice when talking about his music, his teacher and the amazing house he lived in. Inspite of himself, David's curiosity was aroused and he insisted on accompanying George to his next music lesson to Chandini Chowk, two days later.

The teacher's house was located at the end of a narrow street, lined with nearly similar looking houses on both sides. It was an interesting house, taller than it was wider, with an ornate entrance door, above which was hung a small carved weather beaten figure of indistinguishable features. There was a small balcony projecting over the main entrance, giving the house an even more hemmed in feel. A boy of about ten or twelve years came to lead them in, and before following him they took off their shoes in a small vestibule at the entrance. The house was built around an open courtyard, flanked by small rooms on all sides, and it was to one of these that the boy took them. David was surprised at the size of the room; what had seemed to be a small darkish room from the outside, was actually a large hall, long and narrow. It had carved stone pillars and a high ceiling, giving it a somewhat grand appearance, but was sparsely furnished. There was what appeared to be a huge mattress on the floor, with round bolster type of cushions strewn around carelessly. One corner of the room had a niche, in which an oil lamp was lit in front of a painting of a woman, which David guessed was that of a goddess. A man of about fifty years or so was sitting on the mattress, teaching two young boys the sitar, the same instrument that George was attempting to learn.

'Pandit Medha Prasad Mishra, from whom I'm learning music, is a master in his own right. He is one of the leading sitar players of the North, and is also an accomplished singer,' George had told David on the way, with a touch of reverence in his voice. 'It was only after much persuasion by my friend, who is a distant relative of his, that he agreed to take me on as a student,' he added. David was suitably impressed, and not wanting to embarrass his cousin in any way, took care to follow his every gesture, even bowing low and folding his hands in salutation when they entered the room.

They had been sitting for about five minutes, when a girl came into the room. She was young, maybe sixteen or seventeen, with long black hair, and dark flashing eyes. She was fair, not fair like his countrywomen, but fairer than most women he had seen in India so far. After the two boys left, George took his assigned place on the mattress, and introduced David to both his teacher and the young girl. If Panditji was annoyed at this intrusion into his private chambers, he hid it well, greeting David warmly. The girl, whose name was Gayatri, also gave him a smile, and asked him in perfect English, how he was. David's initial surprise soon gave way to curiosity, and on the way back home he could talk of nothing else. Who was she, why was she not in purdah, how was she so fluent in English? George's knowledge of the family was sketchy, but he did know that she was Panditji's only child, born rather late, when he was in his early thirties. Her mother had died in childbirth, and she had been brought up by Panditji and his mother, who had shifted to Delhi from the village to help raise her granddaughter. George's friend had hinted at some family dispute between Panditji and his cousins, most of whom were also music maestroes, whereupon the former had decided to do away with long held family traditions, and had brought up his daughter like a son, getting her the best tutors in Delhi, and refusing to let her go into purdah. She was an excellent sitar player, and had even accompanied her father on one or two occasions, much to the shock and consternation of both family and friends. Her grandmother, unable to bear the snide remarks, and unwilling to live any longer with a son who was bent on tarnishing the family name, returned to the village to live with her youngest son, once Gayatri was old enough to manage the house.

David was even more intrigued, and could not sleep the entire night. In the short time that he had been in India, he had heard enough stories about the sensuous nature and physical attractions of the native women to excite his curiosity. After an arduous and seemingly endless day spent marching to Chitral, his fellow officers would cheer themselves up at night by eulogizing over the various charms of the native women, their rounded limbs, beautiful caramel coloured skin that felt like silk to the touch, almond shaped dark eyes that could look into one's soul, and lustrous black hair. David was sure that much of the bragging was rooted in hearsay, rather than in actual physical opportunity to savour these delights, but after meeting Gayatri he could agree that most of the claims were not exaggerated. Desirous of meeting her again, he insisted on accompanying George to his music class the next day, in spite of the latter's obvious reluctance to take him. 'Panditji may not like you coming along every day,' he said to David. 'I'll be as unobtrusive and quiet as possible, I promise,' begged his cousin. But much to David's disappointment, Gayatri did not put in an appearance the next two times they visited, and he had to sit through George's often tuneless and jarring renditions. On the third visit, which David decided would be his last, he thought of taking a stroll through the area rather than sitting quietly in a corner of the dark hall. There was a very narrow passage between Panditji's house and the neighbouring one, and he had hardly walked along it for a hundred yards or so when he heard the loud cooing and chirping of birds. David was intrigued, the passage was narrow, flanked on both sides by tall buildings, and he could see no trees anywhere. The chirping seemed to be coming from behind a carved door that was half ajar, and peering in he saw nearly half a dozen pigeons and an equal number of parrots, in a courtyard of sorts. The parrots were inside a big cage, while the pigeons were pecking at some grain scattered in a corner. There seemed to be no one around, and feeling emboldened, he walked in. The pigeons were very pretty, with no two being alike, clothed in different shades of brown and grey dappled with white, and reminded him of the way sunlight streamed through the peepal tree in his uncle's house.

Hearing a sound, he looked up and was surprised to see Gayatri emerging from a door on the opposite side. Suddenly, and rather surprisingly, he felt a huge rush of excitement. She was as enchanting as he remembered, with her silken hair open and softly framing her face. There was another, slightly older girl with her, and they were both eyeing him with alarm. Realizing the inappropriateness of walking into the house like he had, he apologized, explaining that it was his curiosity that had made him behave in such a manner. He saw the look of relief on Gayatri's face as she recognized him. 'You are David, aren't you?' she asked. 'Yes,' he answered, 'I haven't seen you in the music class these last two days,' he added questioningly. 'I have been busy with the birds. My father dotes on them, and as the boy who looks after them is on leave, I have to do most of the work,' she replied. The other girl still seemed uncomfortable with David's presence and said something to Gayatri in Hindi, which the latter ignored and turning to him, asked him whether he liked pigeons and kept them at his home. David, sensing an opportunity to continue the conversation, admitted to his ignorance of all thing avian, but quickly added that he would very much love to increase his knowledge. Since it was late and George would have finished his lesson by now, David asked if he could come at the same time the next day, at which Gayatri was quiet for a minute before hesitatingly saying yes.

The next day it seemed to David that Gayatri was looking even lovelier, if possible. The pink saree she was wearing seemed to make her face glow, the colour reflecting off her cheeks and lips. She seemed to blush a little when she saw him, whispering something to her companion, the same girl who was with her yesterday. There were fewer pigeons about today, and picking up one which seemed hurt in one foot, Gayatri asked him to follow her upstairs, to the terrace. The staircase was dark, narrow and winding, and David narrowly avoided hitting his head on the ceiling at one or two places. The terrace, a vast open space on the second floor, was bounded by a brick wall, and had four or five large cages that were full of pigeons. At least two of the cages were of the size of a small room and had bars for the birds to perch on, as well as terracotta dishes for water and grain. David noticed with amazement, that most of the birds were wearing bangles on their feet, some even two or three each. While the other girl, whom Gayatri introduced as her cousin Kamla, filled the pots with water and did the general cleaning up work, Gayatri told him how *kabootarbaazi*, or pigeon rearing, was a favourite sport in the area, and how nearly every well-to-do family had at least a couple of pigeons each. The sport had been popular with the Mughal rulers, who used pigeons to communicate with their officers in secrecy. Pigeon keeping was said to have originated in Agra during Akbar's reign in the 16th century, from where it came to this part of Delhi, called Shahjahanabad during the time of Shahjahan, Akbar's grandson and the fifth emperor in the line of succession. 'My father has more than eighty pigeons and he knows each one by name,' Gayatri said proudly. 'He mixes their feed himself every morning, and gets the best quality ghee and millets and corn,' she continued. 'But what does he do with the pigeons? Surely he doesn't need them to send messages?' joked David, wanting to keep the conversation going as long as he could. Although interested in what she was saying, he was distracted by her nearness, by the faint fragrance of roses emanating from her. 'Of course not,' giggled Gayatri, 'although he does have a couple of those pigeons as well. He trains his birds to participate in pigeon-racing, which lasts the whole of the winter season. He teaches them to fly against the wind, and his favourite are a pair of Kabli's who take a walk with him in the early morning every couple of days, flying alongside loyally, not even getting distracted by the grain scattered about on the road.'

However, before David could answer, Gayatri looking a little worried, asked him to come away from the terrace into a small enclosed space on the landing. 'We have very nosy neighbours, who won't take a second to tell my father about your being here,' she said, adding 'anyway, it's better if you go now.' Resisting the urge to push her tousled hair away from her face, and the even stronger urge to arrange another meeting with her, David let himself out of the building quietly, hoping that no one had seen him. He did not want to cause any trouble for Gayatri, and certainly not for his cousin, who would be furious if he learnt of the days' events.

It was late evening, almost dusk now, and looking up he saw flocks of pigeons flying in perfect formation. It was amazing, he thought to himself, how two hours had changed his perception of these nondescript birds, at whom normally he would not look at twice. But now he noticed the rhythm in their flight, saw them come close, veer really low before flying off again. He wondered how they knew which roof in this sea of similar looking roofs was theirs. He could hear the sound of men cooing, calling, shouting, whistling, encouraging the birds, and remembered Gayatri telling him that the pigeons recognized the voice of their master. Suddenly, everything seemed so alive—the sky, the narrow lanes, the uncomfortably hot air, and he wished the moment would never end.

It was the third week of May now, and nearly half his leave was over. Torn between wanting to see Gayatri again and the futility of doing so, he decided to spend the rest of his vacation exploring Delhi. On his uncle's advice, the next morning he started off for the Purana Quila, or old fort, which was some distance away from the Civil Lines. But neither being used to the terrible heat, nor being able to find any suitable transport to the place, he gave up his quest midway and returned home dehydrated and with a bad headache. Maybe he lacked the adventurous spirit and hardy body of true explorers, and would do best to spend the rest of his time in Delhi in the cool confines of home. 'Don't give up so easily,' admonished George. 'I'll give my music class a miss today, and we can instead take a walk in Chandini Chowk. I have been wanting to do so once before I leave anyway, and as you know, the evenings are not as unbearable.'

'Thank you, that's very nice of you' answered David, wondering at the coincidence taking him back to the area again.

They started in the late afternoon of the next day, stopping on the way to tell Panditji that George would not be attending his lessons that day. Panditji was in a good mood, brought on perhaps by George's gift to him of a brand new harmonium, which had been ordered from the best maker in the city. He told them about the best places to visit and on David's commenting on the number of pigeons in the area, even offered to show them his own, an offer that George politely declined. He had no interest in the silly birds and wanted to explore the area before nightfall. Just as they were leaving, they heard Gayatri calling to them from the small garden near the gate, and on the pretext of asking George something innocuous about his class, managed to whisper to David to meet her in the courtyard the next afternoon. David felt a sliver of excitement course through his body, and spent the rest of the evening in a sort of daze, hardly paying any attention to what George was saying. The latter was telling him whatever he knew about the area, pointing out the beautiful havelis or mansions of the noblemen and the well-to-do, some of which were now in a state of neglect.

Chandini Chowk was part of Shahjahanabad, the walled city that had been constructed by the Mughal Emperor Shahjahan, after he shifted his capital to Delhi from Agra in the mid 1630s. The site he chose by the banks of the river Jamuna to the north had a long history of settlement, and in the following two hundred years or more had seen much change. It had gone from being the glittering capital of a famous empire, complete with a splendid fort and numerous mosques, temples, gardens, markets and huge havelis of the elite, to being a less opulent, congested but culturally still as important a centre, by the time the British arrived in the early 1800s. However, after the uprising of 1857, the changes that took place were momentous and far reaching. The British army took over the fort built by Shahjahan and made numerous alterations to the land use. Needing more land for the military, large areas within the fort were cleared, and barracks constructed, without any thought for the beautiful buildings and meticulously planned gardens destroyed in the process. Land was cleared outside the fort premises as well, to make way for a new railway line and station. The railway line ran from Shalimar Bagh, through a corner of the Red Fort to Chandini Chowk.

As they walked along the shop-lined, main street of Chandini Chowk, George pointed out the Town Hall, municipal offices and European Club constructed on what used to be the serai and garden of Jahanara, Shahjahan's eldest and most beloved daughter. The garden, called the Sahiba Abad Bagh or more simply, Begum Bagh, was, in its hey days, filled with fruit trees and well-ordered flower beds, and was a favorite with ladies of the royal household. A part of the garden housed a serai and a bath. What David found most intriguing was the legend associated with the naming of Chandini Chowk. An earlier canal that transported water from the Jamuna and was built for the purpose of irrigation, was repaired and extended into the city during the reign of Shahjahan. One branch of the canal watered Begum Bagh on its way to the fort, while the other flowed down the main street on which they were now walking. It was said that the alignment of the canal was such that on clear nights, moonlight glinting off the water was clearly visible from the main pavilion of the palace, hence the name Chandini or moonlight. However, the British converted the tree lined canal into a street, which was joined all along its length, at right angles, by narrow winding alleys, often resulting in the formation of small chowks at the points of intersection. The chowk in front of Jahanara's serai was in the shape of a half moon and was bigger in size than the rest and was the original Chandini Chowk, from which the entire market had got its name. Like the main street, the narrow alleys were also lined with shops on both sides. George was explaining at length about the commodity segregation that made this market so interesting; there were some streets selling only clothes, while others sold utensils made of copper and brass, or haberdashery or exotic looking spices. But David was no longer interested, he had seen enough and wanted to turn back. 'You have been unusually quiet,' said George. 'Are you feeling well? The heat can get to the best of us.'

'I'm fine,' replied David, 'just tired.' The evening was indeed very hot, and he could feel little beads of perspiration running down his back, wetting his shirt. Uncomfortable as he was, his thoughts turned to Gayatri, and he wondered how her skin would look glistening with sweat. Would her saree cling to her breasts, or hug her rounded hips, accentuating their fullness? Suddenly, tomorrow afternoon seemed a long way off, and he was afraid that George or his uncle would sense his excitement, or something would happen that would prevent him from meeting her.

But nothing untoward occurred and after a fitful sleep, David got ready early and left the house immediately after breakfast. By the time he reached Chandini Chowk, his mind had subjected him to a plethora of emotions; eagerness, fear, anxiety, guilt—leaving him feeling totally drained. The late May afternoon was punishing, a relentless sun beat down harshly, keeping both man and beast off the roads. The hat he was wearing felt uncomfortable, but at least it would keep him from being recognized. The alley adjoining Panditji's house was deserted and the door to the courtyard was slightly ajar. It seemed Gayatri had been waiting for him; her beautiful eyes lit up as he entered, and he was suddenly reminded of the legend that George had narrated yesterday regarding the naming of Chandini Chowk. He could imagine moonlight being reflected in the limpid pools of her eyes, and tangling itself in her long hair. Fighting back an impulse to reach out and feel its silkiness, David followed her inside and up the stairs to the roof with the *kabootarkhanas*, which were now covered with dark cloth to shelter them from the sun. Gayatri led him to the edge behind the structures, to a low parapet that connected their roof to the adjoining one, which was the portion of the house that belonged to Kamla's parents. David was amazed at the agility with which she jumped over to the other side, her glossy hair billowing after her.

This roof had more built up area, which made it appear smaller and more compact. The room that Gayatri took him to was dark and very sparsely furnished, with only a rickety looking diwan placed along one wall, and a couple of wooden boxes along another. Gayatri's cousin, the daughter of Panditji's older brother, was sitting on one of the boxes, waiting for them. 'Three years ago my uncle and aunt moved to Kanpur to be with Kamla's oldest brother, whose wife has kept very unwell since the birth of their third child. Her younger brother also lives in Kanpur, in a separate house with his wife and child, but his wife is very quarrelsome and refuses to look after her ailing sister-in-law or the poor children, because of which her parents have had to wind up everything and shift.'

'Kamla didn't accompany them?' asked David surprised. 'How could she?' answered Gayatri. 'Kamla and I study here together, so naturally she couldn't go. But they took her younger sister, the youngest of the four siblings with them. Besides, Kamla and I have always been very close, and my father loves her like a daughter, and even when her parents were here she lived with us,' she added. David was intrigued. 'So you both go to school,' he asked, a part of him appalled at being attracted to a school girl. 'No,' giggled Gayatri, as if amused by his ignorance. 'Pitaji has arranged for a tutor who comes home four times a week in the mornings to teach us.' At this Kamla also started to giggle. 'He is fat and totally bald and keeps saying "attention" all the time, as if we are in a parade,' she added.

As their light hearted banter continued, David wondered why Gayatri had asked him to come. Surely it was not just to indulge in idle chit-chat? As if reading his thoughts, Gayatri took his arm and led him from the room to a small enclosure in a corner of the roof. 'My father bought a couple of new pigeons last week, rare brown ones with black wings splaterred with white. They are very strong fliers, and very intelligent, and can carry messages over long distances without being detected. I thought you would like to see them', she said. However, David was barely listening. At her touch a jolt of excitement ran through his body and he felt more alive than he had in a long time. The feeling of happiness stayed with him long after he returned home after duly inspecting the birds, the euphoria fuelled to a large extent by her invitation to him to return the next day.

David had only ten days leave left, and for every one of those days he braved the terrible heat to meet Gayatri. It was the beginning of June, the week of the *nau tapa*, the hottest nine days of the year, and it was believed that the greater the heat, the stronger would be the monsoon. The intense low pressure created by the relentless heat attracted rain bearing winds from the Arabian Sea and the Bay of Bengal, thus bringing much needed relief to both land and man. But as of now, the heat hung low in the eerily quiet afternoons, and it seemed to David that all life was still, no birds chirped, not even a leaf moved. But the room at the top of the stairs in Kamla's house was deliciously cool and it was here that the two of them spent hours talking, while Kamla kept guard downstairs. On David's last day, Gayatri was unusually quiet, and asked him whether he would ever come back to Delhi again. David, torn at the thought of leaving her, promised to return soon, although he was privately not sure when, if ever, that would be. It would depend upon whether he genuinely cared for her or whether what he felt for her was merely a passing fancy, a result of loneliness and homesickness.

But he started to miss her almost immediately, and even before he left Delhi, started planning his return. It was, however, not before the end of July, two months later, that he was able to get a couple of days off. This time he did not tell his uncle or George that he was in town, and instead stayed at the Officer's Mess located very near Chandini Chowk. It was his intention to spend as much time as he could with Gayatri without her father coming to know. But providentially, Panditji was away to Lahore while David was in Delhi, and such was Gayatri's pleasure at seeing him again that she was willing to throw all caution to the wind, even asking him to spend the night in the room upstairs. This he refused, but it was in the same room that he took her into his arms on the final day, whispering to her how much he loved her, and promising to be back soon. He felt Gayatri momentarily stiffen at his words, before she reached up and brushed her lips against his.

It was as if a dam of pent up feelings had burst its banks, the waters gushing, swirling, overcoming all hurdles. Half spoken words of endearments, sobs of joy, sighs of pleasure, all carried along in one huge rush. When it was over, David felt a rush of tenderness towards Gayatri, towards her innocence, her trust in him and vowed to speak to Panditji as soon as the latter was back from Lahore. They could get engaged that very weekend before David returned to his posting, and meanwhile to remind her of him, every single moment, he slipped off his ring and put it on her finger. It was far too big in size but Gayatri was delighted, and the memory of her face, radiant with love and excitement, stayed with him long into the night.

But his joy was short lived. Early the next morning, a messenger brought the news that an emergency had come up in Chitral and he was required to report back to headquarters immediately. A special vehicle had been arranged to carry some important dak, and he could take a lift in it. David was devastated, and for a moment contemplated leaving the army, and staying on in Delhi instead. But sanity prevailed and realizing the futility of such a course of action, he decided instead to confide in his cousin and request him to deliver a letter to Gayatri.

George was shocked and most disapproving. Did not David know the consequences of such a course of action? Did he think Panditji would agree to marry his only child to a foreigner? It would cause a terrible scandal, and worst of all, George would lose an excellent music teacher. But David was desperate, he had to leave in under an hour, and after much persuasion George agreed to deliver the letter the very next day.

Chapter 10

When Gayatri got David's letter, her initial reaction was one of panic. She had heard enough stories of doomed relationships between the *firangis* and native women to justify her worry that this was just an excuse for David to go back on his promise of marrying her. But her optimistic nature took over soon enough, convincing her that David was different from his countrymen, and it was indeed a coincidence, although an unfortunate one, that he had been called back to duty the day after she had given herself to him physically. The memory of it brought a blush to her face, but she felt no shame. In her mind they were already married; she had made him promise in front of her favourite idol of Radha-Krishan and besides, she had his ring to prove it. And his letter was so loving and reassuring. He would be back as soon as possible and together they would tell Panditji about their wanting to spend the rest of their lives with each other. If Gayatri wanted he would even leave the army and they could return to England, where he was sure he could get a decent job. He had also written the address of his parents' farm in Suffolk. It was his only permanent address, and he wanted Gayatri to have it.

But Gayatri was afraid. Afraid of the uncertainty, afraid of Panditji finding out, afraid of David never returning. Her fears were somewhat assuaged on receiving a second letter from David a month later. Delivered by George, it again reiterated his love for her and spoke of returning as soon as possible. David had further written that he had been promoted to the rank of Lieutenant and would be leaving for a very important assignment shortly. But Gayatri was not to worry. As soon as the assignment was over, on the first leave he got, he would be back, and they could get married right away.

However, within a week of delivering the letter, George stopped coming for his music lessons, telling Panditji that he needed to make preparations for his voyage to London. Gayatri was distraught and took this to be a sign that David was never coming back. Why else would George, who was the only conduit between the two of them, decide to leave at a time when he was needed the most? And as the days passed without any news of David, Gayatri became more and more anxious. Kamla was her only confidant, and even her reassuring words could no longer quell the feeling of panic that would cause her stomach to churn several times a day, whenever she thought of her father, the future, David's betrayal. Anger at David would alternate with worry about his well-being. What if he had been injured or wounded, or worse still, had died while on the assignment he had written about? The tension started telling on her health, and she lost the rosy glow that had attracted David to her in the first place. Lack of appetite made her toy with the food in her thali, and she was often distracted during the music lessons with Panditji, something that had never happened before. She was passionate about her sitar and had done *riyaz* every single day for more years than she could remember.

It was now the end of September, and the last of the monsoon clouds had dispersed, leaving the days bright and sunny. The September sunlight, like the one in October, was very sharp, and her grandmother would always say it caused more tanning than sunlight during the hot summer months. The days were getting shorter, but in sub tropical Delhi the change was very gradual. Even so, the dusk came in a little earlier now, and the lamps would be lit well before dinner. This was usually Gayatri's favourite time of day, when the last of Panditji's students had left and the strains of raga Puriya Kalyan, which her father liked to play in the early evening, would fill the whole house. It was a delight to hear him at this hour, it was as if he was playing only for himself, and his mastery over his instrument was astounding. Gayatri and Kamla, who had also been learning for the last couple of years, would join him for their evening practice, and the three of them would play until dinner was served.

But now Gayatri started dreading the evenings. Dusk would bring with it a strange sense of queasiness and nausea, and she almost always had no appetite for dinner. As a result, she would often wake up light headed and giddy in the morning, and no amount of coaxing by Kamla, who would get the cook to make Gayatri's favourite dishes, would get her to eat. This continued for some days, until finally one evening, immediately after dinner, she felt the walls closing in on her and collapsed, only dimly aware of the alarm in Panditji's voice as he called out to her. For more than two days she drifted in and out of consciousness, sometimes hearing voices as if coming from a long distance off, wandering at other times into a dream world with David.

On the third day, she felt stronger and was able to sit up, but sensed immediately that something was very wrong. For a minute she could not recognize her father, who looked haggard and very old, and Kamla, who seemed frightened, refused to look her in the eye. 'The Vaid ji says you are about to become a mother,' Panditji said abruptly, as if forcing himself to say the painful words aloud, voicing them with much effort, each syllable bruising him. Gayatri felt the world shift beneath her feet as she looked at him in disbelief. It couldn't be, it was only that one time, and was that all it took to make a woman pregnant? Where oh where was David when she needed him, needed to tell her father that they were married and that everything would be alright? Fighting back a strong wave of panic and nausea, she tried to explain to Panditji that David would be back any day now, but the very mention of his name enraged her father even more. 'What a fool you have been, child. Did you for a moment believe that the *firangi* really cared for you? These men never marry Indian girls, at best they keep them as their bibi's, which is itself humiliating and impermanent. No, the firangi has had his pleasure and is never coming back,' he said scornfully. 'But we got married in front of the Radha Krishna murti in the room upstairs. I have David's ring to prove it,' replied Gayatri tearfully. 'Stop this silly talk,' shouted Panditji, 'you have

brought shame to our family. My mother was right all along. I
was a fool to have trusted you and given you so much freedom.
She was right in saying that girls from good families do not learn
music and dance like the *tawaifs* do". Before Gayatri could reply,
he sat down abruptly at the foot of her bed, and holding his head
in his hands, began to sob, the sound of his crying, in a way, more
painful than even David's betrayal.

The next few days passed in a miserable blur, a nightmare
from which there was no waking up. Panditji had stopped talking
to her, and all communication was through Kamla, who was, in a
way, bearing the brunt of her uncle's anger and disappointment.
Had he not brought her up like his own daughter, had he not loved
her enough? Was it not her duty to tell him if her sister was doing
something wrong? How could the two of them have connived to
cheat him, their own father?

In a way Gayatri preferred his ranting to his silence, for it
was when she saw him defeated, bent over like an old man, that
remorse smote her the most. What was even more disturbing was
the news that Kamla brought one evening; Panditji had refused
to take on any new students, and had told the older ones that he
was leaving Delhi and would be unable to teach them anymore.
'Leaving Delhi,' Gayatri said, alarmed. 'What do you mean, leaving
Delhi? Who told you this?' 'I overheard him telling the boy who
comes to learn singing in the evening,' replied Kamla, 'I heard it
with my own ears,' she added.

'But I can't leave Delhi. David will be coming any day and he
won't know where to find me,' said Gayatri, fighting back tears.

But Panditji had decided to leave Delhi forever, it being to his
mind, the only way to save Gayatri and the entire family from
disgrace. They would go back to their native village near Lahore,
where he would present Gayatri as a married woman, whose
husband was in the army, away fighting at the present. Later, at
an appropriate time, the fictitious husband would be killed in war,
and no one would ever be the wiser about Gayatri's sordid little
secret. Friends and family would be told that since the groom had

to leave shortly for an assignment, his parents had insisted on an immediate wedding, leaving Panditji with no time to make any arrangements for a big wedding or to invite anyone. Kamla would accompany them, of course, and the three of them would leave as soon as possible, probably in a week's time at the most.

Gayatri was distraught, but for once her pleading and crying left her father unmoved. Still very weak and troubled by an almost daily bout of nausea, she was largely bed ridden and dependent on Kamla for all news. Kamla was equally upset, she had no desire to leave Delhi and move to a small village. She loved Chandini Chowk, its hawkers, pigeons, hustle and bustle, its vibrancy. She would miss her friends and even her silly guruji. She didn't want to leave them all behind for some obscure village, especially since Gayatri was no fun anymore, always remembering David and crying. Panditji also seemed so aloof and stern, talking only when necessary. He had sworn both girls to secrecy, forbidding Kamla from even telling her parents anything of what had transpired.

Things moved very fast after that. Panditji seemed desperate to leave Delhi, convinced that David was never coming back, and it seemed to Gayatri that he had become totally emotionless, showing no regret at having to abandon his city, remaining stony faced throughout. She spent the remaining days in a daze, alternately pleading with her father and crying, and did not sleep at all the night before they were to leave, waiting for everyone to go to bed before tip toeing out of the room she shared with Kamla. Slowly she went from chamber to chamber, knowing her way perfectly in the dark, almost not needing the small candle she held. Lovingly she ran her fingers over every surface, every table and chair, over the carved pillars in the music room, stopping before the idol of Saraswati placed in a niche in the wall. Saraswati, the goddess of music, who would preside over endless silence now, the notes of the sitar and tabla gone forever from the vast hall. Panditji had decided not to take any of his musical instruments with him, and Gayatri didn't know what she grieved over more, David's betrayal or her father's sadness. Music was his life, he had stayed faithful to it all through the years, through the death of his beloved wife, through the long drawn fued with his cousins, through all the days and weeks and months. It was what defined him, but now such was his sorrow that he had not picked up the sitar or played a single note since that fateful day two weeks ago.

In the morning, before they were to leave, Gayatri found the courage to mention it to him and to ask whether he would like to take at least his sitar with him. Panditji's only answer before turning away, was a cold stare. Gayatri was heartbroken, and thought to herself that as long as she lived, she would remember this day of October 1895, whose balmy morning, complete with a light zephyr and the cooing of pigeons, belied the storm raging in her heart. She wondered what her father and Kamla were thinking, and whether they were gripped by the same hopelessness as she was. Kamla was crying, but Gayatri had no doubt that her sadness would be short lived, and that she would soon adjust to her new life. But what about her, Gayatri ? Maybe Panditji was right after all, and David was never coming back. And even if he did, he would not be able to ever find her. Panditji had kept their departure a secret, and not even their very nosy neighbours had got wind of their plans. Fighting back the panic rising in her throat, she quietly followed her father out of the gate, her heart heavy with a grave premonition.

Chapter 11

They reached Chunian, Panditji's ancestral village, in the evening, and in the falling dusk, the place appeared desolate. Smoke from chullahs hung low over the village, draping it in a thin veil, while the road, no more than a dirt track, snaked across the land like a ribbon of white; its fine, white silt settling over everything in a shower of dust. The bullock cart they were travelling in was swaying alarmingly, making Gayatri nauseous and adding to the feeling of unreality gripping her. It was only the look of horror on Kamla's face that convinced her that this was no nightmare, and that they had indeed left Delhi and her beloved David far behind.

The morning was no better and the first light of dawn, which painted the sky a bashful shade of pink, could do little to redeem Chunian , which seemed to Gayatri to be as disappointing as it had been the previous evening. It was a small settlement, and on first glance, seemed to be no more than a haphazard conglomeration of low lying mounds, which she later found out, had been formed by the river Ravi, after a particularly bad flood some hundred years earlier. The river formed the southern boundary of the town, skirting past it in its journey down from the glaciers of the Kangra region in the Himalayas, before flowing past Lahore on its way to Ahmadpur Sial, where it merged with the much bigger Chenab. From where she stood on the first morning at Chunian, Gayatri could not see the river, but fancied that she could feel it's cool breeze on her skin, and wanting to get a shawl, was turning to go back in when she saw Kamla hurrying towards her with a worried look on her face.

'Where have you been?' she demanded. 'Pitaji has been looking for you. You are not to step out of the house without wearing these,' she added, handing her a packet containing red glass bangles and sindoor, in addition to some silver hair clips and a pair of thick payals.

'Why,' asked Gayatri, shocked.

'Because you are a married woman now,' answered Pitaji, coming up from behind. 'God knows I feel terrible at this deceit, and wonder whether He will ever forgive me for using your late mother's things to perpetuate it. She was a very pious lady,' he added, giving her a pained look.

The now familiar tide of guilt and panic washed over her again, burying her under its powerful surge, threatening to engulf her, and from a long distance off, she could hear Kamla's voice and then Pitaji's slightly worried one, but she couldn't make out what they were saying. Her head was full of clamorous voices, reproaching, angry , guilty, but in the midst of all the din, a small whisper of hope. She was indeed a married woman, had married David in the presence of God and had even worn his ring, but had erroneously omitted to do any of the shingar necessary after marriage. She could have worn at least one glass bangle and applied sindoor where it would not be visible to anyone. She had brought this inauspiciousness upon herself, and maybe if she rectified it now, it would bring David back to her. Clutching on to this small glimmer of hope, she wore the bangles and the payal and applied a big sindoor bindi, and went about the routine chores of the house a little more cheerfully.

The house was comfortable in a functional sort of way, being much smaller than the one in Delhi, with three rooms arranged in a line on one side of a small central courtyard, and the kitchen located on the opposite side. Panditji had built it many years ago, after a particularly bitter argument with his cousins which had firmed up his decision to leave for Delhi. But he had spent his growing years playing in Chunian's dusty lanes and hearing stories about his family's long association with it, and wanted to have a home there to return to whenever he wanted. Lonely in Delhi, he would reminisce about it often, first with his wife and then with the girls, telling them about its antiquity and long history.

The region had been inhabited since times immemorial. Lahore, located fifty miles to the south had been founded by Luv, Lord Ram's son, while the even nearer Kasur, a mere twenty miles away from Chunian, was attributed to his twin Kush. Panditji's ancestors had settled in Chunian and Kasur more than 300 years ago, and at least two of them had been court musicians to Akbar, and later to his son, Jehangir. The town had grown in importance during the Mughal period, when it served as a cantonment, but after the decline of the Mughal empire the entire region fell into disarray and suffered numerous invasions from across the border in the north west. But through all the turmoil, Panditji's family continued to live in and around Chunian, and his great great grandfather had even fought and been killed in the historic Battle of Harchoki in 1720. The battle was fought between the Mughals—through the Lahore governor, who was very unpopular—and the combined forces of Chunian and Kasur, and although the latter were defeated, the battle continued to be remembered reverentially and Panditji never tired of talking about it.

Panditji had got an outhouse built in one corner of the compound, initially intended to be his music room, but occupied for the last several years by a family of *malis*, who in return for living there for free, ensured the upkeep of the house. They grew vegetables for a living, originally along the banks of the river, but since the last few years on a patch of land that Panditji had given them. Now that Panditji was back with his family, the wife Chameli had taken on the duties of a maid, cleaning and washing for them. They had two teenage boys, and every morning father and sons would leave for Panditji's plot in the Canal Colony.

Canal Colony was the name given to reclaimed lands in the arid western part of Punjab. Since the 1880s, the British Government had identified and set up colonies in the barren, less fertile districts of the state. The rectangularly cut fields were serviced by a network of canals which drew water from the five major rivers that criss-crossed the land, and were to be cultivated by the peasants directly, preferably without the help of tenants. In addition to peasants, land was given to nomadic camel herders, who were the original inhabitants of the area, and who had, in a way, now been rendered homeless. Land was also given as a reward for military service and for loyalty to the Raj. Prominent families of the state, especially those who had significant social and cultural contributions to their name, were also given land, and it was in this category that Panditji's family was allotted plots in the Chunian colony. Both he and his brothers were given fifty acres each in the new Colony, established only a couple of years ago, and watered by an extension of the Upper Bari Doab canal, which also watered lands in Amritsar and Lahore. The family already owned land between Chunian and Kasur, but it was in an undulating, semi barren stretch strewn with pebbles and small rocks, and was so unproductive that the sons had not bothered to get it transferred to their names after the death of their father. But the new land was irrigated by the canal, and the farmer to whom Panditji had leased out his share had already harvested a good crop of wheat last year, and was making preparation for the next. Panditji had gifted two acres of the land to the family living in his outhouse, both as a baksheesh and with a view to keeping an eye on the tenant. This earned him their everlasting loyalty, along with the services of Chameli, who managed the cooking and all the household chores. Her husband and sons served as the errands men, and were also the daily suppliers of fresh vegetables.

Gayatri liked Chameli, and found her non inquisitive nature soothing. During the day, she enjoyed sitting in the angan, opposite the kitchen, watching Chameli go about her work. The tinkling of her glass bangles seemed to keep tune with some unsung melody, and Gayatri envied her the love of her husband and sons. Her own bangles, on the contrary, seemed to mock her, to remind her of David's betrayal, and as the days passed and the weeks turned into months, the small, last flicker of hope she had kept alive also died. David was never coming back and the thought of spending the rest of her life as a widow, bereft of all happiness, shouldering the responsibility of a child she didn't want, filled her with despair.

Winter added to the sense of gloom, and sometimes the fog would not lift till noon, making the short days seem even shorter. The freezing winds chilled her to the bone, and try as she may, she never felt warm anymore.

To Gayatri, who was used to evenings filled with music and the hustle and bustle of Chandini Chowk, the dark, silent house seemed like a tomb, a tomb built over her still alive body. Panditji had not played a single note since they had left Delhi, and all of Kamla's pleadings about her needing to practice left him unmoved. There was no need for the girls to learn any more music, and indeed it would be better if they forgot the ragas they had already learnt. Kamla protested vociferously, but Gayatri suspected that she was secretly relieved. She had never been a serious student and had found the long hours of *riyaz* very irksome. But, as she confided to Gayatri, anything would be better than the endless monotony of their days spent cooped up inside their small room. It was too cold to sit in the angan anymore, and they never went anywhere, not even for a walk. And although Kamla never once complained or expressed a desire to go back to her parents, Gayatri felt sorry for her. The poor girl was being punished for no fault of hers. The last few months had been very tough on her too, and although the situation was trying everyone's patience, it had brought the cousins even closer, and gradually Kamla became the only person Gayatri could talk to. She spoke about the constant feeling of dread she lived with, about her deep sorrow at having hurt her father, and the sense of despair she felt whenever she thought about her future. But she never spoke about David again; it was as if the certainty of his never coming back made it pointless to talk about him anymore. She knew that Pitaji had not told any of his relatives about their relocation to Chunian, and was just waiting for the birth of the child before announcing the death of his son-in-law. And just like that David's name would be erased from the collective memory of the family. His child would carry the name of a fictitious man, and the woman he swore undying love to would be widowed without ever having been married.

These thoughts tormented Gayatri constantly, but their intensity, she realized, varied with the time of day, and in the morning when the sun rose over the horizon and the house was filled with light, hope would arise in her heart, and she would look out for David surreptitiously, going to the small window in their room again and again. But as the day wore on, so did anticipation, and by the evening, she would be irritable and full of self loathing, berating herself for not accepting the fact that he was never coming back again. But lately, even the optimism she felt in the morning had begun to fade, and despondency became her constant companion, waking her up at day break and going to bed with her at night. And with it, her already tiny appetite reduced further, leaving her tired and listless all the time. Chameli, noticing her increasing pallor, exhorted her to eat well and drink milk at least twice a day if she wanted the baby to be healthy and plump.

'What will Sahib say when he comes to take you back home and finds the baby weak?' she would say, adding, 'he will blame us all and his mother will taunt you about it for years if her grandson is sickly.'

Gayatri, grateful for the concern showed by Chameli, was however, unable to bring herself to eat even her normal amount as the days went by, and in her eighth month, just weeks before she was due, developed a low grade fever, which came on in the evenings and left her virtually bedridden. Panditji, worried at her condition, asked Chameli to request the midwife to shift in with them a week in advance, instead of coming in when the labour pains started.

The midwife was a cheerful, middle aged woman belonging to one of the lower castes, whose dexterity and skill in her profession made her much sought after in the town. She came accompanied by her daughter-in-law, whom she was training to eventually take over from her. The daughter-in-law went home in the evenings, but the midwife stayed back, sleeping with the girls in their room, and during the day, helping Chameli make special *panjeeri* and *ladoos*—full of the goodness of *ghee* and almonds—which were mandatory for a new mother to eat. All went well and five days after the mid-wife's arrival, Gayatri delivered a healthy baby girl in the second week of April, whom Kamla immediately named Amiya after the tiny fruit just beginning to form on the mango trees. Both mother and daughter did fine for the first few days, but thereafter Gayatri developed a deadly fever accompanied by bouts of shivering, and by the time the doctor was called in she had slipped into a coma from which she never woke up, passing away in the early morning hours, before the baby was even a week old.

Chapter 12

Amiya went to live with her massi Kamla in Lahore when she was eight years old, immediately after the death of her grandfather. The year was 1904, it was the start of a new century and the world wore a new look, especially for a child moving from an isolated house in a small town to a bustling city full of people and tongas and big shops.

After about an year of Gayatri's death, Panditji had started looking for a suitable boy for Kamla, and within the next year and a half she was married into an educated Brahmin family settled in Lahore. Panditji, secretly unwilling to shoulder the responsibility of a young girl any more, had wanted Kamla to return to Kanpur with her parents after the thirteen day formalities following Gayatri's death were over. But his brother's wife, a kind and sensible woman who had loved Gayatri like a daughter, refused, insisting that Kamla would stay to look after the new-born baby. Any grudge she bore against her brother-in-law, about not being invited to Gayatri's wedding, she put aside at this hour of need, earning the everlasting gratitude of her husband, who was aghast to see the state his younger brother was in. She herself stayed on for nearly four months, during which time she took complete care of Amiya, bathing and feeding her and in the process teaching Chameli and Kamla the proper way to massage the baby, and what to do when she became cranky. After she returned home, Kamla took over her role, becoming the surrogate mother, spending every moment of the day with the child, who as the months passed, grew more and more attached to her. On the day of Kamla's marriage, when her mother-in-law saw the little girl clinging to her massi, inconsolable at being separated from her, her heart melted and she offered to have her come and stay with them whenever she wanted.

Chunian was not far from Lahore, and over the next six years Amiya was a frequent visitor to Kamla's house, often staying for a month at a time. She was a lovable child, quiet, never making any demands, and quickly won over Kamla's mother-in-law and husband. She had inherited her father's fair skin and also his broad forehead and curly hair. But her eyes were Gayatri's, almond shaped and black, and sometimes Panditji could not bear to look into them. When she was one year old he announced to all his relatives that her father had been killed in the line of duty, and as his widowed mother was too old to look after a small child, the poor unfortunate girl would continue to live with him.

A number of eyebrows were raised and much vicious gossip followed this news. In the first place, why had Panditji married off his only child in such a secretive fashion? What was he trying to hide? After all, even after shifting to Chunian he had not taken the now married Gayatri to meet any of their numerous relatives, preferring instead to keep both her and the baby under wraps. Why had no one from her in-law's family come upon hearing of her death? It was all very strange, and eventually the gossip shifted, in an entirely expected manner, on to the little child. Were her features not slightly different, the forehead too broad and the nose too straight? And who had she inherited that curly hair from? The women in their family all had straight, lustrous hair. The insinuations reached their climax after Panditji's cousin's wife, who lived in Chunian, some distance away in the heart of the town, claimed that on her recent visit to Delhi, she had met someone who had heard from one of Panditji's neighbours about the foreigner who came for music lessons every evening. And how, after he suddenly stopped coming, Panditji gave away his beloved *kabutars* to a friend, packed his bags and left for good. The boy who worked for Panditji was then bribed by the same neighbour with a cup of milk and a few annas to divulge some more insider information. This was then all put together by women who had spent a lifetime honing their predatory skills, and the conclusion reached that the child was a bastard and a half-baked Anglo-Indian at that.

Panditji, fully aware of the talk regarding Amiya, was however, not overly concerned. Gayatri's death had left him in a state of shock, and he became more of a recluse than ever, seldom leaving the house any more. The little girl was looked after by Chameli, who after Kamla's marriage, had gradually started living in the house permanently, even sleeping the nights with the child. But Chameli had work to do during the day, and with a grandfather who had started living increasingly in his own private world, Amiya learnt to be alone. By the time she started going to the small one room school run by the priest of the local temple, she was mature way beyond her years. At only six years of age, she was the youngest in her class, but never once did she cry or complain, even when the older kids bullied her into giving them her brand new mat to sit on. She would quietly take her place under the peepal tree in the corner of the temple, the only girl in a group of more than ten boys. The guruji thought her grandfather foolish for wasting money on a girl, and that too, on one so young, but who was he to complain? The locals were very tight fisted with their money and the *chadava* at the temple was never enough to meet the demands of his nagging wife. Moreover, every once in a while, the girl would be accompanied by the maid, who was a sight for sore eyes. Usually one of the maid's sons would accompany Amiya, and for the two hours she was in school, the no-gooder would play *pithoo* with the other boys in the galli outside the temple, making so much noise that guruji personally had to admonish them. But whenever the maid came, she would wait on the other side of the peepal tree, preening herself, tucking away a stray strand of hair, fiddling with her bangles, thus proving to be a very pleasant distraction for a bored teacher. On those days, guruji was full of good humour, paying extra attention to Amiya, scolding the boys instead of giving them a clip on the side of the head.

Those were the days Amiya enjoyed the most as well. She liked it when Chameli walked her to school and back. The temple was not far from where they lived, probably less than even a mile, but to get to it they had to cross the river, walking carefully across the narrow bridge. The temple was situated on the left bank of the river, at a point where it was at its shallowest, and the flight of steps leading down from it to the water always tempted Amiya, but her grandfather, afraid that she would slip and fall, had forbidden her from going that side. Instead, Chameli was willing to walk a short distance upstream with her, to a place where the river made a sudden bend, the water forming small eddies midstream. Amiya loved this stretch of the river. The sandy banks where Lapwings laid their eggs, the big grey boulder in the middle which the waves circumbulated with such dexterity, the sunlight glinting on the water, all enchanted her and she could have spent hours watching the antics of a kingfisher, who sat surveying his domain from the branches of a nearby tree, but Chameli always insisted they return after a few minutes. This was the place she missed the most when she had to shift to Lahore after her grandfather died, and often at night, unable to sleep in an unfamiliar room, she would imagine herself back at Chunian, temple bells ringing in the distance, the water dancing with the sunlight.

Kamla lived with her family in the Gumti Bazaar area, located in the centre of the walled city. It was an old, almost entirely Hindu neighbourhood, with a very colourful and popular bazaar, famous for *gota-kinari* and *meenakari*. Kamla's house was located in Gali Kali Mata, right next to the temple which gave it its name. It was a densely populated mohalla, with numerous narrow lanes and by-lanes. The house, although two and a half storeys high, was built on a small piece of land, and like the others around it, made up in height what it lacked in width. But tall buildings on either side of a narrow lane made it a dingy place to live in and hardly any light reached the ground floor. To Amiya, it seemed to resemble a cattle shed more than anything else, with almost every family, including Kamla's, keeping cows in the tiny open space outside each house, rendering the narrow lane nearly unfit for walking. Amiya used to country living, blue skies and green fields, found it very constricting, especially since it was filled to overflowing with people; parents and two grown up sons with their families, comprising of six adults and numerous children of all ages, living together as one amorphous fluid mass. Except for the kitchen and the baithak and the rooms of the sons, no other space was assigned to a particular person or purpose. Kamla's parents-in-law never slept together in the same room; the mother-in-law had her favourite charpoy in a small room next to the kitchen, from where, during the day, she kept a strict vigil on the entire family. At night, she would shift to one of the rooms on the first floor, usually with the older grandchildren. Kamla had three children, although by looking at her thin frame one couldn't tell, while her sister-in-law, who was younger to her by a few years had four, the youngest being just a couple of months old. The oldest of Kamla's children, a boy, was born exactly nine months after her marriage, with the other two, a girl and then another boy, following in quick succession. Kamla also had three-sisters-in law, all married and with children of different ages, and when they came to visit, the house resembled a barat ghar, with matresses spread on every available surface. At such times the two designated bedrooms would be given over to the daughters and sons-in-law, for there was no question of making the *damads* sleep on the floor.

When Amiya went to live with them, there were seven children in the house, all younger than her, and she was immediately welcomed as a governess, the harried mothers grateful for any help they could get. Kamla's husband, Ram Swaroop was a quiet man, of medium build, fair, with a head full of unruly hair which he liked to keep slightly long. He taught history at the government high school, the first member of his family to take up a teaching job. His father was the head priest of the Kali Mata temple, where his younger brother and a cousin were the junior pandits. But Ram Swaroop had shown no inclination to pursue the traditional occupation of his family, had indeed even rebelled against it, going on to get a BA degree from the government college instead. He was a poet and a dreamer, lost in a world of his own most of the time, but it was he who had insisted that Amiya come to live with them when her grandfather died, instead of going to Kanpur with her mama, Kamla's eldest brother. And later he was the one who took the initiative to get her enrolled in the school where he taught. Amiya loved him; he was always kind and treated her like his own daughter, and was at times even more considerate than Kamla, who was forever occupied with the demand of a large family.

Amiya was a good student, hardworking and eager to learn. She excelled at school and was a favourite with the teachers. Deeply influenced by Ram Swaroop, she started to write poetry in her early teens, and most weekends the two of them would walk the short distance to the temple, where they would sit on the rustic wooden bench circumbulating the old peepal tree, sharing their latest poems with each other. Sometimes they would be joined by Ram Swaroop's writer friends, who even if they found it odd to hear poetry recited by a young child, never mentioned it, most of them instead, actually encouraging her by critiquing her work. However, Kamla's mother-in-law was most disapproving of Amiya being given such freedom, and would often make snide remarks about her doubtful parentage and the lack of Brahmin blood in her which made her behaviour so appallingly lax. She was also upset with the way her son had insisted on getting Amiya to learn vocal Hindustani music from the masterjee who came home to teach his older son.

'What is the need to teach the girl music at this age? These are not the signs of a good upbringing. And besides, you know very well how expensive Masterji is', she told Ram Swaroop one evening, who in an uncharacteristic display of irritation, snapped back at her. 'You're not paying for her education or these classes, her mama is. And I doubt you would have let her live here all these years without the generous allowance he sends every month.'

Panditji had left behind a considerable amount of money and property, which had devolved on his older brother, Kamla's father, who lived in Kanpur. Since he was getting on in age himself, most family and other matters were handled by his son Rajesh, Kamla's older brother, who being a godfearing man, did not want to either cheat his niece or leave his sister vulnerable to any taunts from her husband's family. Consequently, when Amiya went to live with Kamla, it was decided to give the latter's mother-in-law a fixed sum of money every month to cover her expenses. This amount was far in excess of the money actually spent on the child, and was the reason the arrangement had continued so smoothly for so long. And to further sweeten the old lady, on his last visit, Rajesh had asked her to look for a boy for Amiya, now that she was sixteen, casually mentioning the money and jewellery that had been kept aside for the occasion, knowing fully well that she would look forward to some small amount coming her way as well. But Amiya was not keen on getting married at all and pleaded with her mama to wait until she finished school the next year. Also, of late she was desperate for some answers. Who was her father, and why had no one from his family ever made any effort to get in touch with her? Why was her mother the subject of all gossip in the neighbourhood, what had really happened all those years ago? All her life she had been subjected to snide remarks and barely veiled taunts, had even been called a bastard and an Anglo-Indian. She knew she looked different from the other girls in her class, was taller and fairer and her hair, which she kept tied in two plaits, was stubbornly curly and impervious to the weekly oil massage that tamed beautifully the long tresses of her cousins.

Amiya had tried asking Kamla about her father on many occasions, at times subtly in a round-about way, and at others more directly, but had always got the same standard reply. Her father belonged to a well known Brahmin Bharadwaj family, and had died fighting in the Boer war. Nothing more than that, nothing about her grandparents or uncles and aunts, if any. Once, some years back, she had questioned her mama about their whereabouts, and in a rare candid moment he confessed to having no knowledge of them. He did not know her grandfather's full name or to which village he belonged, or even whether her grandparents were dead or alive, and advised her to stop thinking about them, adding that since she was a girl, they had probably decided to wash their hands off her once her father had died.

This was the same point that Kamla reiterated after Amiya's marriage was fixed when she was nineteen, explaining to her kindly, that henceforth her in-laws would be her family, and that she must never think about either her father or her mother again. The boy she was to marry was ten years her senior, and lived in Gawalmandi, right in the centre of the city. His father was the priest of the Ganesh temple located nearby and he had three older sisters, all of whom were married, and an unmarried younger brother. His mother had died some years ago, and since then the running of the household had been taken over by his grandmother, whose death a few months back had plunged the father and sons into a crisis of sorts, with the younger two daughters, who lived nearby, coming to cook on alternate days. It was unthinkable for Pandit Jeevananad to either accept food from his daughter's homes, or to keep a woman to do the cooking. The first was a huge sin, and the second a sure way to hell, because who knew how contaminated the food would become if touched by an outsider? As a result, either of the two daughters who lived nearby would come in the morning, and do the cooking for the entire day. But this arrangement could not continue indefinitely, and it became imperative to get the older boy, Ishwar Chand, married immediately.

The boy was already twenty-nine, and had been procrastinating about getting married for far too long. For a family of modest means, largely dependent on the generosity of Pujariji's patrons, Ishwar's appointment as a junior clerk in the postal department was a stroke of sheer luck, a miracle, and the former was keen to start enjoying the fruits as soon as possible by getting the boy married to a girl from a rich family. The problem was Ishwar himself. It had been more than four years since he had landed the job, and the line of proposals from eager parents was a long one, but for some inscrutable reason he was adamant about not getting married, and no amount of threatening and pleading and sulking had been able to move him. Gradually, as word of his unwillingness had got around, the number of proposals had reduced, while speculation regarding the possible reason for this strange disinterest had increased. Maybe the boy was suffering from some incurable illness, or even worse, was involved with a woman. However, after the death of his grandmother, Ishwar could no longer ignore the problem faced by the family every day, and so much to the satisfaction of his father and sisters, he finally consented to get married. The family was ecstatic, strange were the ways of the Lord, making good come out of a sad event. And when Amiya's mama engaged the same go-between, a crafty Brahmin, who had a no-fail record to his credit, it was only a matter of days before the two families were in negotiation. The boy's family was in a hurry, worried that Ishwar would change his mind again. The girl was from a good family, had completed her matric, which would be a first for their entire extended family, and what was more, her uncle was willing to spend handsomely on the marriage. She was also pretty, tall and fair with beautiful eyes. Any misgivings about her parentage were assuaged by the go-between, who had drawn up a wonderful, if fictitious, family tree for her. Amiya was not consulted about anything; what did she have to do with it anyway? Her mama, who had been camping in Lahore for the past fortnight, never missed an opportunity to remind her of her astounding luck. To land a clerk in a government department, and that too in such a short time, was nothing short of a miracle. And so, in the October of 1916, Amiya who was nineteen and a half years old, was married to Ishwar Chand, whom she had never set eyes on. Once or twice she had been tempted to ask Kamla what he looked like, but shyness had prevented her from doing so.

Chapter 13

Amiya got married from Kanpur, from her mama's house. Her mami tried her best to make it a jovial occasion, inviting all the women of the mohalla to join in the festivities, strengthening their already close knit symbiotic relationship, in which most of them were anyway hosts to the outstation guests who had assembled for the marriage. The house was large enough, but it already housed Kamla's parents and two brothers with their families, and although Kamla and her sister Nirmala, along with their husbands and children and in-laws, would naturally be staying at home, space constraints dictated that the rest of the family and friends would need to be accommodated in the neighbourhood. The two sons vacated their rooms and shifted into the central living space with their wives and children, and the entire place began to resemble a mela ground.

The celebrations started a week in advance, with each day being earmarked for a different ritual, and almost always being accompanied by singing and dancing to the beats of the *dholak*. This was an all-women affair, and at times songs with double entendre and innuendoes would make Amiya uncomfortable. She was surprised at the atmosphere of laxity and uninhibitedness that pervaded these sessions; old stern looking aunts, mothers-in-law with their *ghunghat* covered bahus, young unmarried girls, all letting their hair down, and joining in the revelry. The actual wedding, was however, a more solemn affair and Amiya was nervous throughout the ceremony. On one occasion she was aware that her husband had lifted his *sehra* to let the pandit apply the customary *tilak* on his forehead, but she was too scared and too bogged down by the heavy ghunghat to even try and sneak a look at him. The entire ceremony, starting from the jai mala to the *sat pheras* and the ritualistic putting of sindoor in her hair, seemed to pass in a blur. The *kanyadan* was done by her elder mama, who was the one who had fixed the marriage, and although Amiya was fond of him, she secretly wished it had been Ram Swaroop. Kamla and her husband had been the closest to parents she had ever known, and the thought of leaving them, especially Kamla, and going to live with perfect strangers filled her with dread.

The feeling of anxiety and disorientation stayed with her throughout the long journey to Lahore, to her in-laws' house, the nervousness persisting even during the customary rituals that started the very day they reached. There was much laughter and merriment and good natured teasing, with Ishwar's sisters taking centre stage, and it was nearly dawn before one of the elder women eventually put an end to the festivities. Amiya, much to her relief, slept in the room where the pooja had taken place, along with Ishwar's eldest sister and some other women. The next morning, she made lunch for the entire family, and as was the custom, all those present gave her some money as sagan, and a separate amount as mooh-dikhai, all of which added up to a considerate sum, but which her sister-in-law took from her in the evening to give to Pujariji, or to keep for herself, Amiya didn't know or particularly care. Whatever she had brought as dowry, all the jewellery and clothes, were displayed on two beds for the women to admire, and it was from this collection that her three sisters-in-law would each pick a saree to take for themselves.

Amiya had not exchanged a single word with her husband, had not even shared a look, and on the one or two fleeting occasions she saw him during the day, his head was bent and she could make out nothing of his face at all, especially through the heavily worked ghunghat she was obliged to wear all the time. She disliked how long it was, covering nearly half her face, and longed for the night, for the isolation of her room, where she could finally be rid of it. But tonight was also the first night that she would be spending with Ishwar, and the nervousness she felt was compounded by the sly, teasing glances her sisters-in-law exchanged with her. However, once alone in the room with him, apprehension mingled with excitement, making her palms sweaty and clammy, and not knowing what to do, she sat down abruptly on one side of the bed. At length, Ishwar who had been standing by the window, spoke 'I'm not feeling well Amiya. I have a bad headache and you must be tired too. Why don't you go to sleep?'

Amiya was surprised, this was not what she had been expecting, but secretly relieved, she just nodded her head and did not reply. However, sleep eluded her for a long time, and when it did come, was fitful and uneasy. Up with the first light of dawn, she looked at her sleeping husband properly for the first time. He was of medium height and build, fair, clean shaven and with his hair parted neatly on one side. His nose was slightly long and hooked and seemed to dominate his face. She felt strange looking at him, this man with whom she would be spending the rest of her life, and promised herself that she would learn to love him, and would be a good wife, just like her massi Kamla.

Getting ready early, she got involved with the daily routine of the household, watering the tulsi plant in the angan, packing lunch for the relatives who were departing that morning, learning to make food the way Ishwar and his father liked. This was the last day of her husband's leave from office, and the whole day she kept a lookout for him, hoping to exchange a look if not a word, anything that would make her feel married and special. But he seemed to have left the house in the morning itself and she did not see him the entire day. He came in just in time for dinner, and after casting a brief look in her direction, sat down to eat with his father and younger brother and the few relatives who were still at home. His father's elder sister, who would be staying with them for a month to help Amiya settle in, must have noticed his absence. 'Where were you the whole day, Ishwar?' she asked, adding 'you have been away since morning.' 'I had some important work to do,' he replied nonchalantly, without divulging any further details. After dinner, he went to his room, where Amiya who joined him after completing the after-dinner chores, found him fast asleep. Not wanting to disturb him, but feeling unsettled, she changed and lay down beside him as quietly as she could.

The next day followed the same pattern, with Ishwar leaving for office in the morning, followed soon after by the remaining guests, who had all gone by the time he came back. Amiya had a pleasant day with bhuaji, who seemed to be a good natured woman, and by the time dinner was over, she felt a rush of anticipation in her heart. These past few days, both Ishwar and she had been very tired, but today the dinner had finished early, and there were no guests to entertain, so maybe she would get to spend some time alone with her husband. But when she entered the room, she found him lying on the bed with his eyes closed. Not knowing what to do, and too shy to call out, she bustled about the room, hoping that the sound of her anklets would announce her presence, and wake him up. It did rouse him but only for a second, and opening his eyes briefly he mumbled something about having a headache, and turning his back on her, went to sleep again. Amiya felt a strong sense of disquiet, but consoled herself with the thought that maybe he really was unwell. However, when the same thing happened the next two nights in a row, she realized that something was amiss. She may be innocent, but she knew that this was not the way a husband behaved with his new bride, so mustering up her courage she decided to talk to him.

'Are you not feeling well? Should I ask Pitaji for some medicine?' she asked, lying down next to him on the bed.

'I will never be fine again,' he said after a small pause. 'My life is finished.'

Startled at his words and forgetting her shyness, she sat up abruptly and put a hand on his arm, shaking him slightly.

'What are you saying?' she asked alarmed, imagining some deadly incurable disease. When he didn't answer for a long time, she shook him again, her heart pounding. Finally, he sat up and looking her in the eye said, 'I shouldn't be telling you this, I suppose, but you are my wife and deserve to know the truth. I am in love with another woman, and I can't imagine having any sort of relationship with anyone else, not even with you.' Amiya felt the blood drain from her face at his words, and unable to open her mouth to utter anything at all, just looked at him in shock. 'She is a widow, and belongs to the baniya caste. I met her three years ago and we are together since,' he elaborated.

'But why did you marry me then?' asked Amiya, feeling her world crumble around her.

'I didn't want to get married, and put it off for as long as I could. But when my grandmother died earlier this year, the pressure from the family became unbearable, and I had to give in,' Ishwar answered.

'So you didn't want a wife at all, only a maid for your father,' said Amiya, dazed.

Ishwar did not answer, just hung his head, as if not wanting to look at her anymore. But Amiya, angry now that the initial shock had worn off, was in no mood to end the conversation.

'You didn't think twice before ruining my life, did you? What am I supposed to do now? Where will I go?' she said, despair making her voice shrill.

'You don't need to go anywhere, this is your home now. None of this is your fault and you have every right to continue to live here as the bahu of the house,' Ishwar replied condescendingly.

His words filled her with a strange sense of self loathing. Did he think that was her only concern, having a roof above her head? Did he think her to be so helpless that she should be grateful for whatever little he chose to give her?

'How can I be the bahu of this house when I'm not your wife in any sense of the word?' she asked, surprised at how sharp her words sounded. 'Does your family know?' she added.

'My father came to know a year back, after one of his friends saw me at Jagdamba's house. He went into shock and his health started to deteriorate, so I had to promise him that I would stop meeting her,' Ishwar answered, adding in an anguished tone, 'I tried, I really tried to do so, but couldn't stay away.'

A sense of unreality had come over Amiya; she couldn't believe that she was having a conversation about another woman with her husband four days into her marriage. Even the mehandi on her hands had not faded yet, nor had its fragrance diminished. Feeling suddenly faint, and not having anything more to say, she lay down in one corner of the bed, her eyes filling with tears and her slender body shivering with shock.

The dazed feeling stayed with her over the next few days. Never had she felt more alone in her life, with nobody to talk to and nowhere to go. She went about her everyday routine mechanically, wearing a new saree, adorning her forehead with the customary bindi and sindoor, cooking and cleaning, but with her mind in constant turmoil, fighting back tears several times a day. There was no way she could ever return to Kamla's house, nor did she want to go live with her mama in Kanpur. The house there was already overflowing with people, with six elders and an equal number of grown up children, besides which, her younger mama's wife was very quarrelsome and was already giving her old in-laws a tough time. Her elder mama's son was getting married later in the year, and he and his wife would also need a room. On the other hand, she could not imagine living this life, day after day, endlessly, just cooking and cleaning and looking after her husband's family. Ishwar himself had started staying away more and more, returning late at night, often after having eaten his dinner. If her father-in-law noticed, he did not say anything about it to her, and she was seriously contemplating writing to her mama about the situation at home, when one evening after Ishwar came back even later than usual, she heard shouting in the hallway.

'What is the matter with you, Ishwar,' her father-in-law was saying. 'You can't treat your wife like this, staying away from home all the time, and not even coming back for dinner.'

'I have work in the office,' Ishwar replied nonchalantly.

'No you don't,' said his father, forcefully,' 'you have just gone back to that wretched woman. Do you realize what will happen if your wife comes to know about it?'

'She already knows, I told her myself some days ago, and if she is alright with it, what's your problem?' Ishwar answered rudely.

'You told her?' her father-in-law said incredulously. 'Have you gone mad? What will I say to her family when they come here to fight with me? Listen to me Ishwar,' he added, when the latter did not reply, 'Amiya is a pretty woman, well versed in household work. She will keep you happy, and once you have a child, you will forget that homewrecker.'

'I don't want another child,' shouted Ishwar. 'I have accepted Jagdamba's five year old son as my own.'

Amiya was stunned by his words, and although the conversation continued for some time more, she shut her door and lay down on the bed, unable to sleep, a thousand fears tormenting her mind. Finally, just as the dawn was breaking, and the birds had started their noisy chattering outside her window, she got up, a strange peace settling over her, knowing at last what she had to do. The following week, she asked her father-in-law's permission to visit her massi, deliberately choosing that time of day when Ishwar would be away at office, and she could go alone. She could see the apprehension on Jeevanand's face at this sudden request, but probably wanting to placate her, not only did he willingly agree, but also sent his younger son along, with instructions to stop on the way and buy some sweets for the children, even insisting on giving her money to give them. At Kamla's house everyone was pleased to see her, including her mother-in-law, who for once gave her a hug and remarked at how well she was looking. Amiya was struck at how deceptive appearances could be, and how a bright saree and some jewellery could perfectly camouflage a troubled mind.

After the initial excitement of her arrival was over, and everyone had dispersed about their duties, she finally got a chance to talk to Kamla alone.

'I want a job, massi,' she blurted out, 'that's why I have come today. I need to talk to mausaji.'

'What's happened?' Kamla asked alarmed. 'I hope everything is fine.'

'Everything is fine, it's just that with everyone away the whole day, time hangs heavily on my hands, and my father-in-law suggested that I could put my education to good use by teaching in a school for a few hours,' she lied.

Kamla was appalled. There was no way Ishwar would ever allow his wife to work. He was earning enough to keep his family in comfort, and besides, no girl from a good family like theirs went out to work. What would her mama, the family, the neighbours say? And most importantly, what would her in-laws, especially her sisters-in-law think about them, her family, for not having instilled the correct values in their daughter? It was impossible, and Amiya was to never talk about it again. But Amiya was adamant, and threatened to visit all the schools by herself to ask for a job, if her mausa refused to help her, and so, eventually Kamla, worried, but helpless in the face of Amiya's determination, gave in and agreed to bring Ram Swaroop to meet her sometime in the coming week. It would have to be in the afternoon when Amiya's father-in-law was away to the temple, and was to be kept a secret, because Kamla was not even sure that her husband would be willing to be party to such a scandalous idea.

However, surprisingly Ram Swaroop was not averse to it at all, and started considering the available options from the moment Kamla spoke to him about it, so that by the time they met Amiya, he already had a small job ready for her. One of his friends sometimes wrote short stories for a weekly magazine for children, which had started only last year, and the publishers were looking for translators familiar with both Urdu and Hindi, and most importantly, with English. Amiya would be perfect for the job, she had a good knowledge of all three languages, and besides, Ram Swaroop thought highly of the poems she used to write at school. And the best part was that she could work from home, and would need to visit the magazine office only once, or maybe twice in a month, the first to collect the stories to be translated and the second time to submit the finished work. But since she was not an established writer, her name would not appear on the translated piece, which would only carry the name of the original author. Amiya didn't mind; any work was fine with her as long as it paid her reasonably well. Tormented by a deep sense of insecurity about her future, fearful that her husband would abandon her one day, or even worse, bring his mistress to live with them in the same house, she was desirous of having some money of her own, enough to enable her to lead a life of dignity, even if all alone by herself. And the money the magazine was offering to pay per story she translated was not bad at all.

'So its settled then,' Ram Swaroop said, interrupting her thoughts. 'I will accompany you to the magazine office this coming Monday in the afternoon, and they will give you a small piece to translate first, as a sort of a test.'

'Thank you,' Amiya said to him gratefully, turning to hug Kamla who was standing in one corner of the room, sulking.

'There is no need to thank your mausa a hazar times,' she snapped at Amiya. 'I am not in favour of this arrangement at all. Your husband and father-in-law are going to be very angry.'

But Amiya was too relieved to mind what Kamla was saying, and on impulse gave her a second warm hug. After a moments' hesitation Kamla hugged her back, and holding her close said, 'you are my daughter Amiya, and I always want to see you happy. Never hesitate to come to me if you have any problem.'

For a second Amiya was tempted to tell her the truth, to lay down her head and just cry, to allow herself the luxury of being comforted, but the momentary weakness passed, and she went into the kitchen to make tea and pakoras for them instead.

Monday dawned bright and sunny, but with a cold wind that blew in from the north, where it had snowed in the mountains intermittently throughout the last week. Ram Swaroop accompanied Amiya to the magazine office, where they met the former's friend, who gave them tea and the work to be translated. The hot beverage, plus the reality of her first job warmed Amiya's heart, and her cheeks turned pink with excitement.

It was now the first week of December, and the winter which had been limping along so far, had set in properly and the mornings were often foggy. Amiya had never really paid much attention to the weather, but now the short, often grey days made her restless and sad. She hated waking up while it was still dark outside, but there was a lot of work to be done and she needed an early start to be able to pack breakfast, and sometimes even lunch, for the three male members of the household, all of whom were very fussy about the freshness and taste of every meal. Amiya bathed first thing in the morning, then hurriedly washed the kitchen and put the food to cook. She was very efficient, the house was always sparkling, the food delicious and her own demeanor impeccable. But her heart was not in anything anymore and she completed all her work mechanically, moving from one routine chore to another, neither stopping to savour the season with its abundance of new vegetables and fruits, nor enjoying her newness as a bride. She had not exchanged a single word with her husband in days, beyond the brief perfunctory greeting, and in spite of her father-in-laws feeble attempts at small talk, the house was as if cloaked in a veil of gloom, the frost inside vying with that of the cold December days outside. The only activity that gave her some pleasure was the translation work she was doing. She liked writing and playing around with words, choosing the right ones to convey the exact meaning the author had intended to, pondering over the more elusive ones as she went about her work. And even though the afternoon sun tempted her with its mellowness, inviting her to sit on the charpoy outside and soak in its warmth, she denied herself that pleasure on most days, knowing fully well that the neighbour's interest in her activities bordered on the obsessive, and that the moment she stepped out, peering eyes would be watching her every move. And she couldn't risk that, not having told her father-in-law and husband about her new job. Kamla had made her promise that she would take Ishwar Chand's permission before starting with the translation work, but in a sudden fit of defiance, she decided against it. Her life was of little consequence to him, he had created a parallel universe for himself, peopled with those whom he really cared about, without sparing any thought for her, the girl he had married. Absolving herself, thus, of any guilt, Amiya spent every spare moment on her writing, submitting her first piece a full week ahead of schedule.

Chapter 14

Pleased with both the quality and the punctuality of her work, the magazine started giving her regular commissions, and by the end of three months she had saved some money, but had still not told her husband about her little secret. It was now the end of March 1917, the severe winter was over, and Lahore was young and fresh once again. Signs of spring were everywhere, mango trees were laden with tiny yellow blossoms, and the neem just behind their house was clothed in tender pink leaves. From the kitchen window she could see two pairs of mynas fighting over a small hole in one of the thicker branches of the tree. It was nesting time and there was much screeching, shouting, tumbling and even physical grappling as each pair attempted to claim it as their own. Occasionally a couple of parrots, with their bright green bodies and red beaks would join in the fray. Amiya loved the parrots, they reminded her of the red and green chillies laid out to dry in the sun by Kamla's mother-in-law.

The old lady had been keeping unwell for the past few weeks, so one day early the next month, Amiya decided to stop by for a quick visit, on her way to the magazine office. But the stopover, peppered with chai and snacks, took longer than she had anticipated, and by the time she reached the office it was deserted, except for the chowkidar and a man she had never met before sitting in one of the inner rooms. Feeling apprehensive, she turned to leave, but the man called out to her.

'What do you want'? he asked in a kind voice, looking at the pretty young woman in a light blue saree and big bindi, who appeared somewhat lost.

'Nothing really, I just came to submit this translation,' she replied, pointing to the papers she held in her hand.

'You can give them to me,' he said.

'But I don't know you,' she answered, 'and besides, I give them to Rashid Khan every time.'

'My name is Imtiaz, and I own the magazine,' the man said jokingly, a smile playing on his face, 'your papers will be safe with me.'

Amiya had heard of Imtiaz and his wife Nafisa, who had together started the publishing house Noor, located on one end of Nisbet Road. Nafisa belonged to a prominent family of Bombay, where her grandfather owned one of the biggest cloth shops of the town. Although uneducated himself, he had nevertheless made sure that his six children, three sons and three daughters, were home tutored by the best teachers in the city. Three of the six later went on to complete their college education as well, with Nafisa's father being one of them, and her growing years were much influenced by his work on women's education and upliftment. She was fortunate enough to marry a man with equally progressive views, and together they started a publishing house which catered exclusively to children, providing them with access to the best quality literature available. Imtiaz was a writer himself, and had recently published a collection of inspirational short stories for youngsters. In addition, Noor specialized in the translation of folk and mythological writings. Stories were translated from Urdu to Hindi and vice versa, and from both these languages into English. Amiya was mostly given work to be translated into English, like on the present occasion, when she had translated a beautiful story from the Panchtantra, which she handed over to Imtiaz, who put it into a drawer without glancing at it. And so, when on her next visit to the magazine office, she was told that he wanted to see her, she was surprised and slightly apprehensive. When she went into his chamber, she found his wife also there, and the meeting with them turned out to be a very pleasant one.

'We liked your work, Amiya. Where have you studied from?' asked Nafisa.

'I did my matric from the government school last year,' replied

Amiya, surprised at the turn the conversation was taking.

'We are looking for women writers for a new magazine we are launching next month,' said Imtiaz, speaking for the first time. 'It will be called *Nayi Awaaz*, and is meant for young adults who have just finished their education. I read the piece you submitted the other day and was impressed by your command over the language and your style of writing. We would like you to write a short story or a poem intended for older children, and if we like it we will publish it in the magazine, and of course, pay you accordingly.'

Amiya felt her heart thumping in excitement, and thanked them profusely. The April evening was hot, but not unbearably so, and standing on the broad, tree lined avenue on which the office was situated, she felt happier than she had in months, and in spite of the rickety state of the tonga and the tardiness of the horse, gave the tongawalla an extra anna. Once home, she hurried through the remaining chores of the day, all the time thinking about what she would write, a poem, a short story, an article. Finally she decided on a short story, one with a message, delivered subtly, so as not to appear too sermonising to the young readers, and although confident both of the plot and of her ability to convey what she intended to, she wrote and rewrote it several times before submitting it under a pseudonym.

The story was much liked by Imtiaz and Nafisa, who promised to publish it in the very first issue of *Nayi Awaaz*, but who were clearly curious about her not writing under her own name.

'You should assert your right as the author of any work you produce, it makes things much easier,' Imtiaz said to her, 'but if this is the way you prefer, we have no problem with it. Continue writing for us under whichever name you want,' he added jokingly, giving her an envelope containing the money for the story. Amiya was delighted at the amount, and before going home that evening, stopped by the temple of Kali Mata near Kamla's house. This was where she had started writing, and it was here under the tree in the temple complex, that she had read out her first poem to her mausa, Ram Swaroop. Maybe it was the Devi's way of having equipped her with a skill she would need later in life, and she wanted to express her gratitude by leaving a small token of money at the feet of the goddess. For a moment she was tempted to walk across to Kamla's house next door to share her excitement with them, but fearing her massi's continuing disapproval, she turned back, suddenly feeling very alone and sad.

Life had not been kind to her, and even when she tried to put right its unfair decisions, she had no one to share her small victories with. The feeling of loneliness was overwhelming, magnifying her insecurities a thousand times, and the first thing she did on reaching home was to tuck away the money securely. God only knew when her husband would leave her, or even worse, throw her out of the house, and she needed as much money as she could save if she hoped to lead a life of dignity. Forgetting her earlier guilt at lying to Ishwar Chand and his father, she resolved to work even harder, aiming to get either a poem or a story published in at least every other issue of the magazine, while also looking for more translation related commissions. And so, after spending every single moment she could spare on her writing, by the end of the year she had more than half a dozen short stories and poems in *Nayi Awaaz* and many of her translations had been published as part of a larger volume of stories.

Success gave her some confidence, and she decided to tell her husband about her work, thinking up various scenarios of his reaction and her defense. But her worry was unnecessary, and in the end it turned out to be surprisingly easy, and while Ishwar Chand was taken aback but quiet, his father did the customary protesting, raising his voice, invoking the family honour and attempting to be the strict patriarch. But Amiya was adamant, she would not give up her writing under any circumstances. Her husband was in love with another woman, was virtually living with her, and yet it was her job that was threatening the family honour? For once, looking her father-in-law in the eye, she offered to call her family for mediation, or if her husband so desired, she was even willing to leave the house and move out. As she had expected, both father and son cowed down under her veiled threat, not wanting to risk Ishwar's affair becoming public and their carefully cultivated standing in the community getting compromised. Besides, there was the added possibility of Amiya's family creating a scene and involving the community elders, or in the extreme case, even taking Amiya back with them. The scandal would most certainly ruin the family, and make it impossible for Ishwar's younger brother to ever get married. It would also leave father and sons without a cook and housekeeper.

Amiya, aware of these considerations, and emboldened by her own boldness and sense of righteousness, gradually started writing under her own name, and within the next couple of years became quite well known in the small literary circle of Lahore. While continuing to write for *Nayi Awaaz*, she started contributing to other magazines as well, and occasionally also to newspapers. She developed her own style, flowing yet effortless, her thoughts penned with consummate ease and her work exploring social issues, discrimination, the position of women in society and occasionally even venturing into the forbidden area of sensuality.

The twenties were a good time to be a writer in Lahore. The city had become an important hub of writing and publishing, both for Urdu and for English, and there was much experimentation with style and content. Plays were staged in colleges, literary gatherings became common and poetry was recited at community halls to much appreciation. Journalists, especially those writing on political issues, could now sway public opinion through their columns in newspapers, more so since vernacular papers were proliferating and reached a much larger audience. Patriotic literature, fuelling the spirit of nationalism became main stream, and although Amiya enjoyed reading the different genres, she herself stuck to writing stories with a social message and also to her poetry and translation work. She was particularly drawn to the concept of free verse in Urdu poetry—which was becoming increasingly popular—liking the thought of writing in an unmetered style, of freeing her words from the rigidity inherent in more traditional forms, and a poem she penned in the summer of 1922, got published in *Makhzan*, a very old and well respected Urdu journal, garnering for her almost instant acclaim. It was a poem about infidelity and longing, simply written but powerful, and paved the way for her work to gain acceptance and more importantly, find ready publishers. She had the added advantage of being able to write eloquently in three languages, and with the starting of some more magazines for children, had no dearth of translation work. This, along with the poems and short stories she wrote for both weekly and monthly journals, ensured her a steady income, which she saved almost in its entirety.

Her needs were few, and with a husband in the government service, money was not a problem. She managed to save some part of the household allowance her father-in-law gave her every month, and this she spent on the occasional box of sweets for Kamla's children, and on the almost weekly tonga rides to the offices of the publishers. She had no desire for new clothes and jewellery. Whom was she to dress up for? Her husband hardly ever spoke to her, and even when he did, kept his eyes lowered and face averted. It was all a sham, the sindoor she wore dutifully every day, her glass bangles, the bells tinkling on her toes. Five years of living a farce. She often had a desire to run away, to leave the house and never come back, to get away from the increasingly vitriolic taunts of her sisters-in-law, each of whom had a child exactly nine months after marriage. Even Kamla was worried and spoke to her about it every time they met, asking probing questions and dropping not so subtle hints about her relationship with her husband. And the last time her mama had come to Lahore, which he usually did for the festival of rakhee every year, he even suggested to her father-in-law that he send Amiya and Ishwar Chand with him to Kanpur for a few days to consult with a famous vaid.

It was at times like this that sadness, her otherwise constant companion, was dislodged by an even stronger feeling of anger. Anger at her husband for putting her into this situation, anger at her mama for not having made enough enquiries before getting her married, and most of all anger at her own self for accepting this life year after year. She wanted to shout from the rooftop, to tell her neighbours and her sisters-in-law and Kamla that it was Ishwar and not she who was responsible for their not having a child. He was the one living with another woman, he should have to bear the cruel smirks and snide remarks, instead of being given the status of the aggrieved one, the poor unfortunate man whose wife was unable to bear him a son. The injustice of it all gnawed at her, but maybe it was her own karmas, the deeds of her past lives, that had returned to haunt her, and maybe it was best to accept without complaint whatever life chose to throw at her.

At least she was economically somewhat secure; the sadness and anger were there as before, the intervening years having done nothing to lessen their burden on her heart, but the feeling of helplessness had diminished somewhat. She may not have any where to go, no parents or brothers to fall back upon, but she had her writing and a growing sense of self-reliance. Writing made her calm, eased the drudgery of long, empty days in an empty house, and transported her to far-off places where she could be whoever she wanted to. Words became her best friends, and the more she played around with them, juggling them to please every new master, the more they got her acclaim, and by the time December rolled in and the year 1924 drew to a close, her work had been published in all the major journals and newspapers of Lahore. Being multilingual, she moved with ease among different cultures and thoughts, adapting her sensibilities accordingly.

Recently, she had written a poem in Punjabi, in the Urdu script, not being adept at the Gurmukhi one, and it had become a favourite with the critics as soon as it was published in *Nayi Dastaan*, an Urdu magazine published from Bhatti Gate. She was already a regular contributor to *Tehzib-i-Niswan*, a magazine for women, and to *Makhzan*, which had carried her short stories and poems twice this year already. In addition, she translated stories by well known English writers into Urdu, and these were printed from time to time in publications of repute.

Seeing her work feature in journals of such literary excellence filled Amiya with a sense of immense satisfaction, but the feeling was always accompanied by a strange sense of loss. Once home from the publisher's office, reality struck almost immediately; the dark house, the empty rooms, hers and Ishwar's on different floors, the hopelessness of daily existence, the never ending loneliness. At times she found it difficult to reconcile the two different women living inside her, the erudite, witty, confident Amiya and her unhappy, resentful, but secretly hopeful twin. She hated herself for looking out for a sign, any sign from Ishwar, hated it when she thought of him while getting ready in the morning, hated the small flicker of hope that refused to die down. On the few occasions when he was home for dinner, she would glance at him surreptitiously from under her *pallu* while serving him, but he would always be looking away. His weekly visits were spent either talking to his father and giving him money, or by himself in his room rummaging through some papers. The younger brother was totally ignored, as was she.

Chapter 15

Over time Amiya started to notice a change in her father-in-law's attitude towards Ishwar, with the old man becoming increasingly short tempered and exasperated with his elder son. Much of this stemmed, no doubt, from the latter's refusal to shoulder any responsibility for getting his younger brother, who was now nearly twenty-five, married and a fortnight earlier, upset at something Ishwar had said, his father got very angry, shouting at him to either shift back and lead a normal householder's life, or never set foot in the house again. Amiya had never seen her father-in-law in such a state, his face red and entire body trembling, and for a moment she was afraid that something would happen to him.

Maybe the incident jolted Ishwar as well, because since that day he was spending most nights at home, and even made an effort to come back from office on time. The house seemed different when he was there, more alive, the gloom less overpowering. Pujariji was also happier, often requesting her to make something special for dinner. The previous night, for the first time in the nearly seven years that they had been married, Ishwar complimented her on the food, calling it delicious. Amiya was startled to hear her name on his tongue, it felt so intimate, so right.

It was late March, the season was changing, and maybe so would her life. She liked the ambiguity of March, and later in the year, of October and November as well, much preferring their mildness to the extreme heat and cold of the other months. But as the days passed, and March gave way to April, the sun didn't seem so harsh this time, and the long days were made unusually sweet by the distinctive call of the Koel, which could be heard throughout the day, and sometimes late into the evening as well. A pair which frequented the peepal near their house started their dusk duet at the exact same time that Ishwar came home every evening, and gradually as the summer progressed, Amiya started looking forward to their song as much as she did to her husband returning from office. She often wondered at his change of heart, and whether he had broken up with his mistress, because Pujariji's getting angry that day did not seem to her to be reason enough for the apparent transformation in his behaviour.

But whatever it was, she was grateful for the renewed chance at happiness that life had offered her and was going to grab at it with both hands. Maybe there was some truth in the hurtful taunts of her sisters-in-law after all, and maybe if she had been more wily, more loving, she would have been able to wean him away from that woman. Not knowing how long his present mood would last, and desperate to make the most of every moment she got with him, she went out of her way to show him her love, taking extra care with her appearance, cooking his favourite dishes, attending to all his needs. And as the days turned into weeks, and monsoon clouds began to gather overhead, she felt a growing familiarity in his behaviour towards her, the routine familiarity between a normal husband and wife, which had been denied to her for so long. He now called her if he needed something, asked her what she had cooked for dinner, rebuked her when he couldn't find his papers in the morning.

Amiya revelled in this attention, and although they still had separate rooms and he talked to her only when necessary, she was content, having willed herself not to think of the past, or ask for more than he was willing to offer. She didn't care that she didn't know anything about his office or who his friends were, or whether he was still in touch with that woman. She was too caught up in the enchantment of the moment, in the newness of happiness to bother about anything else, and so one Saturday in early July, when he suggested they visit Anarkali to buy her a saree, she was overjoyed, and sending a silent prayer of thanks to the goddess Kali, hurried through the household work and was ready immediately after lunch.

It was a sultry, windless afternoon, with dark clouds hanging low over the horizon. Amiya, who didn't look a day older than when she had got married, was wearing a light green cotton saree, with her hair tied up in a neat bun at her nape, accentuating the delicacy of her shoulder blades. A few strands of her naturally curly hair escaped from confinement to softly frame her face, and small beads of perspiration dotted her forehead. Seeing them, Ishwar remarked, 'It is unusually humid today, and I have a feeling it will rain at night.'

'Its long overdue,' sighed Amiya, fanning herself with her pallu, 'the monsoon should have been here at least ten days ago.' However, as she spoke a light wind picked up, making the evening tolerable, even enjoyable. The tonga ride further cooled the sweat off her body, but Ishwar's closeness, his arm and leg brushing against hers, seared her with its unfamiliarity, and by the time they reached Anarkali, Amiya was light headed with happiness, forgetting the purpose of their visit, content just to be with her husband. But Ishwar insisted on buying her a saree, a very expensive one, and some glass bangles to match. Later, they strolled through the galis, looking at the colourful wares on display, before eating a delicious dinner at Nathu's, the famous halwai shop at the entrance to the bazaar.

It was dusk by the time they finished and headed back home, the evening darker than usual due to the clouds, which had now started to gather in earnest. The first drops of rain fell just as they alighted from the tonga, and Ishwar took her hand to hurry her along, half pulling her, both of them laughing like children. At the entrance of the gali leading to their house, he stopped suddenly, and looking her straight in the eyes said, 'I'm sorry'. The words had a strange effect on Amiya, pleasing her on the one hand, while at the same time breaking the mood and bringing her back to earth, reminding her of her place in Ishwar's life. But they also gave her hope, and she carried them as a charm with her for the rest of the evening, and late into the night, drawing a thousand inferences from the two words. Thus lost in her thoughts, she was startled when the door to her room opened and Ishwar walked in, wearing a white kurta pyjama, and looking boyishly appealing. Her heart gave a loud thump, which she was sure was audible to him right across the room, for he came over to where she lay on the bed, and taking her hand in his, said, 'Don't be afraid Amiya, I've just come to ask you to forgive me. I have been a fool all these years.' Amiya couldn't speak, her throat felt parched, but she instinctively moved towards the centre of the bed, making place for him to lie down next to her. He did so, and after a moment's hesitation, took her into his arms, and buried his face in her hair, inhaling deeply of her fragrance, as if this was something he had wanted to do for a long time. They made love long into the night, Amiya fighting her natural shyness, determined to savour every moment, taking pride in the momentary discomfort which finally made her feel like a married woman.

It was raining when Amiya awoke the next morning, a steady monsoon downpour, which continued intermittently through the day. She was only dimly aware of the passage of time, doing all her work mechanically, her mind lost in the pleasures of the previous day. She had a translation to finish for Noor, and an article to write for another magazine, but she was restless and kept her eyes glued on the door, waiting for Ishwar to return from office. The past twenty four hours had been dizzying and exhilarating, like one of those jhoola rides of sawaan, when all the ladies in Kamla's mohalla would gather under a huge banyan tree located in a small open space at the end of their lane, and take turns at the swings that had been hung from the tree. And although Amiya had seldom enjoyed that experience, this ride was one she never wanted to get off from. Her wait ended at last and Ishwar came home earlier than usual, carrying a box of sweets and some pakoras, but it was his smile and the loving look in his eyes that she was most thankful for. She had been vaguely anxious the whole day, wondering whether yesterday had been an aberration, and he would revert to his usual aloof self once again.

But over the coming days and weeks he became more and

more caring, as if trying to make up for the lost years, returning from office on time, spending every holiday at home and insisting on taking her out at least once a week, either to a temple or the bazaar, and on one occasion, even to watch acrobats performing. The monsoon rain, notorious for being unpredictable and fickle minded, arrived in bursts which often lasted a week at a time. The downpour, self willed and playful, would begin and end suddenly, often forcing Pujariji and Jagdish, the younger son, who slept on the terrace of the second floor the entire summer, to rush in with their bedding. Normally, Amiya who slept indoors, would be only dimly aware of the commotion that ensued, but ever since Ishwar had shifted in with her, her nights were young, and very often they would be awake into the early hours of the morning, loving and talking like newly-weds. Stormy nights, when the thunder rolled and the lightning flashed, and which always made her nervous, now became an excuse to cuddle closer. The rain beating down, lashing against the window pane, sounded like music and the slushy lane outside their house, no longer put her into an irritable mood. It was as if she was cocooned in a world of love, insulated from day to day living.

The atmosphere at home was as if transformed magically; her father-in-law looked happier and even the normally reticent Jagdish took the liberty of pulling his older brother's leg once in a while. For the first time since her marriage Amiya looked forward to the festival season, to Teej and then to Karva Chauth, taking special care of her appearance, wearing the saree Ishwar had bought for her. Her sisters-in-law were somewhat mollified at the unexpected amount of money she had Ishwar give them for Rakhee, and a full month before Diwali, she started cleaning the already clean house with a vengeance, tackling every nook and cranny, and when the potter brought the earthen diyas on his donkey to sell, she bought more than half his stock, wanting the house to be lit up as never before. She soaked the diyas overnight in water, dried them and then soaked them again in a bit of oil, making the batis in her spare time. She made gujiya and ladoo at home and sent a box of each to her sisters-in-law and Kamla. The monsoon was long over, as was the short period of heat that followed it, and it was the last week of October now, cool and pleasant, and very festive. Sweets were exchanged and new clothes bought. Amiya's father-in-law, delighted at the change in his son and the wave of happiness sweeping through the house, gifted her with a beautiful pair of earrings which had belonged to Ishwar's mother. Amiya loved them and wore them throughout the festivities, which continued for a full week after Diwali. Kamla came over with her children for Bhai Duj, her sons the only brothers Amiya had known. On Ishwar's insistence she had bought clothes for the children and a loyi for Ram Swaroop, which the latter refused to accept, horrified at the thought of taking anything, even a glass of water, from a daughter's house. Kamla remarked on how good she was looking, and when the two of them were alone, asked her subtly if she was pregnant. Amiya blushed and shook her head, but the thought filled her with a warm glow. She desperately wanted to have a child, not only to silence her critics and reclaim her pride in her womanhood, but also because of a deep-seated conviction that a son would bind Ishwar to her irrevocably.

Even though Ishwar and she had never spoken about Jagdamba, the other woman was always there at the back of Amiya's mind, fuelling a nagging sense of insecurity, which increased as the year wore to an end. Sometimes she caught Ishwar with a faraway look in his eyes which worried her, and everytime he was late from office, which he was with increasing frequency once again, she felt her heart sinking. The December dark came early, and the evenings stretched endlessly, cold and empty, when he was not at home. However, not wanting to appear prying, she never questioned him, although subconsciously she was always looking for signs that signalled a change in his affections. But all seemed well, he was as loving as ever, taking her out on the weekends, buying her gifts, snuggling with her in the same quilt at night. Still Amiya was worried, intuitively sensing that something was bothering him. Something had changed, he was increasingly preoccupied, and although never garrulous by nature, now he spoke even lesser and there were often long uncomfortable silences between them. Try as she might she found it difficult to ignore her misgivings, the thousand nagging voices in her brain not letting her concentrate on her writing, which she had anyway ignored these past few months, afraid of doing anything that might annoy her husband.

On the last day of the year, Ishwar did not come home the entire night. Amiya waited up for him well past midnight, only going to her room when her father-in-law, who was also restless, insisted that she do so. The next day, being the first day of the new year, she went to the temple with Pujariji, made *halwa poori* for lunch and kept up a façade of normalcy, while all the time being consumed by anxiety on the inside. Fear, like a dead weight settled in the pit of her stomach, making all movement arduous. Her father-in-law, after seeing her home, went out again, ostensibly to go back to the temple, but she knew he had gone to look for Ishwar. Suddenly she felt sorry for the old man, this was not his age to have to worry about his errant son. She was aware that he had not slept the whole night either, and anger at Ishwar's behaviour, overtook temporarily, anxiety over his well being.

Ishwar returned home late in the afternoon, gave her a weak smile, greeted his father, and went straight to their room without saying a word. Amiya, whose initial relief at seeing him safe, had given way to anger almost immediately, fought the urge to follow him and demand an explanation. How could he be so inconsiderate, did he not realise how worried she had been for his safety, how many dreadful scenarios had played out in her mind the whole night? Was it not his duty to have stayed and talked to her? By now she was seething with anger, but before she could formulate her thoughts, there was a knock on the door, and without waiting for someone to respond, a woman walked in. She was short, plump and of a wheatish complexion. She wore sindoor in her neatly parted hair and a big red bindi on her forehead. Her red cotton saree was crisply starched, forcing Amiya to cast a furtive glance at her own saree, which looked limp in comparison. 'I want to meet Ishwar,' she said in a confident voice, and Amiya knew at once who she was.

'Who are you?' asked Pujariji, but before she could answer Ishwar came striding out of his room, his face red with anger. 'What are you doing here,' he shouted at her, 'did I not ask you never to come here?'

'You left me with no option,' she replied. 'First you don't come home for several months, and when you do, its only for a few hours at a time. I can't live like this anymore. You are my husband and I have a right to be with you,' she added tearfully.

The silence which met this statement was deafening. Finally Pujariji spoke, 'You are not his wife,' he said in anger, 'Amiya is'. The woman turned to look at Amiya, who was standing quietly, stunned into silence, and then walking up to Ishwar in a deliberate fashion, said to him, 'tell them that I'm your wife, that you married me in the temple, bought me red bangles and put sindoor in my maang.' When Ishwar did not answer, she continued, 'tell them how you promised my mother that you would accept my son as your own, that we have been living together as husband and wife for more than nine years now.'

Pujariji again tried to intervene. 'Such marriages have no value!' he said. 'Marriages which are performed with the consent of the families, within the same caste and following proper customs and rituals are the only true marriages. Ishwar realized this and has, therefore, returned home to his wife,' he added.

'I'll tell you why my husband came back to this hell,' said the woman, raising her voice. 'No Jagdamba, don't,' interjected Ishwar sharply, finding his voice at last.

'You threatened to cut him off from all ancestral property, here and in the village if he didn't return, so we decided it was in our best interest if he came back for a few weeks. But the weeks have now stretched into months, and I don't care about the money any more. I just want my husband back,' Jagdamba said, bursting into loud sobs.

Amiya who had been listening quietly so far, felt the blood

draining from her face and cast an anguished look at Ishwar, who refused to meet her eyes. Not wanting to hear any more, she rushed into her room and bolted it from the inside, flinging herself on the bed and crying till the tears ran dry, her eyes swollen into narrow slits. Anguish at Ishwar's betrayal alternated with anger at her own naivety. She should have trusted the nagging voice at the back of her head that had always suspected Ishwar's sudden change of heart, the sixth sense that she had smothered under layers of hope. To think that she had allowed herself to fall in love with him so completely, filled her with despair. If this interlude had not taken place, life would have continued as it had been doing for the last seven years, with her concentrating on her writing and trying to make the best of the situation she found herself in. But now things were different and for all she knew, that woman and her son would move in with them, or Ishwar would move out again. Either way it had become too humiliating for her to continue living here, and moreover she had no reason to do so any more. The tiny flicker of hope that had sustained her through these years had finally been extinguished, doused by the cold water of reality. Her husband had cheated her right from the start, first by marrying her when he was in love with another woman, and now, even worse, by pretending to care for her only to save his inheritance.

Chapter 16

Amiya did not leave her room the whole night, and by the time morning dawned, cold and misty, she had made up her mind to leave the house for good. Ishwar had left with Jagdamba almost immediately after the quarrel and she knew in her heart that he was never coming back. She may not have anyone to go back to, but years of aloneness had made her self reliant. She was earning enough from her writing to lead a life of reasonable comfort, and although it would create a huge scandal, it was time she told Kamla and her mama the truth.

But it was tougher than she had expected. Kamla and Ram Swaroop were aghast, upset at Ishwar's behaviour, but even more disturbed at the prospect of her leaving home. She was the daughter-in-law of the house and had every right to live there, with or without her husband. No good ever came from taking hasty decisions, Kamla would call her brother from Kanpur and together they would try to make Ishwar see reason. The go-between who had got them married would also be present in the discussions, to put extra pressure on the boy's family.

'But I don't want to live there anymore, massi,' Amiya said in a determined voice, 'there is nothing left for me in my husband's house any longer. I have endured the humiliation of his living with another woman for seven long years, but no more.'

'If you had told us about this right away after your marriage, things would not have come to this. The problem would have been nipped in the bud,' answered Kamla, adding in a matter of fact tone, 'and besides, you know very well that two women of our family are co-existing very happily with their husband's second wives.'

'But I will not do so. A wife is one whom the husband cares for. I will not be able to live in the same house where my husband is sharing the room with another woman,' replied Amiya.

'You are as foolish as your mother, Amiya, not thinking about the consequences of your actions,' said Kamla angrily. 'Where will you go, how will you live alone, or are you contemplating shifting to Kanpur?' she asked in an agitated tone.

But Amiya, who had caught onto what Kamla had said about her mother, was only half listening. So it was true, there was more to her birth than met the eye, and somehow her massi knew about it. But now was not the time to question her, especially in the presence of Ram Swaroop. 'I will send for my brother immediately, and he should be here in a fortnight at the most. He will talk some sense into you.' Kamla said, walking off in a huff.

Mamaji, when he came, did try to make her see reason. No woman from their family, not even one, had ever done such a shameful thing. Marriages were not to be taken lightly, they were solomnised according to the will of God and were for keeps. 'But mamaji, I did try to make my marriage work. I know what you are saying is true, but I cannot live here anymore. My husband left home with that woman that day, and has not been back since. Who should I stay here for?' Amiya pleaded.

'You have a duty to your father-in-law and the rest of your husband's family. Men get involved with other women all the time. That is no reason for a marriage to break up,' mamaji replied in an angry voice. 'Besides which, I am meeting your father-in-law and the go between tomorrow. Together we will sort this out. We will make Ishwar come back home,' he continued.

'He will not come back, and even if he does, he will bring that woman and her son along. Don't you see mamaji? They are his real family.' Amiya said, tears welling in her eyes. 'Please don't make this more difficult for me,' she pleaded.

But it did get more difficult. Ishwar did not return and no one knew where he and Jagdamba lived. A visit to his office also proved futile, he had been on leave for the past one month, and it was not known when he would be back. Mamaji, Ram Swaroop, the go-between, and two of mamaji's cousins came several times to meet Pujariji, but in the absence of Ishwar no solution could be found. There was much shouting and histrionics and veiled threats, but mamaji eventually had to return to Kanpur, and after he had left, the matter died its natural death. Ram Swaroop and Kamla did come to see her a couple of times, and even threatened to take her back with them, but both Amiya and her father-in-law knew that their words were like the empty punches in a friendly wrestling match, not meant to carry any weight or cause any harm.

By now Amiya was desperate. It had been nearly two months since that fateful day, and neither had she found a place for herself, nor was she any clearer on how to go about it. Not knowing what to do, and finding Nafisa, whose publishing house Noor she had been associated with for the past so many years, alone in the office one day, she confided in her. Nafisa, although very sympathetic, initially tried to dissuade her from following such a drastic course of action. Was Amiya aware of the pitfalls of living alone? A young, pretty woman like her would be at the receiving end of much unwanted male attention, and even worse, of much malicious gossip. Why didn't she shift to her family in Kanpur? But Amiya was determined, she had given the matter her utmost consideration and was sure that this was what she needed to do. And going back to Kanpur, in addition to the other problems it would create, would rob her of her financial independence and make her dependent on her uncles and cousins for the rest of her life. Which was unthinkable.

Shortly afterwards, Nafisa told Amiya that she had looked up a room for her with a Parsi couple she knew, whose three children had got married and moved out, leaving them feeling very alone. They were willing to give on rent a room with an attached kitchenette on the first floor, which had its own separate entrance, and which would be an ideal arrangement for Amiya, living with a family in secure surroundings, yet retaining her independence. Amiya was excited and went to meet them in the forenoon of the very next day. They lived on Beadon Road, just off the Mall, and it took her nearly half an hour to get there. The house was the last one in a quiet lane and was almost hidden behind a huge peepal tree, and as she walked up the leafy driveway, trepidation nearly made her retrace her steps, but even though fear gripped her heart, she told herself that there was no going back now. Her husband had left her with no other choice, and so it was with a new found determination that she rang the bell.

The door was opened by a young boy in his late teens, presumably the servant, who ushered her into a big room. Amiya who had never seen such opulence before, gasped in amazement. There were plush sofas with crochet antimacassars, plump floral cushions, beautiful paintings on the walls, and tables laden with photographs in silver frames. It seemed almost too pretty to be real, very much like the woman who walked in a few minutes later. She was probably in her early fifties, plump, short and very fair, wearing a printed floral saree with her head half covered. She greeted Amiya warmly, and gestured to her to sit down, herself taking a seat close by.

'Nafisa tells me you are looking for a place to live. Why?'

The direct question stumped Amiya for a moment, but she recovered her composure quickly and began to speak. She had already decided that she would be honest with her prospective landlords, but even so, she found herself revealing far more than she had intended to. A small voice at the back of her head was telling her to stop, aghast at the ease with which she was opening up to a total stranger. But the flood of words refused to recede, and she spoke about her grandfather and Kamla and Ishwar and having no place to go back to. Her hostess listened quietly, asking no questions and offering no comments. At length Amiya finished, feeling drained and too embarrassed to even look up. After a brief pause, the woman spoke.

'Do you realise we haven't introduced ourselves? I am Khorshed Sodawalla, but you can call me aunty, considering that we are going to be living in the same house.'

Amiya felt a surge of relief at her words, as if a burden had been lifted from her shoulders, and smiling at Khorshed gratefully said,

'I'm Amiya, and I assure you that I'm usually not this presumptuous or bothersome.'

'Don't be harsh on yourself, my child,' Khorshed said kindly, 'I'm sorry you had to go through so much in such a young life.'

Feeling tears pricking at the back of her eyes at this unexpected sympathy, Amiya quickly changed the topic, discussing more mundane things like the rent and when she could shift in. Khorshed took the hint and over cups of hot tea and a delicious sweet which she explained was made from bananas and dried fruits, they worked out the details. Khorshed's husband Adel, who had left for work, would no doubt like to meet the new tenant, but he trusted her judgement and had left the final decision to her.

The room was on the first floor, and had a separate entrance through a flight of stairs built on one side of the house. Although it overlooked the front garden and gate, the long, twisting driveway afforded it privacy from people coming in, and a flowering gulmohar tree hid the stairs from view. The room was fully furnished, as if someone had been living there for some time. Pretty blue and white curtains framed a huge window which opened onto the garden, and a matching coverlet was spread over the cosy bed. Against the window was a small study table and a comfortable looking chair, and Amiya could picture herself sitting there and enjoying the view of the garden as she worked on her writing. The room also had a small dressing table with drawers and brass knobs. Amiya loved it at first sight, it was so grand and unlike any place she had ever lived in before.

'I hope you like the room, Amiya. It has a connecting bathroom and a small kitchen,' said Khorshed.

'It's perfect, aunty Khorshed,' replied Amiya, rolling the unfamiliar sounding words on her tongue.

Amiya shifted in a week later. She could have done so sooner, her clothes and few personal possessions did not require more than half a day to pack, but her father-in-law pleaded with her to stay a few days longer, saying that he had it from a very reliable source that Ishwar would be returning home soon. Amiya knew that

Ishwar was never coming back, nor did she want him to anymore, but her father-in-law had been kind to her, and she felt sorry for him. He seemed to have aged ten years in the last few days, and for the first time she noticed that his hands had started shaking. He even sent for Kamla to try and persuade Amiya not to take such a drastic step, but she didn't come, sending a disgruntled Ram Swaroop instead, who told them in no uncertain words that his family had washed their hands off the entire affair, and would have nothing more to do with any of them, especially Amiya, who was bent upon such a shameful course of action. Amiya was shocked at his words, she knew that Kamla was very angry with her, but had not expected such a severe reaction from him. Had her own mother been alive, would she have abandoned her like this? She felt very alone, but strangely, it was this very feeling that fuelled her determination to become totally self-reliant, to never expect anything from anyone ever again.

She packed her bags that night, and while her father-in-law was away to the temple in the morning, quietly left the house. Sitting in the tonga, she thought about how easy it had been in the end. No weeping, no histrionics, no one to stop her, no one who knew where she was going. The house to which she had come with so much fanfare seven years ago had neither given her a sense of belonging while she lived under its roof, nor had it tried to hold her back when she was leaving. She had come a stranger and was departing a stranger. Maybe the room she was shifting to would be luckier for her.

It was certainly prettier, and she settled in quickly, enjoying the feeling of space both within and without. She did not have many personal belongings, her clothes and writing material was all she had brought along. Most of her jewellery was lying with her father-in-law for safekeeping, but she had carried whatever was there with her, including the bangles and earrings of gold that she was wearing. She had no need for any more, and whatever she wanted henceforth, she would earn for herself. It was a good thing that she had continued with her writing, and had the foresight to keep her money with herself, even in the days of intimacy with her husband. It was that money which had gone towards the advance rent for the month, and for the food. She had no utensils, and had planned to buy some to get her kitchen started, but Khorshed offered her all three meals at a nominal cost. Amiya was grateful and quickly quelled any qualms she had about eating meals cooked in a kitchen which predominantly made non vegetarian food. She was hardly in a position to be picky, and besides this was a new Amiya, one who had left her old life behind, and with it all old conditionings. Moreover Khorshed had assured her that all care would be taken to ensure separation of both, utensils as well as ingredients.

The food was delicious, if a little unfamiliar in taste, but somehow did not seem to be agreeing with her. It was only a week since the servant boy, Pappu, had started bringing the meals up to her room, and already in that time she had been nauseous thrice. May be it was God's way of punishing her, a Brahmin, for eating food cooked in a contaminated kitchen. She remembered the fuss her father-in-law would make about the food, insisting that it be prepared by a woman of the family, after bathing and lighting the diya and thoroughly washing each surface. But she herself, since shifting here, had been eating food cooked by a man whose caste she didn't know, and who probably was not always careful about keeping separate the utensils in which he cooked meat. Not wanting to risk falling sick she refused the food that night, and told Pappu not to bring any for the next few days as well. But the very next morning Khorshed came up to ask what was wrong, and was shocked to see a very pale Amiya lying on the bed.

'What is the matter, my child?' she asked in a concerned tone. 'You look terrible.'

'I've been feeling very nauseous for the past few days,' Amiya replied. 'Must be because of the samosa I ate at Noor's office last week, when I had gone to submit a translation,' she added, not wanting Khorshed to feel that it was the food at home that was making her sick.

'Is your stomach upset?' asked Khorshed.

'No, just bouts of nausea that come and go. I'll be fine soon', Amiya said, smiling weekly.

The older woman looked at her searchingly, taking in her pallor and frail looking body, and was quiet for some time, as if thinking things over. 'I think you are pregnant, Amiya,' she said at length.

Amiya felt her heart give a loud thump of excitement, but the initial euphoria gave way, almost immediately, to a sense of dismay. Hundreds of thoughts raced through her mind, falling over themselves in a chaotic heap. Panic swept over her in ever rising waves, pinning her to the bed, so that it was an effort for her to even sit up. Why had she left Ishwar's house in such haste? What was she to do now?

Dimly, as if from a distance she heard Khorshed calling her name. 'Amiya,' she was saying, 'are you all right?'

'No,' sobbed Amiya, 'what am I going to do now? I will have to go back to my husband's house, and I don't even know whether he will accept me back, or whether that woman and her son have shifted in with him already.'

Khorshed thought for a minute before replying. 'Your uncle Adel can help us, I'm sure. He has friends everywhere.'

'But what can he do ?' asked Amiya, in a hopeless voice.

'He will find out whether that foolish husband of yours has come back, and if he has brought that woman with him. After that you can take a decision,' Khorshed said, giving Amiya's hand a reassuring pat. 'And meanwhile, you must show yourself to a doctor, although my hunch is never wrong.'

The doctor Amiya went to the next morning took less than five minutes to corroborate what Khorshed had diagnosed. She was indeed pregnant, but was very weak and it was necessary that she look after herself. And why hadn't she brought her husband along? He needed to be told to let her rest and not do any strenuous household work. Amiya nodded silently and hurriedly left, not wanting the doctor to ask any more searching questions. On the way back home, she oscillated between hope and anxiety, hope that the child would finally wean Ishwar away from Jagdamba, and anxiety because a voice at the back of her head told her that there was very little likelihood of that happening.

When she reached home, Khorshed was waiting for her, with some delicious snacks she had made herself, and after enquiring about what the doctor had said, broke the news to her.

'Adel sent a very reliable person to your husband's house today morning, but the place was locked, and on enquiry the neighbours told him that the entire family had gone somewhere, and there was no knowing when or if they would be back. They seemed to hint that your father-in-law had shifted with his younger son to some other mohalla or maybe even to another town.' At these words, Amiya felt a wave of faintness pass over her and slumped back in her chair. Khorshed was immediately contrite. 'What a fool I am to have to have sprung this on you so suddenly, especially after you have had such a tiring day. Your father-in-law must have gone somewhere for a few days. I'll have Adel find out again next week. Meanwhile you go up to your room and get some rest.'

Early in the morning of the next day, Khorshed came to Amiya's room with a glass of warm milk. 'I knew you would not have been able to sleep, Amiya,' she said. 'Neither could I. I have been up the whole night thinking about something I wish to discuss with you. Please hear me out fully, and think over it before answering.' Amiya was filled with anxiety, both at the words and the serious demeanor in which they were uttered.

'We have three children, Amiya, all doing well with the grace of God. Both the boys shifted to Bombay two years back to look after a new business that my husband was very keen to start. Our daughter Delnaz, who is the eldest, is married into a very good family of Surat and has a daughter and a son. Both the boys are married too, and the younger one, who got married four years back has two children, a baby girl and an older boy. But it is my elder son I worry about all the time. He has been married for six years but has no child. I have taken Ferzana to every lady doctor, to holy men, to saints of every religion and have tried every remedy suggested to me, but to no avail. My son, who has everything a man could ask for is a pauper. Ferzana is a sweet girl but has been unable to bear him a child. His is an empty life, and it worries me to see the sadness in his eyes. Would you be willing to let him adopt your child?' she concluded in a pleading voice.

Amiya was shocked. This was the last thing she had expected. 'But doesn't your religion forbid adopting non-Parsi children?', she said, asking the first thing which came to her mind.

'It does and is very strict about it, but unfortunately we have not been able to find a new born child from our community whom my son could adopt, which is a good thing in a way because my son refuses to adopt a child,' replied Khorshed, but on seeing the confusion on Amiya's face, added hurriedly, 'it sounds contradictory I know, but the thing is that he doesn't want either the child or anyone else, even his siblings, to know about the adoption. But I'm going to stop here for today, and leave you to think about it. Your mind must be in turmoil right now.'

After she had left, Amiya got up and stood at the window, looking out at the garden. It was March, and the early morning sun, slipping through the trees, cast long fingers of shadows on the lawn. It was a peaceful scene; sparrows flitted about, hopping from bush to grass and back again, flowers bloomed in riotous abandon and a light breeze played in the trees. The calm of the spring morning helped to settle her tortured mind somewhat, and opening the door, she sat down wearily on the top most step, hidden from view by a balustrade of sorts. She had spent the whole of last night talking to herself, sparring with her thoughts, weighing her options, and although she doubted that her father-in-law had left his home for good, she was sure that Ishwar was never coming back. He had left with Jagdamba on the first day of the new year, and had neither returned nor sent any message in the nearly two months she had stayed on after that. And if Adel was right, and her father-in-law had also shifted elsewhere, she would have no option but to go to Kanpur to live with her mamas and their large extended families, and she was certain that she would not be welcome there, especially now that she was pregnant, and they would have to shoulder the additional responsibility of a child as well. On the other hand, the thought of bringing up a child all alone terrified her. She knew only too well the pain of growing up hearing innuendoes and snide remarks, of being questioned about her parentage, and being laughed at because of her slightly different looks, and she would never want her child to face the anguish that she had been through. Khorshed's idea shocking as it was, seemed to be the best solution.

But she would not lose hope just yet, would not take any decision without trying to contact Ishwar, and so, just after lunch almost ten days later, she took a tonga to Gawalmandi, debating with herself whether to go to the temple or to the house first. The temple was on the way to the house and seemed to be the easier option since she was less likely to meet anyone she knew so early in the afternoon, most people preferring to visit later at the time of the evening aarti. It was a Wednesday, and there would be no afternoon *satsang* or reading of the Ramayan either, her father-in-law having fixed Mondays and Thursdays for those activities.

As she had expected, there was hardly anyone around, and after paying her obeisance to the Goddess, she went round to the back, where the young brahmin apprentice, who had joined Pujariji nearly a year back, lived in a good sized room constructed by a rice merchant in memory of his late mother. The room also served as a storehouse for extra grain and for keeping a few mattresses which were used at the time of satsang, and it was on one of those that she found the boy lounging lazily, enjoying the temporary lull in activities. He saw her and immediately jumped to his feet.

'Jai Shri Ram, Gokul. Can I talk to you for a minute?' asked Amiya.

'Jai Shri Ram, bhabhiji,' replied the boy looking startled, as if he had seen a ghost.

'Where is my father-in-law,' she questioned, coming straight to the point.

'Don't you know?' Gokul replied, looking at the ground and shifting his feet uneasily. 'He has moved to Haridwar to be with his brother, who was keeping unwell, and together they manage the Vishnu temple just outside the Har Ki Pauri Ghat, I think, although I'm not sure.'

'When will he be back? And what about my husband and his brother?' asked Amiya, knowing fully well that this conversation with Gokul would be fodder for gossip in their gali for days to come. But she was beyond caring.

'Ishwar bhaiya has not returned since that day when ..he.. you...' stammered the boy, going red in the face.

'And?' prompted Amiya

'He didn't even come when poor Pujariji was leaving, and no one knows where he lives, not even his sisters. Pujariji and I went to his office to find out, but he has left his job, and no longer sends any money home,' answered Gokul, the words coming out in a rush, as if he was relieved to have got them out of the way. 'Tell me more,' said Amiya with a beguiling smile, putting some money in his hand 'and you can have a samosa and milk with malai from the halwai.'

'Pujariji was heartbroken after your departure, and decided to leave here for good. His daughters are also very upset and blame you for leaving and upsetting the household. Ishwar bhaiya's younger brother Jagdish has found a job somewhere and has shifted in with his older sister for the time being. There is talk of getting him married, and it is only then that Pujariji will return to Lahore, and that too not to this house. He wants to sell it and has told me to be on the lookout for prospective buyers,' said Gokul, the anticipation of milk making him suddenly very talkative.

Amiya was silent for a long time, contemplating, grieving. A part of her had desperately hoped that she would find her father in-law-and Ishwar here, and the news that she was pregnant would put everything right. But it was not to be, and there was a sense of finality to the fast approaching evening, and it was perhaps befitting that the closure should have taken place in the presence of the Goddess. She could of course, go to Haridwar or to one of her sister-in-law's place, but there was no point in doing that. No one knew of Ishwar's whereabouts, and the thought of going back to spend the rest of her life with her father-in-law, and later with her brother-in-law and his new wife was unbearable. There was also no reason for her to go to the house anymore, its doors were closed to her forever, the gali leading to it now an unwelcoming, strange place.

Feeling bereft, she headed back home. Although the visit had disturbed her, it had also in a way calmed the turmoil, ended the indecisiveness plaguing her. She knew now what she had to do, and on reaching back, went straight to Khorshed and told her about what had transpired, and that she was ready to let the older son Dinshaw adopt the baby, but was apprehensive because she knew nothing of him and his wife Ferzana, their likes and dislikes, what they were like as a couple, what they were like as individuals. She said this rather hesitatingly, not wanting Khorshed to get defensive, but to her surprise, the older woman nodded in complete agreement. 'Of course you are apprehensive, my child. Anyone would be. I will call both of them to Lahore immediately, so that you can meet them before taking a final decision.'

'Thank you aunty,' said Amiya gratefully.

'No Amiya, it is I who must thank you for giving the matter your consideration,' Khorshed answered with a smile. 'I am sure you will love my son and his wife. They are both very nice, simple people.'

Amiya was somewhat relieved after her talk with Khorshed. The Sodawallas were a much respected family of Lahore and of Karachi, where Adel's brother held a very high post in the Municipal office. Adel himself had a number of business interests in Lahore, two English wine shops, one on the Mall Road and the other in the cantonment area, where the family also owned a very popular provision store, which catered mostly to the British military officers. A few years previously, cashing on the booming cotton trade in Bombay, Adel had bought a cotton mill in that city from his cousin who was relocating to London, and had shifted both his sons there to manage it. The two boys, having inherited their father's trading genes, were astute businessmen and had opened a land trading firm last year in partnership with a prominent bania family, earning more in six months than the cotton mill did in an year. Khorshed was very proud of her sons, and frequently talked about their lives in Bombay, which was how Amiya had gleaned so much information about them in such a short time. But knowing about someone, and knowing them personally was an altogether different matter, and Amiya who had met neither of the boys, was very keen to assess Dinshaw for herself.

Dinshaw and Ferzana reached Lahore at the end of the next week, much earlier than Amiya had expected. They made a handsome couple, Dinshaw tall and fair, with sharp features, and his wife Ferzana, equally fair, but shorter and plumper. Her hair and eyes were the same shade of light brown, giving her a slightly exotic look, making her stand out in a crowd. Although not very pretty, she had a definite charishma and Amiya liked her immediately, finding her soft spoken and easy to talk to. The day they arrived, Khorshed invited Amiya to join them for dinner in the main dining room, and over the predominantly vegetarian meal, cooked keeping her preferences in mind, the conversation ranged from the weather in Bombay to the trade policies of the British Government. There was no talk of the real reason behind Dinshaw and Ferzana's visit, and although Amiya was grateful for the respite, she knew she had to take a decision soon, for the matter would be weighing on their minds as much as it did on hers.

Over the coming days, the more time she spent with them, the more she liked them, and by the end of the week she had reasoned with herself that letting them adopt the child would be in the latter's best interest. He would grow up in a loving family, grounded and stable, and would never lack any material comfort. And most important of all, he would be like any other child, with parents and grandparents and a very strong support system, something she could never give him as a single mother, who herself had no one to fall back upon. And if the baby was a girl, there would be the added problem of her safety, and later of her marriage.

As soon as she told Khorshed of her decision, a wave of happiness swept through the house, carrying her along in its exuberance, giving her no time to either regret or rethink. Elaborate plans were made, the gender of the child guessed and names chosen. 'You are a member of our family now, Amiya' said Adel, addressing her directly for once, 'like our own daughter. You will eat with us every day, and of course you will not be paying any rent from now on.' Amiya was overwhelmed, she knew the Sodawallas were very keen on the child, but she had not expected this kind of acceptance, of inclusion into the family. She looked at Adel properly for the first time, taking in his lanky frame and brooding eyes which gave him an officious look, the slightly drooping moustache and the tiny beard growing from just under his lower lip, the salt and pepper hair he kept covered with a Pheta whenever he left home, and tried to protest, to demur; she could not live with them indefinitely for free, but was firmly overruled. This was her home now, and there was no question of her ever living anywhere else.

The discussions continued well into the night, but once the initial excitement was over, the talk veered towards the more vexatious issue of logistics. Since Dinshaw did not want it known that the child was adopted, Amiya and Ferzana would have to live together somewhere for a couple of months, somewhere where they were not so well known. Not even the other two siblings were to be trusted, for that would raise the matter of the child being born to a non-Parsi mother. Although the plan seemed simple enough, it would have to be executed adroitly, with much dexterity. Amiya was so skinny that she could easily hide her pregnancy for another couple of months. Besides, being new to the area she knew no one, and would not invite any attention to herself, and by the time the baby could no longer be hidden, Khorshed and she would leave for Delhi, where Ferzana would join them later.

Much thought was given to the choice of place where the three of them could live quietly for some months, and which would have the added advantage of a good hospital nearby. Ferzana's parents lived in Surat, where they were prominent members of the local

Parsi community, and although her mother would have to be told the truth, their active social life and the fact that Dinshaw's sister lived in the same city precluded Amiya and Ferzana from shifting there. Eventually Delhi was decided upon as the best option, and the concocted reason for the shift would be that since this was a difficult pregnancy, Khorshed wanted her daughter-in-law to be under the care of Dr Dhall, the best gynaecologist in north india, who was based in Delhi. The Sodawallas owned a small house on Nicholson Road, near Kashmere Gate, which they had bought two years ago, and which had been lying vacant since. There were not many Parsis living in Delhi, and in a bid to encourage more of them to migrate, word was sent out of spacious, newly built flats being available at very reasonable rates in the Kashmere Gate area. Adel, always on the look out for good investment opportunities, bought one, furnished it sparsely and locked it. He was from a long line of shrewd businessmen, and liked the idea of owning property in the capital. Khorshed, in her characteristic quiet manner had expressed some reservations at this unneccesary expenditure, but these were promptly brushed aside by her husband, who was now quick to point out the huge service the flat would be rendering to the family. It just needed some furniture and utensils and would become perfectly habitable, and to procure these he made a trip to Delhi in May, a month before Khorshed and Amiya, along with Pappu's mother, Shanti, were to shift in. The baby was due in August and Khorshed wanted Amiya to be fully settled in and comfortable before the end of the seventh month.

Shanti had been with the Sodawallas for a full twenty-one years, from the day that she shifted into the servant quarters behind the main house with her husband, shortly after their marriage. Her husband was the gardener and a particular favourite with the Sodawallas, and through his hard work had made their garden the best in the neighbourhood. And so, when he died within a year of the marriage leaving behind a distraught wife and a two month old baby boy, they decided to employ her to help in the house. Over the years she had learnt their way of cooking and now made the most delicious Parsi food. Adel had tried his best to get her son to study, but the boy was obdurate and had barely made it to the fifth grade, and was now also employed at home as the gardener and general helper. Shanti's loyalty to her employers was unquestioning, and she could be fully trusted to keep silent about the events in Delhi.

It was the first time Amiya had visited Delhi, and she found it to be much bigger and busier than Lahore. The Kashmere Gate area was especially lively, full of hustle and bustle, although Nicholson Road where they were staying, was quieter. Kashmere Gate was one of the gates built by the Mughal emperor Shahjahan, when he shifted his capital from Agra to the present site, called Shahjahanabad, in the middle of the seventeenth century. The gate lay to the north of the walled city, and had been witness to a lot of history, including most recently, the revolution of 1857, less than seventy years ago, when it was used by both the Indian soldiers and the British as a point of assault against each other. The violence was long over, however, and now it was a flourishing market and an equally busy residential area.

Nicholson Road was located to the north of the market, along the old city wall, and their house, although small, was very comfortable, with big windows to let in the light and air. It was also near the Victoria Zenana hospital to which Khorshed took her immediately on arrival, introducing her to the doctor as the daughter of an old friend. The hospital was located adjacent to the Jama Masjid, and Amiya was struck by the sheer size and grandeur of the structure, the red sandstone building standing stark against the overcast sky. It was July and the monsoon had brought much needed respite from the almost unbearable humidity of the past few days. However, the grey overcast skies and the almost constant drizzle was making Amiya pensive, and as the due date came nearer, she began to seriously reconsider her decision. It was her misfortune that she was having to give away the child she had wanted so desperately, and in doing so was probably also giving up on any chance she had of leading a normal family life with Ishwar.

Khorshed, sensing her mood, tried to cheer her up by having Shanti cook different Parsi delicacies every day, and although Amiya loved the *batasas* and the *nan khatais*, the feeling of melancholy stayed with her, and she started dreading Ferzana's arrival later in the month.

Ferzana had already left Bombay a month back and was now in Surat, where her parents performed the customary Agarni ceremony, gifting her clothes and gold jewellery. It had been an unusually low key affair, ostensibly because Ferzana's father who had been unwell for a long time had taken a turn for the worse. That was also the reason given for Ferzana breaking a long held tradition and going to her in-law's house for the birth of the child, and that too the first child. After all her poor mother had her hands full with an ailing husband, and would be hard pressed to look after Ferzana and the new baby. Moreover, as Ferzana admitted to Khorshed and Amiya later, her mother, who was aware of the deception, was upset at the thought of her daughter bringing up a non-Parsi child as her own, but considering the circumstances had made her peace with the situation.

A few days before Ferzana and Dinshaw were to reach Delhi, Khorshed came to Amiya's room and handed her a small box. 'This is for you, Amiya. Open the packet and see,' she said, a look of excitement on her face. Amiya, filled with curiosity, opened it at once and was surprised to see a pair of thick gold bangles, intricately carved, their every facet catching the light. 'I don't understand', she said in a confused voice.

'These are mine, given to me by my parents when I was expecting Dinshaw, and I want you to have them. We may not be able to perform any of the traditional ceremonies, but I can at least give you these. I have already got new ones made for Ferzana,' Khorshed replied, giving her a hug.

Amiya felt tears pricking the back of her eyes and said in a choked voice, 'there is no need for this aunty. You are already doing so much for me.'

'No Amiya, it is you who is doing us a huge favour, one that we can never repay. Don't you think I know how difficult it is to part with your child, especially the first-born?' Khorshed replied, adding 'now no more talk of this. The only thing I ask is that you keep this little secret between the two of us only.'

Long after Khorshed had left the room, Amiya sat thinking about her, about her large-heartedness and generosity of spirit, about her affectionate nature, which had been inherited by her children as well, and not for the first time felt convinced that she was doing the right thing. Ferzana, when she arrived, further reassured her by promising to bring the child to Lahore at least twice a year, and even asked her to choose a name for the baby, an honour which Amiya declined. She did not want to look upon the child as belonging to her in any way, did not want to give credence to any maternal possessiveness she might feel. All through her pregnancy, she had striven for a modicum of detachment from the child who was growing in her, trying to remain emotionally aloof, knowing that it was the only way she would be able to part with it when the time came.

But when the time actually came she was in so much pain that she just wanted for the whole thing to get over. Khorshed was by her side throughout, not even going home from the hospital to bathe. The doctor had offered to send a midwife home, but Khorshed was adamant that the child be born in the hospital, and so on the 26 August 1926, Ferzana and Dinshaw were delivered of a healthy baby boy, whom the father immediately named Dinsha, after his own self.

Chapter 18

Returning to Lahore was easier than Amiya had thought. She had tormented herself for weeks and months, trying to imagine how going back home, bereft, without the baby, would feel. But it had been surprisingly painless, and had felt utterly natural for Ferzana and Khorshed to leave for Bombay when Dinsha was forty days old, on the same day that she returned to Lahore with Shanti. Coming back was uneventful, and Amiya was sure that no one had noticed her absence. It was easy to slip into the routine of everyday life, but Amiya felt torn, as though there were two women living in the same body, one who lived in this big house in Lahore, woke up in the morning, did some writing, occasionally went to the magazine offices, came back, had dinner and slept. The other Amiya lived in a daze, walking the streets of Delhi, hovering around the house on Nicholson Road, or just wandering aimlessly through the by-lanes of her childhood, pausing briefly outside Ishwar's house, before traversing half remembered pathways along the banks of the Ravi in her grandfather's village. Strolling down the broad leafy avenue on which she now lived, she often thought of the lane leading to Kamla's house, so dark and dingy, the *kutcha gali* behind her husband's home, where the peepal grew, the street on which the office of Noor was located. So many roads, familiar passageways that stitched together the story of her life, but always left it incomplete, the threads hanging loose, fraying at the edges. Roads without an end, leading nowhere in particular, destinations which had never given her a sense of belonging.

Her writing was the only thing that was hers, and it was to paper and pen that she turned for solace, the words tumbling out unrestrained and fast, faster than she could assemble them into thoughts. Since coming back from Delhi, she had started writing a lot more poetry, lines and stanzas coming to her unbidden at all hours of the day. Living with the Sodawallas had given her the luxury of time, and she could write whenever the mood took her, without having to worry about unfinished chores. True to their word, they treated her like family, her room was swept and mopped, her clothes washed and folded, and for the two months that Khorshed was away to Bombay, Shanti brought food up to her room thrice a day. Amiya, unused to this lifestyle, was embarrassed at using their hospitality to such an extent, and mentioned it to Khorshed as soon as she returned in December, insisting that she could at least pay the monthly rent. The older woman was genuinely aghast at the suggestion.

'You would not say such a thing Amiya, if you could see how happy my son is with the baby. He is a transformed man, comes back from office early, is relaxed and looks ten years younger, and has even stopped working on the weekends. And it is all because of you. What you have given to my son and his wife is priceless and we can never thank you enough,' she said.

Amiya was happy at her words, as she was whenever Khorshed told her how much the baby was loved. It gave her a sense of peace, of satisfaction to know that her child would grow up in a loving home, enjoying every comfort that life had to offer. It ameliorated the feeling of loss somewhat, made her sacrifice worth the while, and she comforted herself with the thought that even if she could not be a part of his life, she would at least get to meet him twice a year. But that could not stop the frequent pangs of guilt, the feeling that she had somehow failed in her duty as a mother, and whenever she saw a child his age on the road, in the market, she felt a deep sense of loss and regret. However, at the back of her mind was the conviction that she had done the right thing, a feeling that was reinforced when she saw Dinsha for the first time since his birth.

Adel and Khorshed had gone to Bombay in March to perform the Besna ceremony, which was observed when the child was six months old, and for weeks before that Khorshed and Amiya were kept busy buying new clothes and toys. Five elaborately embroidered Gara sarees were commissioned for the occasion; for Khorshed, her daughter, daughters-in-law and Amiya who, despite her reluctance to do so, was given first choice to keep the one that she wanted. Sarees were also bought for Shanti and her new daughter-in-law, Pappu having got married two months ago. The feeling of festivity lingered even after Khorshed and Adel's return from Bombay and for weeks afterwards, the doting grandparents could talk of nothing else but the baby.

Dinshaw and Ferzana brought Dinsha to Lahore towards the end of July, when he was nearly eleven months old. He was a fair, plump, very pleasant child, who looked more like Amiya than his father, having inherited her curly hair and big eyes. The vague feeling of disorientation she had on meeting him for the first time disappeared soon enough, and she enjoyed spending time with him, holding his hands and teaching him to walk, playing with him in the living room, where the furniture had been pushed to one side and a big carpet laid or even just watching his interaction with his parents and grandparents. True to their word, the Sodawallas treated her like family, including her in every little thing, especially if it involved Dinsha, and when he walked unaided for the first time at Khorshed's prompting, she was swept up in the rejoicing at home. A pag ladoo ceremony was planned for the next weekend, lists of invitees were drawn up, the menu was finalised and Shanti and Pappu set about cleaning and polishing every piece of silver and every crystal vase till the whole house sparkled and shone. Daily trips to Anarkali became a must, new clothes were bought, sarees in sophisticated pastels, crisp kurta pyjamas for the men, new clothes even for the domestic help. It was the first party the Sodawallas were throwing for their grandson, and everything had to be perfect.

But Amiya decided not to attend the function, insisting that she would feel out of place and uncomfortable. Instead she sat, hidden from view, at the top most stair just outside her room, watching the guests—as they drove up the driveway in their fancy carriages and shiny new Chevrolets and Buicks—all immaculately turned out, heavily embroidered garas vying with flashing jewels, Parsi men in their kurta pyjamas and white overcoats and traditional black hats, the British sahibs in their best morning suits. But what struck Amiya the most was the dignified and restrained behaviour of the Parsis, their perfectly behaved children, soft spoken women, and although there was much laughter and merriment, only muted sounds, as if coming from a distance, carried up to her, and she was filled with a sudden sense of pride at the thought of her son being part of this elite class of society. Dinshaw's younger brother visited Lahore twice an year with his family, as did his sister, and never once had Amiya seen any of them raise their voices or get into an argument. She had also long settled in her mind the uncomfortable issue of religion. After all, being born in a high caste Brahmin family had done her no good, and she would much rather that Dinsha grew up in a warm, loving atmosphere, assured of education and financial security. And so when it was time for him to leave, it was with a light heart that she bade him farewell, clamping down sternly on the mother in her who wanted him beside her always, looking forward instead to his next visit in a couple of months.

Dinshaw and Ferzana visited Lahore at least twice a year, once at the time of Navroz, and again just when summer was giving way to winter, and each time Amiya found Dinsha to be more lovable than before, a friendly, well behaved child, who called her ameh, the Parsi word for father's sister, and spent hours playing with her. Holding him in her arms, inhaling his baby smell, she sometimes felt a pang of regret so strong, that tears welled in her eyes, and it seemed to her that she lived only for his visits, her life holding no meaning otherwise.

Through these years, writing remained her best friend and Khorshed her biggest supporter. Dozens of magazines and newspapers were being published in English and the vernacular languages, and a lot of work in new and different styles was gaining acceptance. Over the past few decades, Punjabi writing in Urdu had evolved its own unique mannerisms, which Amiya felt brought a much needed breath of fresh air to both languages, being imbued as they were with the distinct flavor of the region's geography and society. Her own work, prose as well as poetry, became increasingly more liberal and free of restricting meters and regulations. She did not hesitate to use Hindi as well as Persian words to give her writing more depth, and played around with rhyme and verse as it suited her, even though this sometimes exposed her work to criticism from the more traditional writers.

The literary and intellectual society of Lahore had gradually come to be divided into two distinct camps, one comprising of the writers from Punjab, who were supporters of a modern approach to Urdu, and the other of those who were more old school and inclined to follow the writers of the United Provinces, whose work placed greater emphasis on grammar and the purity of language. Both groups were prolific and arguments between them became commonplace in a number of magazines like *Narang e Khayal* and *Paras*, with both sides finding faults with and occasionally even making fun of the other. Within Lahore too, the battle lines were clearly drawn, and a group of writers supporting the Punjabi cause of a more liberal approach to Urdu had formed the Niazmandan e Lahore some years back, and the two factions clashed often, both in print and in person at *mushairas*, and although Amiya thought of herself as being too new to take sides openly, her loyalties lay with Niazmandan, which had as its members most of her favourite writers. But since she was proficient in Urdu, English and Hindi, and could change her style to suit the publication, she had no dearth of work, and over time, all the leading magazines had carried both her prose as well as poetry, often to much literary acclaim. This was no mean feat, as Khorshed always reminded her, for there were very few women writers who had been able to carve out a niche for themselves in a field which remained largely male dominated.

When Dinsha turned five, in August 1931, his parents brought him to Lahore to celebrate his birthday with his grandparents. The morning was spent at home with Dinsha opening his gifts and enjoying his favourite foods, but in the evening the entire family including Amiya, paid a visit to the General Hospital, where Adel made a considerable donation for upgrading the children's ward. Amiya had an inkling of the charitable activities of the Sodawallas, but these were never discussed openly, never bragged about. But the love showered on Dinsha made her say a silent prayer of gratitude, and on impulse she wrote a poem, which was in the form of a prayer, a mother's wish for her child. It was published in a leading magazine to much critical acclaim, and for the first time, garnered for her an invite to a *mushaira*, which was to be held at the house of a prominent litterateur living in Bhatti Gate, Mir Khwaja Baksh, but which, rather than making her happy, filled her with trepidation. She mulled over it for a couple of days before mentioning it to Khorshed, fully intending to send a politely worded letter of regret. But Khorshed was insistent that she go, even offering to come along.

'I know that you are nervous about going, Amiya, and I also know that there will probably be no other woman present. But you are not like the others, you are a strong capable woman, and your work is exceptional. Don't let your fear come in the way of your receiving the accolades you deserve. What is the point of your writing on issues concerning women, if you can't practice what you preach? You must attend and if you want I can come along,' insisted Khorshed.

'There is no need for that aunty,' Amiya replied, looking at the older woman and thinking how lucky she was to have her in her life. There was something so gentle, but so determined about her, and on impulse, she got up and gave her a hug.

'Thank you,' she said 'for always believing in me.'

'You bring so much cheer to both of our lives, Amiya. You know your uncle will not leave Lahore, however much the boys may insist, and if you were not living with us, we would have been a very lonely old couple. But enough of this talk. Shanti will accompany you, and since it may get late, the car will wait there to bring you back,' replied Khorshed.

Mir Khwaja Baksh's haveli stood at the end of a rather narrow, dingy street, which was lined with oil burning lanterns, whose mellow glow hid any imperfections that may have visible in the harsher light of day. The atmosphere was festive, and the huge angan in the centre of the haveli was at the moment overflowing with men, the sight of whom filled Amiya with panic. There was no woman around and the scene resembled a marriage, with the men all formally attired and bursting out of their sherwanis, talking in low, cultured voices, Urdu flowing as smoothly as the sherbet they were drinking. Amiya, not daring to cross the threshold, tugged at Shanti's hand and turned to go back, when out of the corner of her eye, she saw a man walking towards her. 'Aadab, my name is Gautam,' he said, 'quite a crowd today.'

'Aadab,' replied Amiya, walking away.

'Wait, why are you leaving without hearing Mir Khwaja Baksh and Pandit Bhagwan Das, and all the other masters I can see in the crowd?' he asked.

'No reason really,' replied Amiya, torn between her desire to stay and nervousness at the sight of so many strangers, 'its just that..' she trailed off.

'Just that you are anxious because you can't see any other woman,' he said, finishing the sentence for her. 'Don't worry,' he added quickly, before she could say anything, 'you can stay with my friend and me for the rest of the evening. We don't know too many people here either.'

For the first time Amiya turned to look at him. He was fair, of medium height, stocky, with a receding hairline, and round glasses framing the kindest eyes she had ever seen. He smelt of a mixture of cologne and cigarettes and unlike the others, was not dressed formally, but was wearing a simple white kurta pyjama.

'Alright, thank you' she said impulsively, put at ease by his gentle demeanor. After some time his friend, whom he introduced as Ranveer, joined them, and the four of them stood quietly surveying the scene. For the first time since entering the haveli, she noticed that they were standing under a beautiful shamiana, decked with flowers and awash with light. The floor was covered with dhurries, and along three walls were mattresses with bolsters placed on them.

Along the fourth wall was a low, long dias, made plush by plump cushions, and at right angles to that was a smaller dias, partially hidden by a screen of sorts. Both were covered by a red shimmery cloth, and separated from the rest of the hall by a low rope divider. A tall bearded man, followed by a band of respectful flunkies, was inspecting the arrangements.

'That is Mir Khwaja Baksh,' Gautam said, adding, 'it's always a pleasure to hear him.'

At his words, Amiya was overcome by a sudden bout of anxiety. There were too many accomplished poets, connoisseurs and patrons of literature present, and there was no way she was going to be able to recite her poem in front of such a distinguished audience. Besides, in all this time she had been able to locate only one more woman, older than her and appearing quite at ease in the crowd. Wondering frantically what excuse she could give to Gautam for leaving, she thought she heard her name being called out, as if from a distance.

'You must be Amiya Bharadwaj,' said a very polished voice, adding, 'I am Mir Khwaja, your host for tonight. My brother read your poem and was very impressed. It was he who insisted we call you for the *baithak*, and it is our good fortune that you were able to come.' Amiya was tongue tied, shy and flattered and nervous, all at the same time. Hesitatingly, without looking at Gautam, she followed Mir Baksh to the smaller dias by the side of the main one, where she insisted that Shanti sit by her side. She felt a million eyes upon herself, judging her, sizing her up, questioning her morals, and it was only when the other woman came to sit beside her that she heaved a sigh of relief. The woman was accompanied by her husband and young son, and it was the latter who joined her on the dias.

The proceedings began with a flourish, a small lamp was lit and placed before the host or *mezban*, who then passed it on to the poet whose turn it was to recite next. There was also a long drawn out, very flowery speech by the *mezban*, in which the new poets were introduced and the older ones welcomed. Amiya, who was unaware of the tradition of the junior most reciting first and the *mezban* reciting the last, was startled to hear her name called out as the poet who would start the proceedings. Her hands were clammy and her throat felt dry, but pulling on every ounce of courage she had left, she briefly thanked the host and started reciting her poem. There was pin drop silence in the hall, and she didn't know who was more uncomfortable, the audience or she herself. But barely had she recited a couple of lines that the *mezban* started encouraging her with the customary 'wah' 'wah' and 'mukarrar' and soon the others joined in, lightening the atmosphere and making it friendlier. As the evening progressed, the enthusiasm of the crowd increased, and it became a living, breathing entity, very participative, but always bound by its own etiquette, never turning raucous or disruptive. Every poet seemed to have his own loyal band of shagirds, who were the most vociferous in their appreciation, joining him in repeating the couplets, often even drowning out his voice in their enthusiasm. Senior poets or ustads recited their ghazals in tarannum, their melodious voice adding to the magic of their words. Amiya was enthralled, and soon forgot her initial nervousness, although shyness kept her from becoming participative. However, it was getting late and taking permission from the host, she and Shanti left in the interregnum between recitals, and it was only when they were outside, in the anonymity of the dark night, that she heaved a sigh of relief. There were a few men standing around in small groups, and she recognized Gautam and his friend.

'Your poem was beautiful, it had such depth of feeling,' said Gautam, coming up to her.

'Thank you,' replied Amiya, and turning to Shanti, asked her to look for their car. Fortunately, the driver being a smart boy, was standing right next to the gate, and in no time at all they were seated in its plush comfort. Gautam, who had walked the short distance to the car with them, seemed to be in no hurry to let them go, wanting to know more about her work, and eventually even asking her where she lived. Thankfully, he did not ask any more personal questions, although he did mention that he was a lawyer, with a new found passion for poetry.

It was nearly nine by the time they got back, and the October night was very pleasant, with a light breeze playing with her hair and ruffling her saree. On Khorshed's insistence, she had worn a bright pink saree, and done her hair up in a low chignon. Since leaving her in-laws' house, she had stopped applying sindoor, although she was fond of wearing a small black bindi. That and the kajal she wore every day, was the only effort she had made at dressing up for the occasion. But tonight there was a glow on her face, her spirits were high and after a long time she felt a sense of real achievement.

Over the next few months she was invited to recite her poetry at other *baithaks*, but refused them all because most of them started late at night and often continued till the call for the morning Azaan from the mosques. Moreover, inspite of her having enjoyed the shayari and the ghazals at the mushaira she had attended, it had left her feeling very vulnerable, naked almost, and she was unwilling to put herself through that experience again. But in January of the next year, 1933, she was invited to read her work at Bradlaugh Hall, infront of a distinguished audience of the leading intellectuals of Punjab. Bradlaugh Hall, situated on the Rattigan Road, had become a sort of landmark of Lahore, the preferred venue for dramas, mushairas, and even literary discussions. It was also the epicenter of political gatherings, and until a couple of years back, had been the headquarters of the Naujawan Bharat Sabha headed by the late revolutionary Bhagat Singh. It had hosted many singers and poets over the years, including Allama Iqbal, who had recited a poem there in 1919. Amiya had been to Bradlaugh Hall twice, both times with the Sodawallas, once a couple of years ago and more recently, a few months back to see a play performed by a Parsi theatrical company, and the opportunity to recite one of her poems there seemed too good to refuse. Khorshed, who insisted on accompanying Amiya, was delighted at the invite, taking it to be a real measure of her worth, of the appreciation her work was now receiving.

The January afternoon was sunny, but very cold and windy, and Amiya found herself shivering a little as she got into the car with Khorshed. She was wearing a dark blue silk saree, with a black cardigan and a beautiful embroidered shawl that Khorshed had lent her. The cold had turned her cheeks pink, the colour highlighting her kohl-rimmed eyes, while a few strands of her curly, wayward hair had escaped to their favourite place on her cheeks, making her look much younger than her thirty-seven years. She was more confident this time, being one of three women who would be presenting their work, and the audience was different too, receptive and participative, but in a restrained manner, more in keeping with her own temperament.

After the program got over, people milled about, greeting each other, exchanging pleasantaries, absolute strangers coming up to her to tell her how much they had enjoyed her poems. Khorshed knew many of those present, and taking pride in Amiya's achievement, introduced her as the daughter of an old friend, gaining for her an almost immediate acceptance into the elite intellectual society of Lahore. Just as they were leaving, Amiya saw Gautam, and immediately turned her back, hoping he had not seen her, but it was too late.

'Amiya, meet Gautam, the son of very dear friends of ours. Gautam is a lawyer by profession, like his father, but I didn't know he liked poetry too,' Khorshed said jokingly, introducing the two of them.

'We have already met briefly, aunty, at a mushaira at Mir Khwaja's house,' replied Gautam.

'Ah yes,' said Khorshed, 'although Amiya has not been to any baithak since. She gets so many invites, and I keep encouraging her to go, but she's not comfortable with the timing and the fact that there is hardly any other woman present.'

'She can come with us, aunty, and I can even persuade Harjeet to come along,' replied Gautam.

'That would be perfect,' Khorshed said excitedly, looking at Amiya 'You would like that, wouldn't you dear? It will solve the problem of coming back alone at night, and you will really like Harjeet. Such a charming girl.'

Amiya, who was standing quietly all this while, felt a sudden wave of affection for Khorshed, for her unconditional love and support, and not wanting to appear churlish, nodded her head in affirmation, although she had no intention of going for any more mushairas, and especially not with Gautam and his wife. But Gautam seemed to have made the offer in all seriousness, and turned up at their house before the week was over, offering to escort her to another mushaira at Bhatti Gate. Amiya decided to be honest with him and told him how uncomfortable she had been the last time, preferring instead the audience at Bradlaugh Hall.

'In that case, I know just the place for you. My friend Ranveer is holding a poetry reading evening at his house, which is not far from here. He has invited only a few of his close friends with their families, and my wife is also coming along. I'm sure you will find it to your liking,' Gautam said persuasively.

Unable to find a polite way of refusing his offer yet again, Amiya agreed to accompany him the following week, secretly hoping that he would be unable to attend or that he would forget to take her along. She was uneasy about going uninvited to the house of a man she barely knew, and mentioned it to Khorshed, who however, was very pragmatic about the whole thing, and stressed upon the need for her to be seen and heard at such gatherings occasionally.

'You will meet fellow writers, editors, magazine owners and men of influence at such gatherings. This will get you more writing commissions, and who knows, one day you may publish a book of your own,' Khorshed said over dinner that evening.

Her words touched a raw nerve in Amiya, bringing to the fore insecurities that always lurked just beneath the surface, long held fears about her future, demons that kept her awake at night. It was true that the Sodawallas treated her like a daughter, not letting her pay for anything and including her in all their family matters, but one day they would grow old and the control of the business would pass on to the two boys. It didn't take long for relationships to sour, and who knew better than her the unexpected and devastating turns that life could take. She couldn't allow the affection showed by the Sodawallas to lull her into a false sense of security; she needed to be able to earn enough to sustain herself through unproductive periods as well, through old age or an illness, God forbid. And although she was earning a comfortable sum through her writing and translation work, things were getting more expensive by the day and it was just as well that opportunities were coming her way, and rather than shun them, she would henceforth look upon them as a blessing from the Goddess.

As always, reasoning with herself ameliorated the turmoil in her mind somewhat, and brought with it acceptance and a hardening of resolve. And so it was with confidence that she greeted Gautam when he came to pick her up and the momentary disquiet she felt at the absence of his wife, she quelled firmly. His marital relationship was none of her concern, and besides, the gathering was small and informal and most of the other men had brought their wives along. The evening went off well, her poetry was much appreciated and deliberately ignoring the nagging sense of embarrassment she felt at being escorted by a man other than her husband, she attended a few more such meetings over the next couple of months with Gautam and Ranveer, her comfort level with them now firmly established. They were both gentlemen and asked no personal questions, made no inappropriate suggestions, confining the conversation to only poetry, of which they claimed to be ardent lovers.

At these gatherings, she met many distinguished poets, writers, academicians; men of letters who delighted with their knowledge and ready wit. She also met the principals of leading schools and colleges, and hakims who had the touch of God in their hands and lawyers who had never lost a single case. She met powerful bureaucrats and editors of newspapers and well known philanthrops. Through Gautam she was introduced to a Lahore she didn't know existed, a vibrant, lively, culturally active Lahore, one in which she was no longer an outsider, observing life from the fringes; rather she was now an integral part of its pulsating energy.

Gautam was a patriot and a nationalist and made no attempt to hide his revolutionary leanings, taking her to gatherings marked by vitriolic wit and anti-colonial zeal, where every poem and piece of writing carried a social message and an fierce desire for freedom from the British Raj. She read many authors for the first time and reread others from a fresh perspective.

Gautam introduced her to the intensely patriotic poetry of Brij Narain Chakbast and Hasrat Mohani, who had coined the immensely popular slogan 'Inquilab Zindabad' some years back. She read Jigar Moradabadi's shayari and Muhammad Iqbal's 'Taranah-e-Hind,' 'Sare Jehan se Achha'. Gautam lent her his collection of poems by Sarojini Naidu and gifted her Lala Lajpat Rai's *Young India*. She read 'Sarfaroshi ki Tamanna', written in Urdu by Ram Prasad Bismil in the early 1920s, and 'Mera Rang de Basanti Chola', which was made a household chant by the revolutionaries Bhagat Singh, Sukh Dev and Raj Guru when they sang it on their way to the gallows a few years back. Bhagat Singh had also written a body of patriotic, inspiring work and the copy which Gautam lent her was heavily underlined, as if he had marked out his favourite passages. Bhagat Singh's uncle, Ajit Singh, was also a great nationalist and was currently in exile somewhere abroad, and his 'Pagri Sambhal Jata', which was written to motivate the farmers of Punjab to rise up against the oppressive anti peasantry policies of the government, was one of Gautam's favourite works.

Chapter 19

Suddenly it seemed that patriotic literature was everywhere; every magazine carried a piece in every issue, the editors of most English and regional newspapers were openly vocal against the British rule, and politics and literature were sharing a symbiotic relationship as never before. Through Gautam, Amiya was made aware of a sense of national pride and a larger Indian identity sweeping across the country, and it was as if she was suddenly looking at things with new eyes, from a totally different perspective. For the first time in her life she observed closely the passions that drove people, their hopes and aspirations and the limitations that defined them. And although social concerns had been central to many of her works, the patriotic fervor gripping Lahore had largely passed her by, always remaining something that motivated others. She had been saddened by Lala Lajpat Rai's death in the late 1920s, and by Bhagat Singh and Rajguru's execution a few years later, had joined in the euphoria that had gripped Lahore when Jawaharlal Nehru had declared 'Poorna Swaraj', but it was always from the outside, as an onlooker, with a strange sense of detachment. Neither the mohalla where she grew up, nor the one she had shifted to after marriage had ever managed to rouse much patriotism in her. Or maybe it was the preoccupation with her own self and the events unfolding in her life that had made her so oblivious to national sentiment. And the Sodawallas were too anglicized and too business minded to concern themselves with such issues. Although they had never said so openly, she could sense their satisfaction with the British rule. They spoke English fluently, partied with the British and derived their business and money from them. Gautam was the only one from amongst her acquaintances who was really passionate about the nationalist movement, and lately some of his zeal had begun to rub off on her, motivating her to write an article on the impact of the Civil Disobedience movement.

It was September 1934, and Mahatma Gandhi had just called off the Civil Disobedience movement—which he had started with the Salt Satyagraha in 1930—after a tumultuous four years. The intervening years had not been very successful either for the Congress or for the national movement as a whole. The Gandhi-Irwin Pact of 1932 had failed to make any impact and the 'Communal Award' passed by the British Prime Minister later in the same year had prompted a deeply agitated Mahatma Gandhi to go on a fast unto death in protest. The Civil Disobedience movement itself had shown mixed results, and while not winning any major concessions from the British Government towards self-rule, it had made patriots of thousands of Indians, who boycotted British goods and defied unfair laws across the country. Amiya, who was writing a political commentary for the first time, was strongly influenced by Gautam's thinking, and the article leaned heavily in favour of the Congress and Mahatma Gandhi. Gautam helped to get it published in the editorial pages of a leading English newspaper, owned by one of his friends who was a fellow nationalist, and who commissioned her to do more such pieces over the next few months.

Although Amiya's political writing was heavily influenced by the beliefs held by Gautam, it was never violently patriotic, being more in the nature of an intellectual exercise, and over time, as her work became more confident and self assured, so did her relationship with Gautam. In the nearly three years that she had known him, he had become a good friend, and most evenings he would be at the Sodawallas, the two of them sitting in the informal living room. And while she enjoyed his company, and looked forward to their meetings, lately a nagging sense of disquiet had started creeping up whenever he came over, as if they shared some dirty secret. He was a married man and surely her sense of propriety and discrimination could not have plummeted to such a low as to allow her to meet him behind his wife's back. So many people must be seeing him come to Beadon Road, his Victoria and occasionally his car remained parked outside the house for hours. His friend Ranveer knew of these visits as did the occasional guests he met at the Sodawallas, the buggy driver knew and had probably been bribed in return for his silence. And the literary and poetic meetings which they attended together, a married man and an unmarried young woman, were most certainly fodder for gossip, and she would not be surprised if some malicious talk had reached his wife. She mentioned this to Khorshed one balmy evening in early November, the delightful weather making her more talkative than usual.

'Don't you find it odd, aunty, that Gautam is here every other evening? Doesn't his wife ever wonder about his whereabouts?'

'I was thinking of the same thing myself. Not that I mind his coming here, you understand. He is a charming, well-mannered boy,' replied Khorshed.

'What is his wife like, and why does he never bring her along?' questioned Amiya.

'Harjeet is a pretty, educated girl from a very good, landed family of Punjab, and they seem very happy together,' said Khorshed, adding almost meditatively, 'you know men, always restless, looking for new experiences. Don't blame yourself, the evenings he doesn't come here, I suspect he goes with his friend to some baithak or the other. His father is a very well-respected member of the community and would surely have intervened if he thought something was wrong. So don't bother yourself about it.'

'But what about you and uncle Adel? He comes here so often, I'm sure people must be talking about it.' replied Amiya.

'We have full faith in you, Amiya, and know that you will never do anything to embarrass us. But the world is a harsh place for a woman alone. Gautam is your conduit to the baithaks and symposiums where you would hesitate to go alone. And besides, you have no one your age to talk to, so it's a good thing that he comes over sometimes,' Khorshed said, displaying a surprisingly pragmatic streak.

'Sometimes? He is here nearly three days a week,' said Amiya jokingly.

'You are a very attractive young woman, Amiya, and I'm not surprised that Gautam wants to spend time with you. In addition, you are also intelligent, and that makes for a delightful combination,' Khorshed answered.

'I'm also unmarried and that makes me available in his eyes,' Amiya said bitterly.

'Don't be harsh on yourself child. It has nothing to do with you. He comes of his own will. Men are by nature weak and cursed with a roving eye. As I said before, don't let it bother you. And if it really troubles you, I'll give him a hint one of these days,' Khorshed said, passing a loving hand over Amiya's hair.

But it did bother her, making her feel awkward and ill at ease in his presence, and the next time he came over, she blurted out suddenly, 'doesn't your family mind your being out most evenings? Your wife must want to know where you are.'

There was an uncomfortable silence, as if she had touched upon a particularly delicate issue, and it was a couple of minutes before Gautam spoke.

'Everyone is busy with something or the other,' he said evasively. 'Evening is the time when the children have to be fed and put to bed, and my wife likes to attend to these things herself.'

Another long silence followed, with a part of Amiya wishing she had never asked such an inconvenient question, while the other part, seemingly beyond her control, goaded her on further. 'How old are your children?' she probed, as if enjoying his discomfort.

'My daughter Maya is nine and a half years old, while the boy is two years younger,' replied Gautam, seeming discomfited by her persistent questioning, and gulping down the Laganshaala—a typical Parsi vegetable soup—which they were drinking, left almost immediately.

'What did you say to the poor boy, he looked distinctly uncomfortable,' joked Khorshed, walking in just as Gautam had left.

'Nothing aunty, just asked him about his family. Did you know that his children are nearly the same age as Dinsha?' Amiya answered.

'Yes,' replied Khorshed. 'I think they are a year or two apart because I remember attending the havan they did for the boy, which was not long after Dinsha's first visit to Lahore. And that reminds me, Dinsha will be here with his parents next week and we haven't yet stocked up on his favourite foods. We must remember to visit the shop tomorrow morning,' she added referring to the huge grocery store the family owned in the Cantonment.

November-end was the time when both the sons visited from Bombay, within a couple of weeks of each other. The weather was perfect, cool and balmy, the intense winter cold not having set in yet, and for Amiya, who was counting the days to Dinsha's arrival, it symbolized all that was good about life. It had been more than six months since his last visit, and she spent the next few days in a cocoon of happiness, wondering whether he had grown any taller, whether he would like the blue muffler she had knitted for him. Living in Bombay he was not used to the cold and had felt the light November chill keenly last year, insisting on wearing Adel's warm scarf all the time. That was when Khorshed had suggested that Amiya knit him one in his favourite colour, and samples of wool were sent for from Anarkali, and a gorgeous light blue English yarn chosen.

Dinsha loved it, it was soft and the colour suited him perfectly, and throughout the two weeks that he was in Lahore he wore it every day. He was a fair, good looking child, slightly plump, with Amiya's curly hair and the mannerisms of his parents. He spoke slowly, enunciating each word clearly, sounding exactly like Ferzana, while his gestures were all Dinshaw's, and try as she might, Amiya could find no trace of Ishwar in him. Maybe, she told herself, she was gradually forgetting what Ishwar had looked like, her memory blurred by the long years between them. His constant absences from home even when they were living together had denied her the luxury of familiarity, and now nearly ten years later, she was beginning to forget a lot of things. But she still remembered how euphoric love had felt, remembered the excitement of his touch, the joy of dressing up, the ritual of reapplying her bindi and sindoor every day. Sometimes at night, alone in the dark, she would wonder where he was now, whether he was still with Jagdamba, and whether he had fathered any children with her, and sleep would then elude her for the rest of the night, her thoughts turning to Kamla and Ram Swaroop, her mama in Kanpur and even her father-in-law.

About a year after Dinsha was born, feeling sad about the way events had unfolded, she had gone to Kamla's house to tell her where she was living now, hoping that time would have mended some fences. But it hadn't, and except for one occasion a few years back when she had crossed paths with Kamla and her husband while shopping at Anarkali, she had not heard from any other member of the family. It was as if her dead body had been carried out from her husband's home that day, and all memory of her had been burnt on the funeral pyre, along with any sins she might have committed. Ultimately it was the Sodawallas who had given her another chance at happiness and she was grateful for their continued affection. And now she had Gautam for a friend too, and more than anything else, she had her writing.

Her writing was becoming bolder and more experimentative, and since she had only recently started taking an interest in politics, she had no favourites, and was equally disposed towards all ideologies, unlike Gautam who was a staunch supporter of Mahatma Gandhi and the Congress, and for whom any contrarian view was unacceptable. Amiya found his loyalty amusing, and would often engage with him in a light hearted debate about whatever was the current happening. Recently, she had been noticing a growing trend towards socialism, and patriotism in its larger sense, seemed to have moved from simply demanding freedom for the nation to desiring freedom from inequality and injustice as well. Newspapers were critical of imperialistic policies, and there was much debate about capitalism. The growing rural-urban divide, which was so evident in politics, now also found a place in literature, and while the so called urban elite came in for criticism, the struggles of rural India were glorified. Last year, in 1934, some members of the Congress party who had reservations about Mahatma Gandhi's way of thinking, and who influenced by Marxism, felt that the only way forward for India was to adopt the socialist ideology, formed the Congress Socialist Party. This created an immediate upheaval in the parent organisation, with opinion sharply divided as to its utility in the long run, and Gautam siding with Mahtma Gandhi, was very dismissive about it but Amiya, who had been following its activities closely, was impressed.

'I like the idea of socialism,' she said to him one evening in June, when the heat and humidity had sapped the conversation of all verve, and the intervals between desultory sentences were growing longer.

'I think it is a stupid idea we have copied from the Russians', replied Gautam angrily. 'Our circumstances, our ideals are all different. Who can be more welfare oriented than Gandhiji?'

'I like that socialism focusses on the welfare of the downtrodden and weaker classes, and am thinking of writing an article on it myself. And besides, Jawaharlal Nehru himself seems to be a strong proponent of the system,' said Amiya.

'Nonsense,' answered Gautam angrily, 'Gandhiji does not agree with socialism as a concept because he finds it to be too violent and divisive. He wants the collective good of all, irrespective of class and creed. And don't forget that even Jawaharlal Nehru has not joined the new Socialist party.'

'He may not have joined them, probably because he doesn't want to break up the Congress, but there's no denying that he is a socialist at heart,' retorted Amiya.

'He may be in his personal capacity, but he certainly doesn't have the support of the Congress Working Committee. Are you forgetting the commotion of the last two months? It was only Gandhiji's astute thinking and personal charisma that saved the party. Certainly Nehru didn't think twice about tendering in his resignation,' replied a very indignant Gautam.

'No need to get so agitated, Gautam,' Amiya said laughingly, 'relax and enjoy your tea. There is another matter that I have been wanting to discuss with you, which I will do the next time you are here, hopefully in a better mood.'

But on his next visit almost ten days later, Gautam seemed preoccupied and sat silently on the sofa with a faraway look in his eyes, making no effort to start or sustain any conversation. This was most unlike him, and after a few minutes, Amiya asked gently, 'is everything alright Gautam? You look a bit worried.'

'My wife is always fighting and putting me down. I try to keep out of her way as much as possible, but even that doesn't please her. Nothing I do pleases her,' Gautam replied in a bitter tone, the words coming out in a rush, as if he had been waiting for Amiya to ask that very question.

'Maybe she wants you to spend more time at home,' offered Amiya tentatively.

'It is precisely because my presence irritates her that I started to keep away in the first place. My mother and she don't get along and are forever involved in some argument or the other, and it's not fair for Jeeto to expect me to take her side every time. I know my mother can be unreasonable at times, but Jeeto should give her the respect an older woman, especially a mother-in-law, deserves,' Gautam said agitatedly, lighting his third cigarette of the evening.

Amiya was taken aback at his frankness and struggled to find the proper response, but once he had started there was no stopping him, and it was almost as if he didn't actually need her to answer or to participate in the conversation. He told her how uncared for he felt, how nothing he did ever made his wife happy or managed to stop her constant complaining. His parents had been married for so many years, but his mother still respected his father and anticipated his every wish. But not his wife. Her family owned many hundreds of acres of land in Punjab where they were very respected landlords, and since there were just the two of them, Jeeto and her brother, the latter pampered her no end. Jewellery, clothes and whatever else she wanted. He brother had even wanted to buy her a Ford for her personal use, but Gautam put his foot down. He could afford to buy his wife two cars instead of one if she so desired, and certainly did not need money from his brother-in-law for that.

Amiya could see that Gautam was genuinely upset, and long after he had left, his words kept playing in her mind, and she wondered what his wife was like and why she didn't care for him. He seemed be a very gentle and likeable person, and the fact that he was a lawyer himself and belonged to a very well known and rich family, should have further added to his appeal. But apparently it was not enough for his wife, he told her on his next visit, setting the tone for the next few months, and as summer turned to winter and spring and back again to summer, his visits became more frequent and their talk more intimate. It was as if his talking about his personal life had propelled them beyond an invisible threshold into a land of deep familiarity. She told him about her childhood, Kamla and Ram Swaroop, her marriage and how it had ended, how she had slowly built a career for herself and what her plans were for the future. But she stopped at that, never mentioning Dinsha or the reason for her closeness to the Sodawallas. That was one secret which would die with her.

Gautam was more forthcoming, discussing with her every small detail of his life, explaining why he delayed going back home as much as he could after finishing office, how he had found something to look forward to after he met Ranveer and discovered a love of poetry. His relationship with his wife was still difficult, and although he had started to sleep in a separate room once the children were born, he had of late even stopped visiting her at night. Even his parents, especially his mother was getting increasingly unreasonable and irascible, finding fault with everything he did. She disliked Ranveer and considered him to be a bad influence, and was so rude to him on a couple of occasions that the poor man had stopped coming home. When he met Ranveer outside, they had a problem with that too, and were most disapproving of mushairas and poetry symposiums. Really, the only thing that gave him any pleasure these days were his children, who unlike their mother, enjoyed being with him, but with whom he was not able to spend as much time as he would have liked to. He was tired of the humdrumness of his life and of his father's old cronies coming home to discuss politics every day and of his wife's friend, Rukmini, and her perfect husband, tired even of the food cooked at home by Bacchu, repetitively day after day, dal and subzi and mutton or chicken. The only bright spot of his days were the evenings he could come to meet her, Amiya.

Amiya usually kept quiet during these tirades, having realized that Gautam was not particularly concerned about her participation, needing only to vent his frustration. She was also becoming increasingly confused about what her response should be. With the passage of time her guilt at Gautam's coming to see her so often was lessening, and she no longer berated herself over it. But she was sometimes bewildered by the dichotomy she sensed in herself, by the disunion between the two women living in her, the older one who remembered how shattering infidelity could be and had always done the right thing in life, and the other, the new Amiya, whom she almost did not recognize, the Amiya who was curious about what lay beyond the confines of her everyday life, who wanted to test her boundaries, and maybe push them a little.

In the endless battle between the two, the winner was decided by the hands of the clock. At night, lying alone in the dark, all her old insecurities would return, and then afraid, she would turn to the comfort of familiarity and routine, wanting life to continue the way it always had, fearful of change, of crawling out from underneath the covers. With day-break, however, came optimism and confidence, and as the sun rose higher so did her spirits. She enjoyed Gautam's company, and if he wanted to spend time with her, she would certainly not give him any lessons on morality. It was for his wife and parents to do that. As long as no one came to know of his frequent visits and there was no gossip, especially involving the Sodawallas, she was alright with the situation. She never took him up to her room or met him clandestinely, all their meetings were either in the living room or, weather permitting, in the garden or the covered verandah at the back of the house, with either Pappu or Shanti or Khorshed always around. She never asked him to come, had not done so even once, and never asked him to stay longer than he wanted to. It was true that he was a married man, but who could define the boundaries of infidelity, the sacred line beyond which the relationship between man and wife was forever defiled? Was it physical intimacy, or the joining of hearts, or the meeting of minds, or something else altogether, like her relationship with Gautam, to which she could give no name?

Whatever it was it felt good, and she looked forward to his visits, missing him when he didn't come, especially if she had written something that she wanted him to read. Although mildly apprehensive about her growing dependence on his approval of her work, she nevertheless liked the intimacy of sharing her thoughts with him, enjoyed the ensuing debate, using it to sharpen her ideas. And so on one of his subsequent visits, she told him of her desire to join the Progressive Writers Association. 'I really like Munshi Premchand's writing, and am thinking of joining the PWA,' she said.

'I like Munshi Premchand too, but liking the President is hardly reason enough to join an organization,' answered Gautam, with amusement in his voice.

Although the All India PWA had been set up in Lucknow only a few months ago in April this year, Amiya had been following the workings of its predecessor, the Indian PWA movement, since its inception four years back in 1932. Started after the publication of *Angare*, a collection of short stories by four Muslim writers, that had been banned by the British Government in the United Provinces the very next year, the movement continued to gather momentum, and last year the 'Indian PWA' was set up in London. And although Gautam disliked the word 'progressive' taking it to be very left oriented, the economic crisis the western world had been plunged into during the recent years, coupled with the rise of fascism and the refugee problem, had given to the word a sort of undeniable power, power to provide freedom from oppression and exploitation. In April this year, Sajjad Zahir and Ahmed Ali, two of the writers of *Angare*, started the AIPWA in Lucknow, and Amiya, who got a chance to read part of its manifesto, was very impressed. Whilst using literature as a means of highlighting social problems was not new, she liked the deliberate drawing of attention, through writing, to poverty and exploitation and backwardness, and resolved to do more such work herself. The manifesto also reiterated the demand for independence from the British and condemned the repression of civil liberties, but for Amiya, the biggest attraction was the women involved with the association, especially Rashid Jahan, one of the co-founders and a fire brand writer.

Born into a very progressive Muslim family of Aligarh, Rashid was a doctor by profession and had served all over north India, but it was her writing that had brought her into the limelight. She had contributed two stories to *Angare*, bold and women oriented, which had created a lot of controversy, but which had deeply influenced Amiya, forcing her to think about her own desires and what she wanted from life. It was after reading them that she changed her attitude to Gautam and his coming over so frequently, deciding that she would allow herself this self centred pleasure. Another early member of the association was Hajra Begum, whose life story, Amiya felt, would make excellent reading by itself. Born into a well to do family, and married into an even more affluent one, she found the feudal attitude of her husband and in-laws stifling, and following disagreements with them, had divorced her husband a few years ago. And the very next year had the courage to sell her jewellery, take her two year old son and go to London for higher studies. In London she came in contact with some Indian students who had very strong leftist leanings, and influenced by their ideology became a communist herself, continuing her association with them even after returning to India and taking up a job in a girl's college in Lucknow. The Communist Party of India had been banned the previous year, but that did not stop her from helping the party whichever way she could, and she played an important role in organizing the first conference of the AIPWA. Her life and struggles and the way she had overcome them struck a chord in Amiya, who had of late, started taking some pride in her own unconventional life, in her writing, in the body of work she had built up single handedly.

She therefore, found Gautam's condescending attitude to her wanting to join the AIPWA mildly annoying, disappointed that he let politics colour his world view to the extent of rendering it irrational. Surely Munshi Premchad's inaugural speech, in which he said that literature should satisfy the spiritual need of the society, while remaining force giving and dynamic at the same time, was totally apolitical and had universal appeal. But Gautam was not convinced. 'Sajjad Zaheer is a well known communist leader, as are many of the other members. Besides, do you realise that apart from Munshi Premchand, there is no other Hindu writer in the entire organization? You will be a total misfit, so don't even think of it, at least not for another six months or so, by which time things will become clearer,' he said, and before she could respond, started telling her about the India Coffee House near the Mall Road, where he had gone with Ranveer last week, and which had enamoured him so much that he had been back there twice already. Amiya, annoyed at the casual way he had dismissed her desire to join an organization she thought highly of, nevertheless found her interest piqued, especially since Gautam was her window to the outside world.

'It's a wonderful, lively place, Amiya' he told her excitedly. 'I wish I could take you there with me. Lots of intellectual discussions and debates and literary critiques. And you never know who you will end up meeting there. Yesterday we met Chirag Hasan Hasrat, can you believe that! He was sitting on the table next to ours and sensing my interest in his conversation, invited us to join him.'

Gautam started to enjoy his visits to the India Coffee House more and more as the months passed, and was there at least twice a week, cutting down on the number of mushairas and poetry gatherings he attended. He also became a regular at the India Tea House located nearby, which had a similar crowd, and recently Ranveer and he had started frequenting the Arab Hotel, which had become another popular venue for such literary gatherings. Located on the Railway Road near the Islamia College, it had immense locational advantage, although from what Gautam told her, it was a very mediocre place otherwise. Gautam, who was used to Stifles and the Gymkhana Club, found the tables greasy and the food very average, but these shortcomings were more than compensated for by the stimulating discussions and the heated political debates. Besides, as he said to her, the food was cheap and the staff friendly, and you could sit for hours nursing the same cup of coffee, now ice cold, without being asked to leave.

Over the years many such places had sprung up all over Lahore; small hotels and eateries where the quality of discussion and debate was much superior to the quality of the food served. But few cared about that and as Gautam explained to her, it was the excitement of meeting like-minded people; distinguished men of letters, passionate freedom fighters, political commentators, idealistic young college students, that made the stale chicken sandwiches taste delightfully fresh. From unpretentious restaurants, often consisting of only one room, to much grander hotels, in Anarkali, Mochi Darwaza, and localities near colleges, these venues became popular with writers, and many articles and short stories were born there, among the noise and the comings and goings and the empty cups of tea littering the tables. Occasionally, in celebration of a poem or stanza having been finished satisfactorily, another round of tea was ordered and the piece read out to much applause. Nagina Bakery near Anarkali was one such place, and whenever Gautam attended a literary gathering there, he brought back delicious cakes and pastries for them to have with their evening tea. The bakery, located near the Government College and the Panjab University, was the natural choice for such discussions. Khorshed loved their fruit cake, and always saved up some to have the next day.

Gautam, who was finding conditions at home increasingly irksome, was by now, spending nearly five evenings a week outside, either with Ranveer or with Amiya, and any hints she threw about the importance of family, he deliberately ignored. He was caught in a vicious circle; the more he stayed away from home, the more difficult it became for him to go back. His daughter Maya was nearly twelve, a big girl now, and son Inder was two years younger, almost the same age as Dinsha. She longed to tell him how bereft she felt without Dinsha, that it was not sufficient to say how much he loved his children if he did not make an effort to be part of their lives. She sometimes compared him to Dinshaw and found him wanting, the former spending every possible moment with Dinsha, even teaching the eleven year old the basics of running a business, and the proper way to hold a cricket bat.

Chapter 20

Amiya's son was growing into a fine Parsi boy; he spoke the language fluently, wore the traditional attire effortlessly on special occasions, relished *sev* and *malai na khaja* and to her mind, even looked like his parents. Amiya sometimes marveled at how seamlessly everything had fallen into place, all the pieces of the jigsaw coming together to form a beautiful picture. She had been living with the Sodawallas for nearly twelve years now, and never once in all this time had their affection waned. She ate every meal with them, showed Adel and Khorshed all her articles before sending them out to be published, took part in every family discussion and had, subconsciously, even picked up their genteel mannerisms. Her taste in sarees had evolved to become exactly like Khorshed's, understated and stylish, she knew how to hold her own at the dining table, knew the difference between a wine glass and a champagne flute, even though she had never tasted either. And twice a year she met Dinsha and was able to reassure herself of the enduring wisdom of the decision she had taken so many years ago. She could never have afforded him the lifestyle he now enjoyed, travelling in a Ford, studying at the best school in Bombay, learning cricket from the most reputed coach in the city, having his every whim catered to, and she wondered if her love alone would have been enough recompense for the manifold love and security that a stable family provided.

One evening towards the end of August, Gautam came over, very excited. 'Amiya, do you remember the play you wrote some months back, the one you were not sure about?' he asked.

'Yes I do,' replied Amiya ruefully, 'considering it's the only play that I have ever written.'

They were sitting in the verandah at the back of the house,

leading out from the drawing room. The bamboo chicks installed to keep out the heat of the midday sun had been rolled up, revealing the monsoon sky, a vast patchwork of white and grey interspersed with azure. A light breeze had sprung up, playing with her hair, teasing it out of the confines of its plait and frolicking with the pallu of her saree, the peach colour of which was reflected in the glow of her cheeks. 'You are a very beautiful woman, Amiya,' Gautam said suddenly, looking at her intently, 'your husband was a fool to have preferred anyone else over you.'

Taken aback by the personal comment, Amiya was quiet, unsure about how she should react. Should she thank him or get angry or just ignore it? The silence stretched on between them, but before it could get uncomfortable, Gautam spoke.

'Yesterday I met my friend Vijay Arora, who was with *The Tribune* for many years. He has just changed jobs and joined the All India Radio in a senior capacity. He was telling me that a number of writers are submitting their poems and dramas to be read out on the radio. I told him about you and he seemed very interested. I'll show him your play and if he likes it, you can meet him personally to discuss the details,' he said in an excited voice.

Khorshed, who had just joined them, spoke up before Amiya could respond. 'That would be wonderful, Gautam,' she said, 'I believe the AIR pays well, and it will do Amiya a lot of good to have her work aired on a new medium.'

'I agree aunty,' replied Gautam, 'she is already well known in the literary circles, respected for her command over whichever language she writes in, and this will make her even more famous,' he added in an indulgent tone.

Amiya who was listening to the discussion, trying to get a word in, felt a sudden rush of happiness. These were two people who genuinely cared for her, and while Khorshed's affection she took for granted after so many years, it was Gautam's sweetness that touched her, and impulsively she gave his hand a squeeze as he was leaving.

'Thank you,' she said softly, wishing she could give him back the compliment he had paid her some time ago, by telling him that his wife was a fool not to appreciate him, and although she said nothing, she did not move away when he took her other hand in his, and looking straight into her eyes said, 'you deserve so much more Amiya, after having have spent the better part of your youth working, when you should have been leading a life of comfort.'

Amiya felt tears smarting at the back of her eyes, and long after he had left, continued to sit outside in the verandah, gazing out at the rapidly darkening day, at the dusk turning to night. Moths had started swarming around the lights which Pappu had switched on, and she wondered what spell the glow cast on them, that heedless of the consequences, they strove to get ever closer to their annihilator. Surely they could see the singed wings of their brethren, could see how ruthlessly the light had treated them? Yet they came back for more. Maybe it was the way of all life, to be forever doomed to desire that which was beyond reach, and to be fatally wounded in the process. Maybe that was why she had waited for Ishwar all those years, inspite of knowing that he was in love with someone else, and maybe it was the same restlessness that drove Gautam to come to her everyday, instead of being with his wife.

Gautam returned two days later with the news that his friend had really liked the play, but wanted some minor changes in the dramatization that would make it sound better on the radio. The radio was something of a marvel for Amiya. She loved it and had bought herself a small receiver the very week it had started in Lahore, last year in 1937. She had been reading about it for the past some time, following its progress, and two years ago when the Indian State Broadcasting Service became AIR she was delighted, especially since Gautam told her that the next station to be opened would be in Lahore. Within the first year itself, the radio had attracted talent from all over Punjab, and now Shamshad Begum and Mukhtar Begum sang Punjabi folk songs, while Din Mohammad Qawal enchanted with his soulful qawalis. There was something for everyone, Dhrupad and Thumri and Khayal by the maestro Bade Ghulam Ali Khan, and bhajans which played every morning. There were even two raagis, one of whom travelled all the way from the Golden Temple, Amritsar to recite verses from the Gurbani. But Amiya's favourite were the poetry reading sessions by well known poets, and also the daily news broadcast by the Central News Organisation. The artists recruited by the department of dramatics were already well known performers, and brought every play to life almost magically, and it was Amiya's endeavour to hear every single one of them.

Amiya's own play, when it was aired, received excellent reviews and encouraged by the response, she contributed another two in the following two years, and was eventually put on the list of approved artists by the All India Radio. At the same time she continued writing for several magazines and newspapers, and for the first time had a short article published in *The Tribune*, highlighting the good work being done by the All India Womens Conference. Gautam's wife was a member of the organization, and it was on his suggestion that she wrote the piece, focusing on the role of women in the struggle for independence, and since the editor of *The Tribune* was a personal friend of his, it was published almost immediately. *The Tribune* was an important English newspaper of Lahore, started nearly sixty years ago by a leading philanthropist of the city, Sardar Dyal Singh Majithia, and Gautam was surprised that Amiya had not contributed any writing to it so far.

At the office of *The Tribune*, where Gautam had gone to meet his friend and give him the article Amiya had written, he met some members of the Progressive Writers Association, including Rashid Jehan, and although their political ideology was totally different from his own, he was most impressed by their passion and the work they were doing. 'They are so committed to the cause of social upliftment, so forward looking in their thinking, that I realized immediately my mistake in asking you not to join them, and without discussing it with you first, have taken the liberty of telling them about you and your work and they seem very keen to meet you,' he said, slightly sheepishly.

Amiya was happy. She had been feeling slightly low the past couple of months, especially since Dinsha's last visit, and perhaps doing something new would take her mind off the dark thoughts that threatened to consume her. Was this the way that the rest of her life was going to play out, always waiting for her son while living alone in a room at the top of the stairs, with nothing to look forward to except writing the next article, commenting on the latest political happening? At forty three she was beautiful, had never looked better. Age and self reliance had given her confidence, and while the former did not show on her, the latter was apparent in the way she carried herself, in her demeanor. Her skin had retained its youthful luminosity, which coupled with her thick hair and slender figure, made her look much younger than her years. The only bit of makeup she wore was kajal, which she made herself once every year, following a recipe she had learnt from Kamla's mother-in-law. The process involved the dipping of a thick piece of cotton wool in ground herbs and neem leaves before lighting it in ghee and then collecting the soot in an upturned vessel. This she stored in powder form, adding a few drops of ghee to bind a small portion at a time, and the prepared kajal was then kept in a tiny silver box she had bought from a jeweler in Anarkali, who had also made her a double tapered silver applicator, with three ghungroos hanging from the centre, which tinkled prettily every time she picked it up. For most of the year she wore crisply starched cotton sarees, shifting to silk only during the colder months. Khorshed had, over the years, gifted her with gorgeous chiffons and elaborately embroidered garas, and these she wore on special occasions, like the weekend in late September when the Sodawallas insisted she have dinner with them at the Gymkhana Club.

Khorshed was always keen that Amiya accompany them on their visits to the club or to watch a play or a cricket match, and although Amiya enjoyed the latter two activities, especially after the stifling summer months were over, she was not much enamoured of either the Cosmopolitan or the Gymkhana club, finding herself to be a misfit among the perfectly turned out women and their equally smart husbands. But not wanting to hurt the Sodawallas by always refusing their invitation, she went along sometimes, especially when there was a special occasion to celebrate, like Adel's birthday the coming weekend.

The day dawned bright and sunny, with a light breeze, the perfect morning for Khorshed and Adel to visit the Fire Temple, after which the two of them enjoyed a sumptuous lunch of Adel's favourite dishes, while Amiya relished the vegetarian papeta nu salan and the fried bananas which Shanti now cooked better than many Parsis. In the evening, Amiya took special care with her appearance, tying her hair in a bun low on her nape, and wearing an emerald green chiffon saree which Khorshed had gifted her some months back, and as she walked into the Gymkhana, she made a striking figure, tall and slender, with soft curls framing her face. Being regulars at the club, the Sodawallas knew almost everyone in the room, the Indians as well as the Britishers who were sitting slightly apart, along the side of the room which had windows opening onto the garden. As they were being showed to their table, Amiya, startled to see Gautam sitting in a largish group directly opposite from them, fought a momentary twinge of panic, afraid that he would greet her in his customary familiar fashion. And so when Khorshed and Adel stopped by at his table, she hung back, smiling a vague greeting at everyone, only paying attention when Khorshed introduced her to Gautam's wife, who looked a vision of loveliness in her bright pink salwar kameez and long ruby earrings. She was tall, with beautiful eyes and a regal demeanor, and Amiya wondered why Gautam did not spend more time with her and their children.

Perhaps, she thought to herself, it was what men were conditioned to do, generation after generation—to concern themselves exclusively with things outside the home, leaving the cooking of food and raising of children to the women. And if, in the course of this duty, they happened to meet a woman they liked, it was perfectly within their right to forge a relationship with her. After all, they were providing for the wife and children, and often for old parents too, and what they did outside the house was no one's concern but their own. The more Amiya thought about it, the more she was convinced that there was no concept of love between a husband and wife and that marriage was a contract of convenience, a relationship between unequals, in which the woman was supposed to bear children and serve her husband and his family unquestioningly for all of her life, in return for food and a roof above her head. That is why there were so many stories glorifying dutiful sons like Shravan Kumar, who served his blind parents till his death and even Lord Ram who, ever the devoted son, accepted banishment willingly to help his father keep his promise. The scriptures were full of legends about conscientious brothers willing to do anything for their sisters, and about men who looked upon their older brothers as fathers and their bhabhis as mothers. It was the ultimate utopia, one in which the wife was supposed to fit in seamlessly, into the slot allotted to her, supporting her husband in his service to the family, and indeed even surpassing him at times. But nowhere had Amiya ever read a story glorifying conjugal love. The moment a man started paying attention to his wife, he was labelled a 'joru ka gullam', and the woman was portrayed as a devil, the destroyer of the large, happy, extended family. That was why her family had been so upset at the thought of her leaving Ishwar; it was almost as though he was only incidental to the marriage, and even after he had moved in with another woman, it was her duty to stay back and look after his family. What other explanation could there be for a man like Gautam, well educated and successful, finding it perfectly normal to spend several evenings a week with another woman?

However, of late, Gautam's visits to the Sodawallas had decreased somewhat, especially since he had officially joined the Congress party and had been given a post of some importance in Lahore. Of his own admission, Gautam had stopped taking an interest in national politics for sometime, but was back now with a vengeance, busy attending seminars and meetings, helping to draft the minutes and rendering legal advice. Subhash Chandra

Bose's resignation from the Congress in 1939, soon after getting re-elected, had plunged the party into a crisis of sorts and Gautam was kept busier than ever. The issue of Indian support to the British Government in the war against Germany, which had commenced the previous year, had created sharp divisions both within and among political parties. Within the Congress, the difference became apparent when Bose was re-elected as President by the more radical members of the party—who were against India lending any help to the British—despite Mahatma Gandhi wanting Pattabhi Sitaramayya for the post. However, later distressed at the Mahatma's unhappiness at this defeat, several members of the Congress Working Committee resigned, making it difficult for Bose to stay on as President.

At the national level, the Congress wanted an assurance from the British Government about complete independence for India before cooperating in any war efforts, while the Muslim League, headed by Jinnah, wanted an assurance that the Muslims would be equal party to any constitution that would be formulated for the country in the future. Not getting the required promise—and outraged at the Viceroy's announcement that India was automatically at war, without having first consulted any of their leaders—all the Congress ministeries at the centre resigned in protest in November 1939. On the other hand, the Muslim League, which had also initially set forth some demands, now offered unconditional support to the British, as did the Unionist government of Punjab. However, what angered Gautam, as well as most Hindus, was Jinnah's call to the Muslims to celebrate the resignation of the Congress ministries as 'Deliverance' day.

'Maybe the Congress should have held on to its political posts, and found some other way of protesting against India's inclusion in the war,' Gautam agreed grudgingly, when Amiya questioned him about it on one of his visits to the Sodawalla's in January of the next year. 'We have just strengthened the Muslim League by resigning. Look at the way Jinnah has started reiterating the League's unrealistic demand for a separate country. I tell you Amiya this is a conspiracy by the British, a way of thanking Jinnah for his support to the war,' he added bitterly.

The demand for a separate Muslim country grew shriller as the year progressed, with Jinnah giving a formal call for one in March, at a meeting of the Muslim league at Lahore. Newspapers and magazines carried opinions and counter opinions and much venom was spewed at gatherings. The Muslim claim to even the Hindu majority parts of Punjab was met with anger both by the Hindus and the Sikhs, the latter, under the umbrella of the Khalsa National Party, having declared in March itself that there was no question of the Sikhs ever parting with their holy land. The atmosphere got further vitiated as the weeks passed, and the declaration by the British Government that the interest of the minorities would be fully protected in any future government that would be formed in the country, only added fuel to the fire. The Sikh leader Master Tara Singh jointly addressed an anti-Pakistan conference with a Hindu Mahasabha leader from Maharashtra at Lahore in December, ending a year that had shaken Punjab and dislodged many preconceived notions of nationality. The year-end saw another development. Mahatma Gandhi and the Congress declared a nation wide Civil Disobedience movement to convey to the British Government their displeasure over India's participation in the war, and much of the top leadership of the party courted voluntary arrest for a period of one year.

For Amiya, the year had been full of disquiet, and a strange lethargy had come over her, making her ambivalent towards her work as well, and so when Gautam offered her a chance to get an article published in the editorial page of *The Tribune*, an opportunity she would have normally jumped at, she refused. The article was to be based solely on the reasons for Mahatma Gandhi's strong disapproval of the idea of a separate Muslim nation, but Amiya, who had steadfastly refrained from writing on the issue the whole year, felt that she would have nothing new to add to the acrimonious debate. Besides, she was herself confused. Long discussions with Adel over dinner would reassure her that the idea of two separate nations was just that, an idea, which had been around for nearly ten years now, and which would never see light of day. But the reality appeared otherwise. Over the course of the year, the status of Jinnah and thus of the Muslim League had steadily risen and the former's statement that he would give his life for a Muslim state had made him a hero in his community. Amiya, unwilling to even think about the possibility of two countries, with her son living in one and she in the other, was becoming increasingly apprehensive, and longed to discuss her fears with someone. She looked forward to Gautam's visits, and to the inside information of what really was happening, but of late he seemed very preoccupied, and the last time he had come to meet her, a couple of days ago, he only discussed his father's failing health.

'My father is rather unwell. He has a low grade fever which comes and goes. Dr Bowry says it's nothing to worry about, but I am still concerned,' he said, worry tinging his tone.

'I didn't know that', replied Amiya, 'but Dr Bowry is very good, and if he says that it's nothing to worry about, you should believe him.'

'It is not the fever alone, he has become very weak and seems to have lost interest in everything. Just lies listlessly on the bed all day,' replied Gautam. 'And in the middle of all this, suddenly my wife seems to have developed an interest in politics and whenever she sees me, asks me about the possibility of a separate Muslim country. Strange.'

A week later they got news of Lalaji's death, and Khorshed and Adel, who went to offer their condolences, told her about how shattered Gautam looked, but how well he had risen to the occasion, managing his nearly hysterical mother, as well as attending to the guests.

As expected, Gautam did not visit them for some weeks after his father's passing away, but Amiya, who was busied by the arrival of Dinsha and his parents, barely noticed his absence. Dinsha was now a handsome fourteen year old and her heart swelled with pride everytime she saw him. His height had shot up in the last couple of years, and he stood nearly a head taller than her, but he was still her baby, and would remain so till the end of her days. He was in her every thought, every prayer, and it was as if her heart, having left her body, hovered over him as he slept, followed him to school, played cricket with him in the evening and snuggled with him in bed at night. Dinshaw and Ferzana had brought him up to be a very loving, kind child, respectful of his elders and generous with his friends, and try as she could, Amiya could find no reason to regret her decision of so many years ago. But sometimes, lying alone in her bed in the dark, she wondered what life would have been like if she had kept him with herself, if he called her 'mother' instead of Ferzana, if he woke up sleepy eyed next to her every morning, if he demanded that she cook him his favourite food. The circle of thoughts thus created was distressing, and kept turning on itself endlessly, and respite would come only with the first rays of dawn.

If only she had a friend, someone who could lighten her mood, someone with whom she could explore all the interesting places Gautam told her about. Living with the Sodawallas had, in a way, cut her off from people her own age, cocooning her in a sheltered, sanitized world, replete with every comfort, but one in which she was basically an outsider. But then, she had been an outsider even at Kamla's house and an interloper in her husband's, living in a sort of no mans' land, haunted always by a deep sense of longing for something unknown and far away. She knew she was attractive to look at, with her wavy hair and slim figure and had been subtly and not so subtly propositioned several times over the years, but rich, middle aged men, looking for some fun outside their marriage disgusted her. Nor was she looking to get married herself, and even though Khorshed had discussed it with her after Dinsha's birth and even made some attempts to get her to meet prospective grooms, she had shown no interest. She would do nothing that would entail her leaving the Sodawallas, and consequently her son, the person she loved most in the world. And she didn't need too many friends either, intimacy would require a certain amount of honesty, a sharing of secrets and she was not prepared for either. She had many acquaintances, men and women whom she met at every literary baithak, her colleagues at work and the small group of poets who met every fortnight at a different member's house. The latter were all Gautam's friends, but over time she had become comfortable enough to attend the meetings without him. And then there was Gautam himself, with whom she had a friendly, easy going relationship, one without any expectations. He was her window on Lahore and brought news of all the latest goings-on; fresh society gossip, who got married to whom, the latest books that had been published, which new restaurant served the best food, all the political developments since his last visit and the inside news of what was happening in the Congress.

Chapter 21

After his father's death, Gautam did not come to see her for nearly two months, which was most unusual, and Amiya, much to her own surprise, missed him and was also getting somewhat anxious. She knew Lalaji's death had put the burden of the entire law practice on his shoulders, and could well imagine how demanding his mother would have become, but two months was a considerable length of time, and she had never known him not to visit her for so long. Every day saw a new political development, Jinnah was getting stronger and now had the upper hand on Sikander, the Punjab Premier. At the same time, the Akali Dal, in a retraction of its earlier stance, had decided to support the British Government in the war, and the fact that Gautam had not even been over to discuss these developments worried her, and irrationally, made her jealous. As always, she was the outsider, who could lay no claim on anyone, could ask no questions, and as the days passed her worry turned to anger, and when he finally did come, at the end of yet another week, she acted aloof, wanting to show him her nonchalance.

Khorshed did most of the talking, asking about his mother's health, remembering Lalaji, and throughout the half hour she sat with them, Amiya was mostly quiet, while Gautam spoke in monosyllables. Dusk was falling and Pappu brought some tea and biscuits, after partaking of which Khorshed excused herself. An uncomfortable silence followed, and just as Amiya was deciding what to say, she heard the unmistakeable sound of sobbing, and looking up was startled to see tears rolling down Gautam's cheeks. Forgetting her anger, she rushed to where he was sitting, and taking his hands in hers, tried to dab at his tears with the serviette that Pappu had brought. 'Losing a parent is very difficult, and I know how much you loved him,' she said to him softly. He did not reply immediately, but at length composed himself and said, 'It is not

about my father's death. Something much worse has happened.'
Amiya was alarmed at his words, but before she could speak he
continued, bitterness lacing his voice.

'Do you know what my wife has been doing for the past several
years? Having an affair with a Muslim, and if my daughter, my
Maya had not seen them together, I would never have learned of
it.' So saying, Gautam started crying again, while Amiya looked
on in shock, not knowing what to say.

'I'm sure there must be some mistake,' she said, rather inanely,
'your wife would never...'

'Never what?' interrupted Gautam, 'never have a relationship
outside marriage, never cheat on her husband? Well you're wrong!
That's exactly what she has been doing, for God knows how many
years now. Maya saw them together upstairs in the guest room
last month, when I had gone to leave my mother to her brother's
house in Karachi. My poor traumatized child. I don't know what
hurts more, Harjeet's unfaithfulness or the look on my daughter's
face when she told me.'

'Did you question your wife then?' asked Amiya.

'Not immediately,' replied Gautam. 'I was in shock for two
days, didn't eat a morsel or sleep a wink. When I did confront
her, she denied it at first, but Maya had seen them with her own
eyes, so when I threatened to bring mother–daughter face to face
she confessed.'

'That's a terrible thing Gautam, I don't know what to say,'
said Amiya.

'There is nothing anyone can say or do,' Gautam murmured
in a low voice, 'she has promised not to meet that man again, but
neither do I believe her, nor do I particularly care any more. And
of course, I cannot ever leave her, my children will be shattered
and my family put to shame. Besides, my son, who is unaware of
the entire sordid saga, will come to know,' he continued, adding
ruminatively, as if talking to himself, 'many times over this past
month I was tempted to tell my son, but I couldn't bring myself to
hurt him. I even felt like telling my mother that all her misgivings

about Harjeet had turned out to be true, but stopped myself. What is worse, I'm sure Rukmini and her husband have known all along, and maybe their friends too. Harjeet has made me a laughing stock. And to think that I welcomed that double dealing man in my house for so many years, even going for outings with him. The rat,' he concluded bitterly.

But Amiya was in a different room now, in a different lifetime, listening to another man confessing his love for another woman. Twenty-four years. Was that really how long it had been? Life, which had seemed so new, so full of possibilities, had not waited for her, the days, months, years had marched on relentlessly, as everything ensnared in the grip of time must, and watching the grown man sobbing in front of her only reinforced her long-held belief that love was an overrated emotion. It made the strong weak and the wise foolish, eventually destroying all those who fell into its trap.

Gautam was still speaking, and the sound of her name being called interrupted her brooding abruptly. 'She had the audacity of accusing me of having a relationship with you,' he was saying agitatedly, 'God knows how long I have dreamt of that, how much I love you, but never once have I behaved inappropriately or done anything wrong. I wish now that I had.'

Amiya was shocked at his words, shocked by his confession of love and even more disturbed at the thought of his wife knowing about her. She certainly didn't want to be the reason for the turmoil in Gautam's marriage, and anger, both at herself and at him, swept through her, alternating with a sense of panic. What if the Sodawallas came to know about it, or worse still, Harjeet came to confront her? Although she had known all along that his visits to her could hardly be kept a secret, she had never been overly concerned, believing that the platonic nature of their relationship made redundant the need for any furtiveness. Obviously, she had been very naïve, and guilt smote at her. 'You must stop coming here Gautam', she muttered, saying aloud the first thought that came into her mind.

Now it was Gautam's turn to look shocked. 'What are you saying Amiya?' he asked. 'Haven't you heard a word of what I have been telling you? That man has been coming to our house for years, probably from long before I met you. Pretending to be a friend of the family. The bastard. And is that your only reaction to what I just said, about my being in love with you?'

'Please don't say such things, Gautam. Right now you are very hurt at your wife's behaviour, and this is probably a reaction born out of that pain, but you know fully well that we can never be more than friends. I'm not that kind of woman, and you love your family far too much to ever do such a thing,' she replied.

'You are probably right about that,' Gautam said at length, 'but you are wrong about what you said before. This is not some sort of a reaction to what Harjeet has done, I really do love you, have done so for years, but respected you too much to ever tell you.'

So saying, he hung his head as if in defeat. Amiya, feeling a rush of affection for him, went over to his chair, and lifting his face, cradled it in her hands. 'You are the nicest man I have met in my life, Gautam, and I am very lucky to have you as my friend. I'm sure things will turn out well and your wife will realise her mistake and stop meeting that man,' she said in a comforting voice.

Gautam didn't reply and left shortly afterwards. Over the next several weeks, he became obsessed with moving the children out of Lahore, making arrangements to get Maya, who was in her last year of school, to shift to Delhi. He wanted her admitted to Lady Irwin College, founded nearly a decade back by the All India Women's Conference, and counting among its patrons Lady Dorothy Irwin, wife of the then Viceroy, and several prominent nationalists like Sarojini Naidu. Rukmini and Harjeet had been to the college a couple of times to attend seminars and talks, and were greatly impressed by both the infrastructure and the calibre of the teachers, which was why, Gautam told Amiya, the latter agreed to send Maya there, even though Lahore boasted of an excellent college for women, the Kinnaird College, where Rukmini would be sending her daughter once she finished school. Harjeet's brother's elder son, unwilling to shift to the village and take up farming for a few years more, was working in Delhi, and it was with him and his wife that Maya would be living initially, before moving into the college hostel. Gautam did not want her to be living alone immediately after the shock she had undergone, and as he said to Amiya bitterly one day, he secretly hoped she would tell Harjeet's brother about her mother's behaviour. 'My wife is so proud of her brother and cousins and their children, but I tell you Amiya, should something happen to me they won't even look at her twice, won't even offer her a glass of water,' he said to her, his voice laced with scorn. 'I have decided to send my son to England with my brother whenever he visits next. He will have finished his schooling by then, and can continue his further studies there. I don't know how I will live without my children, now that my father has also gone, but I have no other option,' he added.

'Is your wife in agreement with your plans?' asked Amiya.

'She has no choice in the matter,' he replied angrily, adding, 'and besides, if she had her way she would have sent them to Mussoorie for schooling, so obviously she won't miss them. I'm sure she finds their presence at home a hindrance. And we know why.'

Amiya sympathized with Gautam, she knew how devastating infidelity could be, but as the months wore on she got increasingly tired of his tirade, and wished he would revert to his old, cheerful self. The country was going through difficult times, the failure of the Cripps mission had plunged the Congress party into a crisis of sorts, and everyday brought a new development. Sir Cripps had been sent to India in the last week of March 1942 to try and negotiate Indian cooperation for the war, but despite hectic parleys with both the Congress and the Muslim League, and promises by the British Government of full dominion status for the country once the war was over, no headway could be made. A senior Congress leader from the south put forth the suggestion that a national government be formed jointly by the Congress and the Muslim League, with the former acknowledging the latter's claim to certain Muslim majority areas. This too was rejected by the Congress. A few months later, in July, at the Congress Working Committee meeting in Wardha, a resolution was passed demanding complete independence for the country, and the very next month Mahatma Gandhi gave a 'Quit India' call, which was followed by widespread violence, anti war speeches and the arrest of nearly the entire Congress leadership. Although the Muslim League had also rejected the proposals put forth by Cripps, unhappy that there was no clear concession on a separate Muslim nation, it nevertheless rejected the Quit India movement and decided to cooperate with the British. At the same time, the Hindu Mahasabha as well as the Communist Party, which had been banned by the British Government, also decided to boycott the Quit India movement, the former for fear that any unrest during the war might compromise internal security and the latter in an attempt to get the ban lifted.

Gautam was upset, undercurrents of dissonance had crept into the Congress as well, and while ambivalent about the Quit India movement himself, chose to keep his feelings to himself, bristling at the thought of any opposition to his beloved Gandhiji, and when the latter's wife Kasturba died in February 1944, while her husband was still in prison, he was genuinely upset and wanted Amiya to write an article on the sacrifices made by Mahatma Gandhi, which although she promised she would, she had no intention of doing. Mahatma Gandhi was released from jail in the summer of the same year due to his poor health, but his illness did not prevent him from trying to work out an agreement with Jinnah, whom he met several times in Bombay a few months after his release.

The talks failed and speculation was once again rife, newspapers carried diverse opinions and there was much debate as to which of the two men had emerged stronger, with both the Hindus and the Sikhs as well as most members of the Congress believing that Jinnah had gained the upper hand. A few months later the British Government, as a gesture of good will, decided to free the Congress Working Committee members still in jail and sent the proposal for the same to England, leading to all round perception that this would be a precursor to India gaining independence.

But Amiya was filled with disquiet, and behaving like the proverbial pigeon which shut its eyes at the approach of a cat, believing that what it couldn't see could do it no harm, had stopped reading the editorial page and had taken to writing more about social issues than political ones. A part of her wished she could just stick to writing stories for children, but no one seemed interested in that anymore. It was as if the idea, the very possibility of two separate nations had consumed Punjab, like a river in spate overflowing its banks consumed field and village till everything became water as far as the eye could see. Even the Quit India movement, which had so impassioned feelings elsewhere in the country, had not impacted the state much, where the only topic of discussion seemed to be the rapidly widening Hindu–Muslim gulf. Gautam had been telling her about how the lawyers from the two communities sat in different parts of the Chamber at the High Court, how the coffee houses and clubs were getting polarized. There were other signs too, subtle but unmistakeable, like editors favouring writers from their own community. People were becoming more religious, almost fanatically so, overnight. Visits to temples and mosques increased, the fragrance of aggarbattis wafted from stores owned by Hindus and groups of Muslims congregating to demand Pakistan now became commonplace.

Amiya was terrified about the outcome of the country getting partitioned, and it seemed to her sometimes that she could feel the repercussions in her heart already. It was unlikely that the Sodawallas would be impacted much either way, Parsis being friends to both Hindus and Muslims, but what about her future and her access to her son? For how much longer could her life continue the way it was, cocooned in a bubble of safety? Tired of these tiresome questions to which she could find no answers, she desperately looked for something else, anything else to divert her mind and so when in December of that year, writers Ismat Chugtai and Sadat Hasan Manto were summoned by the Lahore Court for alleged obscenity in their writings, it provided a welcome distraction from the usual newspaper headlines. Ismat Chugtai and Manto were members of the Progressive Writer's Association, and she had read both the stories for which the case had been registered, 'Lihaaf' by

Chugtai and 'Bu' by Manto, and could find nothing objectionable in either. Ismat was one of her favourite contemporary writers, she admired her free spiritedness and the attitude of total fearlessness she brought to her work and was relieved when, after the initial hearing, the case was adjourned for another date some months away.

The entire episode, and the way the two writers had handled it, made her feel that maybe she had let fear and the dread of what the future might bring bog her down for far too long. She was not faint hearted by nature and had weathered many a storm before and besides, everyone else, including the Sodawallas seemed to be going about their lives as usual, far removed from the turmoil on the streets. Adel left for work in his car every morning, at his customary time, to attend to his businesses; Khorshed met up with her friends and bought exquisitely embroidered garas; Shanti continued to cook Parsi delicacies; and letters from Bombay arrived regularly, bringing news of Dinsha and his parents. Whenever she was with the Sodawallas, Amiya felt secure, lulled into comfort by the familiarity of her surroundings, the sameness of the sofas in the drawing room, the delicate floral curtains, the gentle domesticity of the household, the clockwork precision with which Pappu brought in the afternoon tea, everyday things that reassured her about the predictability of life. The Sodawallas were unapologetically loyal to the British Government, they had prospered under its patronage, had opened stores and set up factories, had mastered English customs and manners, and had no desire for such a benevolent system to change. Amiya had always felt that they were too anglicized to fit in with the local middle class of Lahore, and attributed it in part to their being intrinsically outsiders to this land themselves, foreigners who probably found more affinity with other foreigners. But Gautam disagreed with her.

'It is because they are outsiders that they are insecure, and unsure about their future with either the Hindus or the Muslims. They feel safer with the present government, with whom they have a very profitable arrangement. I tell you Amiya, economic security is their overriding concern. They have no patriotic feelings for the land that took them in,' he said to her one day towards the end of the year. It was a beautiful winter afternoon out in the garden, the sun was warm and the breeze cool, and Amiya who had taken a leisurely bath rather late, had left her still damp hair open. The shadows would soon start lengthening, and as if on cue Pappu would appear to shift their chairs into the patch of sunlight still remaining. This was a quotidian activity with him, and inspite of Amiya telling him repeatedly that she was perfectly capable of moving her own chair, he would be there even before she needed him. She mentioned this to Gautam, adding jokingly that the Sodawallas had spoilt her for life. 'It takes very little to please you, Amiya,' he replied with a smile, and then suddenly leaned towards her till his arm was nearly touching hers, and said in a serious tone, 'marry me and you will spend the rest of your life like a queen.'

For a moment Amiya thought he was joking, and was about to answer with a smart quip, when catching sight of his expression, she stopped short. There was an earnest look on his face, an almost pleading one. 'Don't be silly, Gautam,' she rebuked him sharply. 'I don't like this talk, even in jest.'

'What makes you think I am joking? I have never been more serious in my life. I love you and want to spend the rest of my life with you. Please marry me Amiya, and we can shift to my other house, in Model Town. I promise you will never regret your decision,' he replied, speaking in an uncharacteristically bold manner.

Amiya was angered by his talk, and any hidden pleasure she felt at his words, she pushed to one side. 'What sort of a woman do you think I am, Gautam, and what sort of a life would we have if I accepted your proposal? Always hiding like fugitives. And what about your family? What would you tell them?' she said, and without waiting for an answer, got up and walked off.

Long after Gautam had left, and dinner had finished, Amiya lay awake in her bed, going over the events of the day. A part of her was flattered, Gautam was rich and well educated, and would provide her with every comfort in life. And, inspite of what she had said to him, she knew it would not be difficult for them to live together without too many people coming to know. His daughter was living in Delhi, and his son he planned to send to England with his brother. That left his old mother and his wife, and the latter was in too compromised a position to say anything to him anymore.

The problem was with her. Try as she might, she was unable to bring herself to think of Gautam as anyone other than a friend. She did care for him deeply, but in her own way; her affection always contained within the walls of propriety, always constrained, never allowing her to cross self imposed boundaries, so that even when she was alone she never imagined that they could ever be anything other than good friends. Maybe Ishwar had something to do with it.

Memory was a strange thing, she thought sometimes, blurring into a haze things it didn't want to remember, while polishing to a rich gold, events that were precious to it. Ishwar and those years in his house had all tangled together into a shadowy, indistinct mesh, making it impossible to break off and examine separate bits and pieces. All except those brief months of togetherness which the intervening years had imbued with a special glow, so that she still vividly remembered his touch, the way his eyes crinkled when he smiled, the smell of rain on the parched earth when the monsoon broke, the colour of the saree he had bought for her, how ambrosial the tea had tasted on their first visit to Anarkali. Had the brevity of that time, the sheer impossibility of ever repossessing it, made recollecting it so sensual a pleasure, or was it the Devi's way of protecting her from making the same mistake again? Because the train of thoughts so set in motion inevitably lead to the heartache that followed, to the years spent in anguish, for although she no longer thought about her husband, and had long gotten over any residual bitternes, something or perhaps some guardian angel had kept her from falling in love again. Even with someone like Gautam, whom she had met almost every day for the past several years. And for that she was grateful. Neither did she want the guilt involved with getting into a relationship with a married man, nor could she afford to do anything that might put into jeopardy her access to her son.

Her son was now nearly nineteen years of age, a handsome boy, tall and well built, with the beginnings of a beard staining his cheeks. The last couple of years had seen him shoot in height, so that he now stood taller than both his natural and adoptive parents. He had finished his matriculation from one of the best schools in Bombay and was preparing to start college in the same city. The choice of college had been taken after much debate in the family, with Adel and Dinshaw wanting to send him to England, and Khorshed and Ferzana insisting that he was too young to leave home just yet. Ultimately it was decided to get him admitted to St Xavier's in Bombay, much to Amiya's relief; the mother in her wanted him to stay close, to never leave. His visits to Lahore were the highlight of her year, and even though she knew that their frequency would ultimately decrease, as he grew older and got busy with his own life, she wanted time to stretch itself out as much as it could, so that the months and days of her life continued to be counted by his coming and going. She found comfort in the conduct of the Sodawalla's other grandchildren; the younger son's two boys and the daughter's three children, all of whom were older than Dinsha, but still found time to visit their grandparents.

Amiya often mused over the ethos which defined families; Kamla's traditional household with its time honoured way of life, rebellious Ishwar and his hidebound but helpless father, the close bond of love shared by the Sodawalla's, Gautam's troubled relationship with his wife. Gautam and Harjeet seemed to have reached the stage of an uneasy truce, not fighting but not talking to each other either. Their son Inder was to leave for England towards the end of the year, and as the time for his departure drew nearer, Amiya noticed a change in Gautam's attitude towards her. He became more possessive, uncharacteristically so, reiterating his feelings for her whenever he got the chance, once even going so far as to tell her that he was willing to let his wife marry her lover, thus leaving him free to marry her, Amiya. Such talk filled her with consternation, and she was relieved when he got busy with his son's departure, accompanying him to Bombay and staying back with Maya in Delhi for a fortnight, before returning to Lahore.

Chapter 22

By the time Gautam returned to Lahore after seeing off his son to London, the results of the general election in Britain had been announced, and the Labour party had won with a landslide majority. One of the first things Prime Minister Attlee's government did was to announce general elections to be held in India in the winter of that year, 1945. Gautam, in an unusually pensive mood since his son's departure, was convinced that the Muslim League would win in all the Muslim dominated areas, and would thus sound the death knell for any hopes of a united India. And he was proved right. The Muslim League won in all the Muslim constituencies, and even though the Congress emerged as the single largest party winning in more than half of the seats, it was actually a victory for Jinnah. He had succeeded in uniting Muslims across the country over the issue of Pakistan, thus further cloistering both communities into their respective citadels. The Muslim League was growing in strength every day, drawing to itself not only those Muslims who had no political ambitions hitherto, but even those aligned with rival political parties like the Congress and the ruling Unionists. This was attributed to a very aggressive and effective election campaign, which was believed to have been directed by Jinnah himself, and which resulted in the same pattern being replicated in the provincial elections that were held a month later in January 1946.

In March, barely two months after the elections, Premier Attlee announced that Britain had decided to leave India and that an interim national government would be put in place shortly. Three ministers from the British cabinet came to India to work out the details, and the proposal they put forth was very half-heartedly accepted by the Muslim League and the Congress, and an interim government headed by Jawaharlal Nehru was installed in September.

But, following a call by Jinnah in August for direct action by the Muslims, violence broke out in Bengal and Bihar in September itself, in which several thousand Hindus and Muslims were killed, and there were reports of hundreds of Muslim households flying black flags to protest against the government taking charge under Nehru. The issue of Pakistan had, by now, become a hugely emotive one, and the interim government was reduced to a battlefield between the Congress and the Muslim League, with blame, distrust and anger plaguing it from the very start. The situation on the ground was also worsening day by day, forcing the British Government to impose a public safety ordinance in November.

Amiya was bewildered. Things were moving very fast, too fast for her to be able to compartmentalize and slot them into their proper grooves in her mind, so that the whole thing had become a disarrangement of rumour and gossip and anxiety. There was a palpable sense that freedom was near, but by now Punjab had become a boiling cauldron of hatred, violence and killing, the flames fuelled by snippets of news and unsubstantiated reports. Newspapers, which had for years prided themselves on their ethical coverage, now became openly partisan, printing blatantly one sided versions of the violence that was consuming the state. Religious organisations turned hardline overnight, and citing danger from the other community, began actively seeking enlistments. Speeches at public gatherings became more and more vitriolic, there were reports of both communities collecting swords and knives for self-defense and rumours were rife that the growing demand for daggers and lathis had far outstripped production, with each side exhorting its members to be prepared for self-defense at all times.

The reality of partition was everywhere, staring Amiya in the face wherever she looked, constantly nagging like the dull ache of a chronic wound, never debilitating, but always there, festering under the surface. What would she do if Lahore was given to Pakistan, as it probably would be? Although she had been living with the Sodawallas for nearly twenty years now—and it was taken for granted that she would continue to do so—she had increasingly started worrying about her safety in a Muslim majority country, and also about her ability to get any work in the present atmosphere of hatred. Dinner-time conversation at the Sodawallas had, for the past few months, centred almost exclusively on the spectre of two nations, and what it meant for them as a family and as a community. But still she was unprepared when one evening towards the end of November, Adel said suddenly, 'I think we should shift to Bombay.' It was a very pleasant night, a cool breeze wafted in from the window left slightly ajar, carrying with it the heady fragrance of the jasmine flowers growing just outside. The bird song had died down, but it was by no means quiet, and the silence which greeted his words magnified every sound, so that the distant hooting of a car horn seemed to be coming from next door, the chirping of crickets resonated unusually loudly, and the wind in the trees outside roared like in a storm. Even the clatter of the spoon on her plate was deafening. Eventually Khorshed spoke.

'What are you saying? Why should we leave our home? What will happen to the shops and the business?' she asked incredulously.

'We will sell the business', Adel replied. 'I have been mulling over this for quite some time now and have made discreet enquiries. The Baltiwalas would be keen to buy the business. Cyrus has been hinting to me for some time to take his son-in-law on as a partner. The poor chap has no stable occupation. And with the money we get, we can set up another cloth mill in Bombay. The details are not important, however. What is important is that Punjab is on fire, and the situation will only worsen.'

'You have always been a worrier,' Khorshed reprimanded her husband softly. 'I am sure things will get better.'

'No they won't,' replied Adel. 'Do you think the partition will be smooth? The Muslim League will want the maximum area it can get, while the Hindus and the Sikhs will not agree to part with so much land. There will be bloodshed I tell you', he added in an uncharacteristically sharp tone, his voice several decibels higher than usual.

'But we are Parsis, friends of both communities. We have

nothing to fear even if Lahore goes to Pakistan,' said Khorshed.

'That may be true, but you can never trust inflamed passions, especially in a mob like situation. The *aandhi* that blows in the summer sweeps up everything in its fury, not stopping to differentiate dead leaves from the fresh ones. If Punjab burns we burn too. And Punjab will burn, mark my words,' Adel answered, and turning to look at Khorshed, addressed her directly, 'We are not getting any younger Khorshed, I am already seventy-two, and remember how we have always discussed that sooner or later we would like to move closer to the boys? After all how many more years of working life do I have left? I get tired now and would prefer taking on a lighter responsibility. And it will be very unfair of us to expect them to move, they have worked very hard to establish the business, and anyway it is much more profitable than ours. But most importantly,' he said after a pause, 'have you thought about Amiya's safety if we decide to live in a Muslim country?'

His words had a strange effect on Amiya; she was quiet for a moment before bursting into tears, and through the misty veil covering her eyes, could see the look of consternation and confusion on his face. Impulsively, she got up and gave him a hug, the gesture conveying her gratitude at the implications of his words. The niggling feeling of insecurity about her future vanished in an instant, to be replaced by a rush of thankfulness for the Sodawallas' continued love. Her relationship with them was a symbiotic one, with each segment nourishing the whole and gaining sustenance in return. Over time, as they grew in years, their dependence on her for company, for liveliness had also grown; they waited for her to return from her evening walk before having their tea, insisted she accompany them to the club on weekends, read every article and short story she wrote, even got Pappu to learn how to make her favourite samosas at home. Their children, both sons and the daughter, welcomed her presence in the house and in their parent's lives, especially as they grew older. For her part, she had genuinely grown to love Adel and Khorshed, and cherished being part of the family, especially one that included her son as well, and the realization that they were willing to shift from Lahore for her safety, humbled her and made her love them even more.

But later that night, in the solitude of her room, the true import of Adel's words sunk in, and with a start, she sat up in bed. Shifting to Bombay would entail leaving Lahore and all that was familiar, all that meant home to her, and not even the promise of Dinsha's proximity could lift her spirits after that. Khorshed seemed to be suffering from the same pangs, for she brought up the subject first thing in the morning, even before Pappu had served them tea, alternately reasoning and pleading with her husband, who although inflexible at first, agreed to give the matter some more consideration. But as the weeks passed, events started overtaking them, episode by episode, one hateful speech after another, one violent act too many, till it became impossible to look away from the reality of Punjab anymore.

The situation was worsening day by day and the new year, 1947, Amiya thought to herself, was neither new nor auspicious, as hardly two months into it violence broke out all over the state, in response to the declaration by Britain in February that it would be leaving India positively by the June of next year. The transition would be overseen by a new Viceroy, Lord Mountbatten, who would be replacing Lord Wavell. The wave of happiness that swept across the rest of the country at the promise of freedom transformed into an ugly surge for power and one-upmanship in Punjab, with each party trying to outdo the other. The resulting violence, that lasted for over a month, left thousands dead, most of them Hindus and Sikhs from rural Punjab where they were in a minority. The Muslim League, sensing an upper hand intensified its agitation for Pakistan, blocking trains and hoisting the League flag on government buildings. The coalition government in Punjab collapsed and the Prime Minister Khizr Tiwana resigned in the first week of March, prompting the firebrand Akali leader Master Tara Singh to brandish his kirpan on the steps of the Punjab assembly building in Lahore the very next day, declaring that 11 March would be observed as 'anti-Pakistan day'.

Gautam, who joined them for dinner that night, stunned them with the news that he too would be leaving Lahore and shifting with his family to Delhi within the next one month.

'It has not been an easy decision for me to take, to leave my flourishing law practice and move to a new town and start afresh. But I know for a certainty that the country will be partitioned and that Lahore will go to Pakistan, and I want to leave before that happens. A lot of our friends are moving too, but some like my wife's friend Rukmini have a ready made business to go back to in Amritsar and so won't mind the transition as much,' he said somewhat bitterly.

'That's exactly what I have been telling these people, that the time for thinking is over. Good that you came today, Gautam, it has helped me firm up my mind. I shall talk to Cyrus about the business tomorrow itself, and next week I can visit Bombay to finalise the plan with the boys. We are lucky that we will be moving from one home to another, not everyone has that option. And we have the added luxury of Shanti and Pappu wanting to come along,' Adel joked, looking at Khorshed.

But his program had to be put on hold for a few days because violence broke out in Lahore and the rest of Punjab the following morning. Thousands of Hindus and Sikhs were massacred in towns and villages all over the state in the bloodshed that lasted for a full three days, and thousands others abandoned their homes, in what seemed to Amiya to be a well orchestrated attempt at ethnic cleansing. What was even more disturbing was the brutality and the ruthlessness of the attacks, and the lack of will on the part of the British Government to combat them. The local police, which consisted mostly of Muslims, had become totally partisan by now, and the army when called, either came too late or not at all. The situation, which seemed to have reached a breaking point, prompted the Congress Working Committee, at a meeting in Delhi a few days later, to formally ask for a partition of Punjab into two provinces, and the very next day a worried Adel left for Bombay.

The inevitability of leaving Lahore smote Amiya like a blow.

Lahore. Her city, the only place she had ever known. It had witnessed silently the drama of her life unfolding in its bosom, never interfering, never judgemental. It's spring breezes, balmy and mild, had warmed her after a particularly harsh winter, its summers had scorched her but filled her days with the fragrance of the jasmine and the mogra. Mellow winter afternoons, spent half dozing in the sun, with a shawl covering her face, had an ambience of timelessness about them, as if the dappled shadows cast by the neem on the grass and the walls would endure forever.

It had been kind to her, this jewel among cities, offering her another chance at happiness, generously allowing her to search for livelihood in its plenitude, giving her sanctuary in its leafy avenues. Sometimes it seemed to her that there was something in its air, an intangible glow, almost ethereal, that made it shimmer, like summer haze in the distance on a very hot day. Maybe it was magic dust, an elysian benediction that made its buildings glimmer and its minarets shine, that gave to its bazaars their prosperity, and to its residents the love of music and poetry, so that on a walk along one of its lanes and by-lanes you were sure to hear some melody wafting from half open windows.

Her Lahore, with its crowded gullies and broad avenues, the Devi temple near Kamla's house, the cry of the milk man every morning, woodsmoke rising on cold winter evenings, the half a kilometre walk to the tonga stand and the swaying tonga ride to the office of Noor. Visiting Anarkali with Khorshed and coming home to excitedly open the shopping. Samosas and jalebis from her favourite halwai at the corner of the market, the kites of basant and the chillums of the mystics, the gulmohar tree outside her window which held every season captive in its canopy, balmy evenings at the Gymkhana Club, the quotidian hustle and bustle of the bazaars.

Over the years she had visited several towns and cities, had accompanied the Sodawallas on holiday to Simla and Murree and even to Calcutta once. She had travelled to Karachi and Amritsar to take part in poetry symposiums, and to Delhi where she was often the guest speaker at literary gatherings, and even to Kanpur twice, both times driven by an unsuccessful desire to mend fences with her mama and his family. But each time she was happy to be back home to Lahore, to her small room at the top of the stairs, never for a moment imagining that she might be forced to leave it one day.

But the evil wind that was blowing through Punjab had overrun her beloved city as well, discolouring half burnt buildings with the soot of hatred, paving every street, every gali with malevolence, making beasts of men and criminals of the upholders of justice. Its diabolical rumour laden touch made foes of lifelong friends and incited normally placid people to acts of unspeakable violence. Sloganeering by mobs, usually Muslims demanding Pakistan, would reach them several times a day from the nearby Mall Road, and these would be countered almost immediately by the rallying cries of Hindus and Sikhs. Cloth balls, dipped in fuel before being set on fire were flung by both sides on enemy houses and shops. Arson and looting, sometimes several times in a day, became commonplace, the flames ignited by hearsay and a faster than light intelligence network so that mobs collected in seconds, ready to go on rampage at the slightest provocation. Long standing friendships were torched in the inferno of revenge, with erstwhile friends being the informants in most cases.

Adel was kept busy the entire April and May, either travelling to Bombay or spending long hours at his office, winding up his work and settling the accounts. Following discussions within the community, he hung a plaque stating 'Parsi' in bold letters on the front gate of the house, and another two outside each of the shops, as a sort of talisman against any untoward incident. Several of their friends were moving to Bombay or Surat, but several others were staying back, confident of their inherent ability to appease whichever community was in power, and it was to them that Adel planned to entrust the house and the car till such time as he was able to dispose them off. The business had been sold to Cyrus for a neat sum, lesser than what it would have fetched in normal times, but enough to keep them in comfort for the rest of their lives. The shops had not found any buyers, probably because of the uncertainty over the future of the liquor business should Lahore go to Pakistan, but Adel had been able to lease one of them out to a friend, whose reputation for shrewdness was justified by the hard bargaining he did over the monthly rent. He also reluctantly agreed to oversee the running of the other shop, which was located in the cantonment, leaving Adel very pleased with the arrangements he had been able to cobble together at such short notice.

He was also satisfied with the deal he had struck in Bombay for an apartment located on Marine Drive whose owner, an old Parsi, was moving to Baroda to live with his son. Adel loved it at first sight, loved its proximity to the sea and the novelty of having coconut and palm trees growing right outside the building. It was also big enough to accommodate the three of them plus Shanti, while Pappu and his family would be staying for the time being with Dinshaw who had a house nearby. If Adel had any pangs at leaving the city he had lived in all his life, he hid them well, and in a bid to make the transition easier for his wife, told her repeatedly how excited he was at the thought of living with the children.

Chapter 23

Adel's enthusiasm about shifting to Bombay did lighten the atmosphere of melancholy somewhat, but there was something Amiya needed to do before she left Lahore, and so, on a Saturday morning towards the end of April, she took a tonga to Kamla's house, without even knowing whether her massi still lived there or not. In the past decade she had visited Kamla thrice, the last being more than four years ago, each time with a desire to mend fences with the woman who had brought her up with so much love, but time seemed to have overtaken them as it had overtaken everything else, so that on every occasion she had felt like an outsider, and couldn't wait to get out of the house. The chance meeting at Anarkali had been equally frosty. But this visit was different, it was probably the last time they would be meeting and she had deliberately chosen a weekend when the entire family, especially Ram Swaroop, would be home.

The morning was pleasant, but the day would soon become hot and as the tonga swayed along, picking up passengers and dropping them off, she was suddenly overwhelmed by a rush of rememberance. For the past several years now, on Khorshed's insistance, she had started using the Sodawalla's Victoria, and sometimes even the car, whenever she needed to go somewhere, and this reacquaintance with the sounds and smells of the tonga stand;the driver soliciting passengers, children crying, hawkers peddling their products in a sing song voice, luggage vying for space with the owners, filled her heart with nostalgia. She took her time walking the short distance to Kamla's house from where the tonga dropped her, stopping to take in the changes the intervening years had wrought-new houses, some tea shacks, a well stocked kirana store; the narrow galis the same, but different somehow. It was as if the violence and the hatred that had wracked the city had sucked out the warmth, the essence from the land, so that the roads, the bricks, the very air felt cold, and she gave an involuntary shiver and pulled her saree pallu a little tighter around her shoulders.

But rounding a corner, she came to the Kali Mata temple, and suddenly her disquiet of a moment ago settled somewhat, and as she stepped in for darshan, a deep peace enveloped her. Maybe what Gautam said was his wife's favourite explanation for everything was true after all. Our entire life, from the moment we are born to the day we die, every experience, every instant, is written on the wind, which like a sorcerer acquires different names in different lands and different seasons; Karma and Bhagwan and Kismet. The wind is omnipresent, it knows every thing about us, the past and the future, right upto eternity and there is little we can do other than to let it blow as it will, surrendering to the gales and reposing in the calms, all the while trying to learn the acceptance it seeks to teach us. The same wind that had swept her away from these streets of her childhood, and tossed her around like a leaf caught in a squall, was now taking her elsewhere, to a different world, to new sights and sounds and smells, and she would trust in its wisdom.

It was thus, in a much calmer frame of mind that she knocked on Kamla's door. The front yard had changed somewhat, and although still tiny, showed signs of prosperity, having been tiled and bounded by a newly constructed wall. Kamla and Ram Swaroop had changed too, the passing years had added silver to their hair and cobwebs under their eyes, and imparted a certain fragility to their appearance and to their spirit, so that they welcomed her unusually warmly. Life had been good to them, all their grandchildren were married, and the oldest grandson had just been blessed with a daughter, who was sleeping on the bed next to Kamla. The scene appeared changeless, like a tableau frozen in time. Only the actors had changed, with Kamla having taken her mother-in-law's place in the front room and Ram Swaroop his father's chair in the living room. But underneath the gloss of familial happiness was a reality tarnished by fear and uncertainty.

'You don't need to leave Lahore, Amiya. The Parsis are friends with the Muslims, and anyway there is no certainty that Lahore will go to Pakistan,' Kamla said disdainfully.

'I think that from all accounts Lahore will go to Pakistan, since it has a Muslim majority,' Ram Swaroop contradicted his wife gently, and turning to Amiya addressed her directly. 'We are ourselves thinking of shifting to Jullunder. Do you remember my older sister who was married there? Her sons are running a very successful school in the city, where my brother's son has joined as a teacher, and where I hope our son, Anuj, can also take up employment if need be. My sister has already looked up a house for us. You are welcome to come with us if you want,' he added kindly.

'You say the silliest things sometimes,' Kamla reprimanded her husband. 'Why will she want to live with us poor folks? Those rich Parsis are her family now.'

Amiya was taken aback at the barb, at the superfluity of it on what was probably their last meeting, and not wanting to get into a nasty duel of words with her, got up to leave.

'Wait a minute, Amiya. Your massi has something to give you,' said Ram Swaroop, and turning to his wife, looked at her expectantly, 'Kamla?'

'Oh that!' Kamla said dismissively, 'I'm sure Amiya won't be interested in such old trivia.'

'Yes she will' countered her husband in an unusually stern voice. 'If you don't tell her, I will.'

At his words, Amiya felt a sinking feeling in the pit of her stomach, and sat down back abruptly. 'What is it, what is the matter?' she asked Ram Swaroop anxiously, realizing instinctively that he was more inclined to tell her the truth than her aunt.

'Last year while getting the house whitewashed, I found a letter written by your father to your mother in an old trunk, and also an old ring he had given to her. I was shocked on reading the letter and felt that we should give it to you immediately, but your massi didn't agree,' he replied.

'For nearly fifty years I kept the secret,' Kamla said tearfully 'only because I wanted to protect you, Amiya. I had even forgotten about the letter and would have torn it if I had found it first, but your uncle insisted on keeping it to give to you. Don't judge me harshly, I did what I thought was the best. I didn't want the truth to hurt you in any way, but ultimately your mother and you both met the same fate in love, although under very different circumstances.'

Filled with a deep sense of foreboding, Amiya took the letter out of its time worn envelope and quickly went through it, her head spinning as the import of the words she was reading sunk in. She felt her childhood flash before her eyes, the taunts and innuendoes and whispers, all of them based on the truth, she realized with a shock. Everything fell into place, the total absence of any relatives from her father's side, her fair complexion and the curly hair and the height. There were so many questions she needed to ask, a lifetime of curiosity to satisfy; what her father looked like, why he never contacted her mother again, what made her grandfather rush them all out of Delhi immediately; and as Kamla answered them, dusk began to fall and shadows lengthened on the street outside. One of the daughters-in-law had brought in lunch, and sometime later tea, but Amiya could not eat a morsel, her throat seeming to have closed up. Eventually it was Ram Swaroop who urged her to leave before it became too dark, and despite her protests insisted on sending the younger son to drop her home.

'These are bad times Amiya, and I absolutely cannot let you go anywhere alone at night,' he said, and turning to Kamla, handed her a pamphlet of some sort. 'Read this,' he said, anxiety making his voice shrill, 'it's a warning to Hindus and Sikhs to leave Lahore or face dire consequences. Madan, our neighbour found it placed prominently at the cross road just outside the mohalla, and is going around showing it to everyone.'

'What will we do now?'' Kamla said worriedly. 'Maybe we should shift to Jullunder immediately. We can stay with your sister for the time being.'

'Don't panic like this, let us see what happens. Right now what is important is to get Amiya home safely,' he replied and turning to Amiya added, 'God knows where life will take us Amiya, but I want you to know that I have always looked upon you as a daughter, and I would like us to remain in touch. Please send us your address once you have settled in Bombay, and in the unfortunate circumstance of our also having to move, I will inform you. In any case you can always find out about our whereabouts from Kanpur.'

Amiya, overcome with emotion, just nodded in consent, and hugging both of them, said her goodbyes, strangely detached from what was happening around her. It was as if she was watching everything from a distance, and the slim woman in a yellow saree walking on the darkened street with a much taller man, was not her, but one of the characters from the movies she loved to watch. The night seemed surreal somehow, and she was only dimly aware of reaching the tonga stand, and then the journey back home, her mind struggling to comprehend the enormity of what she had learnt, alternately vacillating between shock and disbelief. And anger. Anger at Kamla for hiding the truth all these years, at her father for abandoning her mother, at fate for always putting happiness just that little bit beyond her reach.

A part of her wished the journey back home would never end and she could lose herself forever in the obscurity of the night. In the course of a few hours she had become unfamiliar to her own self, and the physical features that were supposedly given to her by a quirk of fate, her height and fair complexion, now had a more sinister reason, and as she entered the street leading to the Sodawallas house, she was suddenly assailed by an anxiety so severe, it stopped her in her tracks. How would Adel and Khorshed react to the news, would they still want her to live with them, would they love Dinsha a little less, the fact that his mother was born out of wedlock, and as these phantasmic thoughts played themselves out in the gloom of her mind, the night seemed to grow darker and close in around her. In a fit of panic, she decided to never tell them the awful truth she had learnt that day and entered the house as silently as she could, climbing the stairs to her room almost surreptitiously, telling Pappu, when he came to call her for dinner, that she had eaten and come. Alone at last, she took out the letter to read once again, taking her time over every sentence, trying to reconstruct that day from long ago, consumed by the mystery of it, so that a knock on the door nearly made her jump out of her skin, and before she could react, Khorshed walked in, looking concerned.

'What happened Amiya, what took you so long? Did your aunt say anything to upset you? It's not like you to come to your room without telling me that you're back,' she said.

The room felt stifling, the air heavy and dimensionless, and drained of all will to reshape her fate, she wordlessly handed the letter to Khorshed, and slumped down low in the chair with her eyes closed. From a distance, as if from another space and time, she could hear Khorshed's voice, shocked and concerned by turns.

'I don't understand, Amiya', she said.

'My father,' Amiya replied baldly, her voice shorn of all pretence.

'Oh my dear, I'm so sorry. Did your aunt give you this today? Khorshed asked, 'no wonder you're looking so pale.'

At her words, and especially at the kindness with which they were uttered, Amiya felt herself relax a little, and over the next hour told Khorshed what she had learnt from Kamla, all the time on the lookout for any hint of disapproval in the older woman's reaction. To her relief, she found none. Instead Khorshed, ever perceptive, bought up the topic herself.

'I know what a terrible shock this must be for you Amiya, to be told so abruptly about your parentage. But it happened a long time ago, to people whose life stories you know nothing about; strangers you were born through, not to. Don't think too much about it,' she said in a comforting voice, clasping Amiya's hands in hers.

'That doesn't change the fact that I was born out of wedlock to a man from another religion. That makes me a bastard,' Amiya said tearfully. 'I can understand if you and uncle don't want me to live with you anymore.'

'Don't talk nonsense, child,' Khorshed reprimanded her, 'we can neither choose our parents nor the circumstances of our birth. You are our daughter, and will always remain so. And besides, it doesn't matter where you come from Amiya, because that is beyond your control. It is where you end up, who you become that defines you, and it takes great courage and strength of character to beat the odds like you have done, and we are so proud of you. Although your father may have had a hand in that glowing complexion,' she added jokingly.

Amiya was overwhelmed by the older woman's wisdom and sagacity, and in a rush of relief said the words she had not once uttered in all these years. 'You have been more than a mother to me always, Khorshed aunty, and I can never thank you enough for all the love you have shown me.'

'You know Amiya, I always consider that I have four children and have done so for years,' Khorshed replied giving her a hug. 'But to come back to the letter. We will never discuss it again, unless you want to. And there is no need to tell anyone about it either, not even Adel. Who knows, maybe one day, after you have come to terms with it, you might want to write to your father at the address given in the letter, and if he is alive, and more importantly still lives there... well anything could happen,' she trailed off.

Amiya slept like a log that night, the events of the previous day having totally drained her, and when she woke up, the sun was draping itself over the grass like a carpet, and birds were flitting about in the canopy, imparting a freshness to the morning that was at total variance to what the newspapers were reporting. Mahatma Gandhi, who had largely withdrawn from active politics for some time now, preferring instead to spend time in Calcutta and Bihar, in an attempt to bring peace to those troubled provinces, was against the idea of partition and over the last couple of months had desperately tried to prevent it, even urging Mountbatten to offer the premiership of an interim government of the entire country to Jinnah. However, by now Nehru, the Congress president, and

Vallabhbhai Patel, his deputy, as well as the Viceroy himself, were convinced that partition was the only way to stop the country from descending into a complete civil war. Over the weeks the Sikhs, distrustful of the Muslims, but not wanting to lose their religious places either, had held discussions with the League off and on, but mutual distrust had cleaved a wide unbridgeable chasm between the two communities and nothing came from the talks.

Matters reached a head on 3 June, when in an evening broadcast on All India Radio, Viceroy Mountbatten announced that the British would leave india by 15 August of the same year and that the provinces of Punjab and Bengal would be divided, thus putting an end to months of uncertainty and failed negotiations. This news, welcome as it was, generated conflicting emotions in the state, because independence for the country meant partition for Punjab. What was startling was the preponement of the independence by almost an year since the British had earlier declared that they would transfer power by June 1948, and there was much speculation that this step had been necessitated by the Viceroy's apprehension that any further delay could result in escalating violence and even a civil war.

Amiya, who had made a very reluctant and fragile peace with herself over leaving Lahore, was strangely relieved at the thought of partition, preferring to blame fate rather than her own cowardice for the loss of her beloved city. For even though partition was an open secret, hearing it spelt out in black and white made it a reality and overnight the decision had been snatched from her hands, because there was a very real chance that Lahore would go to Pakistan. But if the announcement calmed her, it had the opposite effect on Adel, who overcome by a sense of urgency, insisted they leave for Bombay within the next fortnight, carrying only their clothes and jewellery with them. He would come back for the rest of their belongings once the situation had normalized somewhat.

There was a sense of irreversibility about the days now, as if they were living on borrowed time, the house, the garden, the trees-some of them older than the man made boundaries surrounding

them seeming to stand under an alien sky, stained an ominous
pewter, instead of the familiar cerulean. The air, heavy with sadness,
hung low and listless, finding its echo in everyone it touched. It
made Shanti cry several times a day, reminding her of the village
she grew up in, while to Khorshed it whispered of abandonment
and loss, for despite Adel's promise of them returning to collect
their belongings and meet their friends, she knew there would be
no coming back.

Amiya spent the weeks before their departure in a sort of
daze, occupying herself with sorting and packing, squirrelling away
thousands of memories in a corner of her heart, true coordinates
that would bring her back to her beloved city in spirit if not in
body. She looked forward to Gautam's visits in the evening, to their
ritual of having tea together in the drawing room, even though
most of the room, like the rest of the house, had been packed
away. Ordinary tasks like walking in the garden and looking for
the first flowers on the gulmohar, had taken on the special lustre
that permeates things that although taken for granted for years,
are now being snatched away by fate. Even the daily pleading by
Gautam seemed endearing rather than annoying, his efforts to get
her to shift to Delhi in a couple of months time, no longer eliciting
an angry response from her. He was leaving for Delhi with his
family next month, in June, just as they were, and she knew how
swamped he was with work, having to single handedly wind down
his practice and arrange to shift their belongings to the house he
had rented in Delhi. He had been more methodical in this than
Adel, choosing a house and moving most of their stuff within a
fortnight of taking the decision to leave Lahore. He had started to
dislike the city, he told Amiya, convinced that his wife's affair, which
he suspected was still continuing, had made him a laughing stock
with everyone, and had no intention of ever returning, especially
since she, Amiya, would no longer be there.

'I will have no reason to return Amiya, and will probably have
no time either, what with trying to set up my practice and looking
after my mother who has not regained her health since my father

passed away. The decision to shift to Delhi has upset her even further, and since I am not confident that my wife will look after her, I will have to restrict my movements somewhat. Although Maya will be living with us now,' he said, his face lighting up at the thought of his daughter. 'The only thing missing from my life will be you Amiya. Please please promise me that you will come to live in Delhi after a few months, even if only for a fortnight at a time,' he added.

'How do you manage to think of such things at a time like this, Gautam?' Amiya asked jokingly. 'What with the packing and your party work and the hectic parleys currently on between the Congress and the League and Mountbatten you must be very busy.'

'The talks are being held at the highest level only, and the situation is so fluid that even senior party leaders don't know what is happening. Besides, ever since Gandhiji has been marginalised, I am very disillusioned and have stopped attending party meetings,' replied Gautam.

'How can you say that, Gautam? This is the moment that thousands of Indians like you and your father have fought for. An independent India!' answered Amiya, in an emotional tone.

'This is not independence, this is partition, painful and bloody, like severing a limb from the body. Tell me Amiya, how can you split the collective memory of generations, allocate some portion to you and some to me, so that each one is left with a meaningless, disjointed piece of remembrance? Are my children to become strangers to the land of their forefathers, and to the river which flows through it and also through me? I may have my personal reasons for wanting to leave Lahore, but the fact is that the wind that blows through these streets tonight is the same breath that blows through my blood, and I have to leave it all and run away like a fugitive in the night. No, this is not the independence I visualized, not this sundering apart of my world,' Gautam said passionately, his face red with the strength of his emotions. 'And what will I do with this freedom which is taking you away from me? Adel has given me your Bombay address, and I have given him mine. Not that you can write to me on that. My wife keeps a hawk's eye on everything I do, the little cheat. Write to me on the other address that I have noted in your dairy.'

'You have told me that a hundred time already, Gautam,' Amiya said, rolling her eyes, 'and I have promised you a hundred times that I will, as soon as we reach Bombay.'

They were leaving for Bombay in the last week of June by the Frontier Mail, the tickets for which Adel had procured with much difficulty. All trains were running full, with Hindus and Sikhs migrating by the thousands, leaving behind friends, houses, shops, businesses and a lifetime of memories. Those who could not get tickets were travelling by bullock carts, although the journey through rural Punjab had become very dangerous, and everyday brought fresh reports of killings. Gautam had already sent his car with the driver to Delhi, piling it high with their remaining belongings, and it would be there to pick them up from the train station when they reached.

With the violence escalating every day, it had become too unsafe to leave the house, and the hours hung about them like a shroud, heavy with melancholy. No one came to meet them, except Gautam and a few friends of the Sodawallas, and a part of Amiya wished that they were already in Bombay, having somehow bypassed these difficult days. The radio had become their constant companion, and what it omitted to disclose was told to them by Gautam or the driver. But even the radio sounded different. Most of the Hindu and Sikh broadcasters whose voices had become familiar, like those of old friends, had left Lahore, and the new ones who had taken their place sounded alien.

The All India Congress Committee, which met in the middle of June to vote on Mountbatten's plan of partitioning the country, endorsed it with a comfortable majority, and although Mahatma Gandhi expressed his unhappiness, he went along with the decision. Two days before they were to leave, on 22 June, the afternoon was suddenly eclipsed by huge columns of black smoke billowing from the Hindu mohalla of Shahalmi. Muslim mobs had set it on fire, and the sound of gunfire and bursting crackers reached them dimly, shattering the stillness of a city already hushed with fear, but it was the sooty pillars of smoke, distended and puffy, assembling in a funereal procession, that signaled to her that Lahore was finally dead. The next day, the Punjab Legislative assembly also voted to divide the province. Partition had become a reality.

Amiya was up before dawn on the day of their departure, after a night during which it seemed to her that she had re-lived her whole life, watching the events unfold on a giant movie screen, herself the actress and herself the audience. She saw the faces of those she had loved and those who had loved her back, saw her husband and his wife, saw her son grow into adulthood, saw Gautam who cared so much for her. Each adumbration flashed for a second before departing forever. All night, tossing about in her bed sleepless and on edge, she traversed the streets of Lahore like a phantom, her fancy taking her along familiar pathways, to old buildings, where peering through windows she listened for echoes from the past, searching for herself in the catacombs of memory. Finally bleary eyed and exhausted from grieving over the past and anguishing about the future, she left the bed and went downstairs to make tea.

There at the sight of their bags all neatly lined up, she felt a current of melancholy wash over her, followed inexplicably by a counter current of happiness at the thought of meeting Dinsha. A flood of affection for Gautam as he walked in some time later, followed almost immediately by a rush of regret at losing him. And as the time of their leaving drew nearer, and both the Victoria and the car were lined up in the driveway, and a tearful Gautam took her in his arms, pleading for the last time that she join him in Delhi after some months, she found herself whispering back a hesitant yes. After all, it was a time for endings and new beginnings.

Chapter 24

December 1948, Bombay

New Year's Eve. A year and a half since they had shifted to Bombay.
A year marked by euphoria, but also by violence and tradgedy.
Mahatma Gandhi was assassinated on 30 January by a Hindu zealot,
as he was on his way to conduct a multi faith prayer meeting,
plunging a stunned nation into mourning. Shockingly, Muhammad
Ali Jinnah also did not live long enough to enjoy the new country
he had fought to create, dying of lung cancer in September. Amiya
wondered sometimes what the outcome would have been if he
had died an year earlier, or if the partition had been postponed for
that duration. Would there have been a partition at all, or would
they still be living in Lahore ?

As it was they were lucky to have left Lahore when they did,
before the carnage and the massacres reached horrific proportions.
The violence at the time of partition was unprecedented, leaving
more than half a million dead and more than ten million homeless.
Madness seemed to have gripped people on both sides of the border,
and not even the places of worship were spared. Mosques and
gurudwaras become death traps, parents were killed in front of
children and children in front of their parents. Rape and murder,
arson and looting became commonplace. It was as if there was
no God, no mercy, no place to hide. Entire mohallas were burnt
down, with not even friends being spared. Women were snatched
by armed goondas from columns of people marching towards the
border or the railway station, raped and then murdered. Or they
were killed by their own menfolk before such horrors could be
perpetrated on them. Roads were littered with dead bodies, as were
the railway stations, and survivors reported of having to step over

the corpses to reach the trains. Many trains themselves reached their destination often with not a single survivor. Assailants prowled the land in mobs and there was no escaping them, because evading one invariably meant being caught by the other. As the survivors gradually reached refugee camps, increasingly gruesome stories of their ordeal started trickling out, and Amiya shuddered to think what would have happened if they had stayed back in Lahore, which as was expected, had been allocated to Pakistan.

Soon after their departure in June last year, a Boundary Commission was set up under the chairmanship of a British jurist, Sir Cyril Radcliffe. The commission had four other members, two judges nominated by the Congress and two by the League, and all four heard arguments from both sides, but could not reach any consensus due to their own prejudices. So it was left to Radcliffe, who had never visited India before and who was not even present at the time of the arguments, to give his own dispensation, and although he did stick, by and large, to the principle of religious majority and even took into account other variables like roads and irrigation systems, he was both ignorant and short of time to be able to do justice to the task he had undertaken. As a result, neither side was completely satisfied with the award he passed, which was not made public until two days after Independence, by which time the Sodawallas and Amiya were well settled in Bombay, and were somewhat cushioned from the grief of losing Lahore.

Adel had bought a three bedroom apartment in south Bombay, very near where the boys lived. It was located on Marine Drive, just two buildings away from the younger son Delawar's apartment, in a largely Parsi dominated neighbourhood. Dinshaw and his family lived nearby on Malabar Hill, where their house was located on one of the highest points of the hillock. It was set in a large plot amidst coconut and palm trees, and enjoyed a spectacular view of Backbay, a shallow expanse of water which merged into the Arabian sea, and from which Marine Drive had been reclaimed more than thirty years ago. This was the first property that the Sodawallas had bought in Bombay, and both the brothers lived there until some years ago, when the children started demanding more space, and an apartment was bought on Marine Drive. It was Adel's intention of demolishing the existing structure, which was old and cramped, and building a three floor apartment complex in its place, complete with a badminton court and servant quarters.

Marine Drive was a promenade constructed on land reclaimed from Backbay, and ran all along the coastline in a C-shaped formation. For the past two decades it had seen much development; new art deco style apartment buildings, cinemas, hotels, clubs; and was now a vibrant place, especially in the evenings, when lights were switched on along the road, justifying the moniker of 'queen's necklace'. Nearby Churchgate street, with its bars and restaurants and jazz clubs, was walking distance, as was the Hindu Gymkhana, which contrary to its name had been offering membership to Parsis and Muslims also for many years now, ever since the British Government had taken over the premises of the Islam and Parsi Gymkhanas during the second World War. Both Dinshaw and Delawar were members of the club, and it was here that Dinsha had learnt to play cricket.

The Sodawalla's apartment was on the third floor of a swanky new building overlooking the Marine Drive and had an unhindered view of the Arabian sea beyond. Amiya who had never seen the sea before in her life, fell in love with it at first sight, finding its energy exhilarating and its vastness soothing. She was enthralled by its many moods, by the hundred shades of blue, by the tidal ebb and flow of the water every twelve hours, by the storm surges of the monsoon with their white foam and glittering crests, by the moonlight forming a highway on the water at night. She spent hours studying its every whim and fancy, saw the mist hang low over the water on rainy days, obscuring everything in view, watched pastel coloured sunrises and fiery citrus hued sunsets and marveled at the light. Especially the light, magical and luminous, unlike anything she had encountered in land locked Lahore. Ferzana, with whom she walked most evenings along the sea front, told her that it was always the same, and was the reflection of the sunlight on the ever dancing waves. The walks had become a favourite part of her days in Bombay, especially since they seemed to be perfectly timed with the breeze which blew in from the sea every evening and brought the temperature down several notches. The sea breeze, which smelt salty and exotic, played with the street lights along Marine Drive, making them flicker and twinkle, before swooping low to whistle in the hollows and chase dry leaves down the road, until tired at last, it lost itself in the clothes and hair of the passers-by.

Life in Bombay—after a few initial surprises—had settled into a comfortable routine. The city was very different from the picture she had in her mind, and the first thing that had struck her about the place was the humidity. She had started to perspire as soon as they got off the train, little rivulets of sweat trickling down her body. The June day was oppressive and very hot, a dark overcast sky stretched from horizon to horizon and not a leaf moved, but fortunately the rain started as soon as they reached Dinshaw's house, blowing curtains of water in every direction.

The monsoon had broken over the city a fortnight back, nearly five weeks before it would arrive in Lahore, and the next three months saw almost incessant rainfall, with the sun sometimes not putting in an appearance for a week at a time. It was a strange feeling, this waking up to dark rainy mornings, and going to sleep while it was still pouring, and by the end of August Amiya was tired of being cooped up indoors and wished it would stop. Ferzana had told her that the temperature and the humidity would remain by and large the same throughout the year, but even so she was unprepared for how warm the rest of the year was. There was no winter, no cosying up in a quilt at night, no fragrance of woodsmoke lingering on bleak winter evenings, and even on the rare cold January days, she could manage with just a shawl. But however uncomfortable the day might have been, the evenings were always redeemed by the cool sea breeze, which would start coming in from the late afternoon onwards, freshening everything it touched.

The two brothers made her feel very welcome, and if the younger one felt it old that she had shifted with his parents to

Bombay, he hid it well, his wife and he always affectionate. With Dinshaw and Ferzana she enjoyed that special bond which only a deeply personal shared secret can beget, and while the former was slightly shy and formal around her, his wife had become a good friend, and had taken it upon herself to show her around Bombay. Amiya liked to attribute some of the closeness between them to her cautious handling of her relationship with Dinsha, who was now a smart college going boy, tall and fair. Everytime she saw her twenty one year old son her heart filled with joy, but she was careful not to get overfamiliar with him, always thinking of him as Ferzana's son, reminding herself that any claim she had over him, his time and love, she had relinquished the day she gave him up for adoption. Besides, time had healed old wounds and the years had brought acceptance and peace.

Within a month of shifting, she had written to her relatives in Kanpur and also to Kamla at the Jullunder address, and while she received no reply from the former, Ram Swaroop wrote back, informing her that the family had left Lahore in the nick of time, and were now well settled in their new home. True to his word, Gautam wrote to her every week, and sometimes as she stood looking out to sea, she imagined it stretching north all the way to Karachi, imagined herself travelling from there to Lahore, making the endlessly long journey by bus, entering her city through one of its majestic gates, pausing outside Kamla's house, before going onwards to Ishwar's and finally to her little room at the top of the stairs. A wave of homesickness would then wash over her, and she would long for familiar sounds and smells, the sea and the glittering lights of the Marine Drive no longer so appealing. The melancholy that would grip her at such times always made her think about Gautam and how much she missed him.

She was worried about him, his letters although informative and chatty, always had an underlying streak of sadness. He had rented an apartment on Sujjan Singh Park in central Delhi, like some of his other friends from Lahore, but it was much smaller than the house he was used to living in, and he felt cramped for space, especially since his daughter had also moved in with them. He had applied for compensation and rehabilitation under the Displaced Persons Ordinance, but given the number of refugees, it was a mammoth task and he estimated that it could be months, and possibly years before he got something. Unwilling to take a risk so soon after moving to Delhi, he had decided to defer setting up his own practice and had joined a senior lawyer as a partner instead. But he didn't feel well, he wrote to her every time, either physically or mentally, complaining of tiredness and a general sense of lethargy.

The tone and tenor of the letters bothered her, and she replied inviting him to Bombay for a few days, secretly deciding that if he didn't come, she would make a trip to Delhi towards the end of the year to meet him. It would be a change for her too, and maybe a change of scene would alleviate the sense of vacuity that threatened to overwhelm her at times. She had not written a word since shifting to Bombay and she missed putting ink to paper, missed the alchemy of disjointed letters transforming into something meaningful. Over time, writing had become more than just a livelihood, she needed to paraphrase her thoughts, needed for the words to wash over her, drown her in their passion, make her bleed on the paper. But inspite of Adel's efforts, she had not been able to get any assignment of interest in the local newspapers and magazines. Everything was too new and too unfamiliar. Bombay was nice in its own way, and had welcomed her into its capacious fold, but she was a stranger to its customs and habitudes, and its history, though rich and varied, held none of hers. She knew no Marathi, knew nothing about local issues and most publishers had not read her work. Any illusions she had about being a well known writer, were just that, she thought wryly, and it had only needed a change of place to show her the truth. Maybe she would hire a tutor to teach her Marathi, she thought one desultory day, or maybe she would write a book.

It was a stray thought, the idle rumination of an empty mind, but it stayed with her, popping up at unexpected moments, like the recalcitrant snatches on an old song which play on and on in the head. Finally, fatigued by its insistence, she discussed the idea with Khorshed, and was pleasantly surprised at the older woman's enthusiasm. Within a day Adel had heard about it, as had the rest of the family, and she was soon swamped with storylines and plots, ranging from the commonplace to the bizarre. None of them were really useful, the story she wrote would have to be hers alone, but she revelled in the sense of inclusion into this large and loving family.

Maybe some good would come out of this moving to a new place, she thought, looking out at the ships in the distance, which looked like pin points of light in the gathering dark. It was New Year's Eve, and all of them would be going to the Gymkhana in some time, and unbidden, the memory of another New Year's Eve cropped up, from so long ago and so far away that it seemed like a different lifetime. She recalled vividly, the knock on the door that had changed her life irrevocably, remembered her husband walking out with another woman. But almost immediately her mind took her to other joyous celebrations, and it was as if the ups and downs of life mimicked the ebb and flow of the waters of the sea, the tide coming in with a rush and going out again, leaving the sands bare. And so the *Jawahar Bhatta* would continue till eternity.

Epilogue

16 October 1949

News of Gautam's death reached Amiya on a very pleasant evening in March. Outside the sun had set in a blaze of multihued glory, and the clamour of birds getting ready for the night was raucous, but she saw nothing, heard nothing. It was as if a giant hand had blighted the light and shrouded her in a funereal silence. How could he be dead, her gentle, kind Gautam, when even now she could see him sitting in his favourite arm chair, smoking his Rothman's and blowing perfect circles of smoke in the air? Gautam, so dear to her for so long and such an integral part of her life. Their last meeting was more than one and a half years ago, when he had come to see them off at the station in June 1947, but never had she imagined that it would be a final goodbye. Grief engulfed her, just as the relentless march of the night had engulfed the day, and as if from a distance she was aware of Khorshed getting up to switch on the light. What was she to do now? The teherveen was next week, but there was no point in her going to Delhi to attend it, she would be an outsider and probably an unwelcome one, given that Harjeet had suspected her of having an affair with her husband. No, there was nothing for her to do other than mourn from a distance and bemoan her kismet which took from her, sooner or later, everything that she held dear.

The death affected her profoundly, and a couple of months later, when the shock and the grief had calmed, and the storm had abated somewhat, she started noticing small changes about herself, insignificant but pertinacious. A strange angst chased her the entire time, a mixture of sorrow and guilt and regret, causing her to brood and shun activities that normally gave her pleasure.

In almost every letter Gautam had mentioned feeling unwell, but she had attributed it to general tiredness and worry, never for a moment thinking that it could be serious enough to cost him his life. If only she had visited him in Delhi once, insisted that he see a doctor, if only she had told him how much she cared for him.

One evening in the third week of May, after spending several hours mulling over the plot of the book she planned to write, and making no headway, she excused herself from dinner feigning a headache and went to her room. The day had been overcast and gloomy, heat and humidity adding to the general feeling of inertia that had plagued her since the morning. To make matters worse, a storm broke just as she was getting into bed, and the lights went off, plunging the house into darkness. Too tired and dispirited to get up, but too uncomfortably hot to sleep, she dozed fitfully, drifting in and out of a disturbed dreamland. Finally, sometime after midnight the power was restored, but by then all sleep had deserted her, and leaving her room, she stepped out into the balcony. The night was surreal. The storm had abated, and she could hear the waves lapping gently on the shore, their fury of only a few hours earlier having left them. The moon rode high in an indigo sky, and the wind was low. Moonlight flooded sea and sky from horizon to horizon, silvering the water and rippling on the waves, making them appear like floating wisps of tinsel. Then crossing the road, which it gilded in a patina of chrome, the light varnished every leaf on every tree before bathing the balcony in irridescent moon dust. Amiya could feel the magic glitter settling on her hair, her arms, her whole body, making her glow, filling her with exhilaration.

There was life in the water and life beyond it, stretching into eternity, and in the coruscating glow suffusing everything in sight, for a moment she felt as if she was the light and the light was her. In the journey through life, she had encountered both good times and bad, had lived through heartbreak and happiness, and in a flash all these experiences merged into the present moment, and although the spell passed almost instantly, it left her with a heady sense of freedom. She felt light, as if a weight had been lifted off her chest and on impulse went inside and taking out her father's letter, wrote to him not knowing whether he was still alive or not and whether he still lived at the same address. Next morning, before she lost her nerve, she slipped out of the house and posted it, telling Khorshed about it when she returned. The older woman, who had been worried about her these last few months, ever since Gautam's death, was delighted but cautioned her against expecting a reply anytime soon.

'I'm sure if your father is alive he will reply to your letter Amiya, but what is more wonderful is the fact that you plucked the courage to write to him,' she said.

'I don't want my story to end like poor Gautam's did, incomplete and full of bitterness. If I had not written to my father now, who knows a couple of years later, I might've regretted it,' Amiya replied, 'but now, even if I don't get a reply, I am satisfied.'

The two of them were alone in the living room, sitting on a couch overlooking the sea. This was their favourite spot in the house, where they would have their mid morning tea, catching up on all neighbourhood gossip. Amiya was wearing a printed chiffon saree, her hair tied in her customary bun low on her nape. Her eyes were rimmed with kajal, and she wore a small black bindi. Khorshed, who had put on weight over the years, was also wearing a saree, a dark navy blue embroidered one. The window was open and a pleasant breeze floated in, smelling of the sea, and Amiya felt the beginnings of a plot take shape in her head. It was a tiny germ of an idea, but over the next few months she nurtured it, forcing herself to write at least a page a day, till the story began to captivate her, the characters developing minds of their own, stubbornly resisting any attempts to slot them into pre-determined grooves. The weather became her collaborator, louring clouds and pelting rain of the monsoon months forcing her to stay indoors and write. Her days began to follow a pattern, with early mornings and afternoons kept aside for writing, and the rest of the time spent with Khorshed or some or the member of the family who was sure to drop in.

In the comfort of an everyday routine, she forgot all about the letter she had written to her father, and was surprised to see a small registered packet addressed to her lying on the dining table one day towards the end of August. It took her a second to realize where it had come from, and she rushed with it to her room, tearing it open on the way. It was a beautiful letter, an outpouring from the heart, and as she read it, tears started to roll down her face. Her father had addressed her as 'my beloved daughter' throughout, writing about how much he had loved her mother and how distraught he was to find her gone when he returned after his assignment. He spent a week in Delhi, travelling to Chandini Chowk every day to try and find out her whereabouts from the neighbours and the shop-keepers in the gali, but no one knew where the family had gone. They had just vanished overnight. Tormented by thoughts of what could have happened to her, it did occur to him that her father, chancing upon the letter, may have got her married to someone else. What he could never have imagined was that Gayatri was pregnant with his child. Confused and saddened at losing the one woman he had loved, he returned to the army, vowing never to get married. Finally, after serving all over the world, he had retired to his house—in a village in Sussex—some years back, where he now lived with his two faithful dogs. He had enjoyed a long career in the army, earning name and fame and considerable wealth, which he had no one to spend on. So, it was his pleasure to send her a ticket to London for the month of October, the earliest he could manage though a friend in Delhi, whom he got in touch with the very day he received her letter. Of course, he could not force her to come, nor would he want to do that, but it would give to him some of the happiness and peace that had eluded him all his life, if he could meet her once.

After reading the letter, Amiya looked in the envelope and found a plane ticket for 16 of October, less than two months away. Gripped with a sense of panic, at this totally unexpectecd turn of events, she wondered what to do. While she did want to meet her father, she had no desire to leave her familiar surroundings and fly half-way across the world. Finally, finding Khorshed alone after lunch, she took the letter and the ticket to her.

'So your story does have an ending, Amiya,' she said after reading the letter. 'You will be going to meet him, of course.'

'But I don't want to leave you and go all the way. What if I don't like it there? I know absolutely no one in England,' replied Amiya, worry clouding her face.

'How can you say that, Amiya? After reading the letter, I feel like your father is an old friend of mine,' Khorshed joked, adding in a more serious tone, 'and never let fear of the new and unexperienced stop you from doing what you should. Meeting your father will help heal the scars of childhood that you carry around with you to this day. You really must go, if only for a few weeks. That ticket will have cost him nearly 2,000 rupees. You can't let that go waste,' she said, with a laugh.

'But what will we tell everyone? And how will I come back?' Amiya asked in an anxious tone.

'We will tell everyone the truth, that your father who lives in England wants to meet you. You have nothing to be ashamed of. And if you're worried about coming back, why don't you take a return ticket with you? Uncle Adel will get it done for whichever day you want,' Korshed suggested.

'That will be perfect, aunty,' Amiya said, cheering up, 'that way I won't be so nervous about going.'

'That's settled, then. Now we have to get you some warm clothes, maybe a coat,' Khorshed said reflectively, looking her up and down, 'and something nice for you to take along as a gift.'

'But I'm not sure that I really do want to go,' Amiya interrupted her.

'Nonsense, child' Khorshed said dismissively. 'I knew we should have brought our woollens along from Lahore, but your uncle didn't listen to me, insisting that we wouldn't need them in Bombay and that he would anyway be going back to get the remaining things. But of course, he will never be able to do that, and there is no point thinking about it anymore.'

The remaining days passed in a whirlwind of activity, exchanging letters with her father, shopping and packing, but as the time for her departure came nearer, Amiya grew more and more nervous. Air India International, jointly owned by the Government of India and the Tatas, a prominent Parsi family of Bombay, very well known to the Sodawallas, had been operating flights from Bombay to London since June last year. The journey took twenty four hours, with the plane making two stop-overs for refuelling, one at Cairo and the other at Geneva. Amiya didn't like the thought of being in the aircraft for a whole day, and no matter how much the others envied her, joking that the flight would be full of celebrities, and maybe even Mr Tata himself, she did not want to leave Bombay and her predictable life. But in the onward march of time 16 October did arrive, and as she stood on the tarmac of the Santa Cruz airport, her palms clammy with nervousness, she was sure her co-passengers could hear her heart beating loudly. It had been a hot day, but the evening was pleasant, with a light breeze picking up as it did every day at this hour. Khorshed, Ferzana and Dinsha had come to see her off, the latter because he wanted to see an aeroplane from up close, but somehow his nearness gave her a sense of calm.

All her life she had done the unconventional, had followed her own star. She had left her husband, moved in with strangers, found the courage to give her son up for adoption, worked hard to make a name for herself in a predominantly male dominated field. And although she had been afraid at every turn, apprehensive of change and anxious about its outcome, she had never allowed fear to stand in her way, had recast herself into a stronger version of herself each time, accepting the pain and letting it flow through her, weaving all her stories, the sad and the joyous, the drab and the colourful, into a single fabric.

And now the winds were calling her once again, daring her to cross the vast ocean with them, and explore what lay beyond the horizon where sea and sky became one. And she had never been one to give up on a challenge.